DRIVING STANDARDS AGENCY

the official DSA
THEORY
TEST
for Motorcyclists

16
Approved by
Plain
English
Campaign

London: TSO

Written and compiled by the Publications Unit of the Driving Standards Agency (DSA).

Questions and answers are compiled by the Question Development Team of the DSA.

Published with the permission of the Driving Standards Agency on behalf of the Controller of Her Majesty's Stationery Office.

First published 2000
Sixth edition 2006

ISBN-13 978 011 552750 8
ISBN-10 011 552750 8

A CIP catalogue record for this book is available from the British Library.

Other titles in the Driving Skills series

The Official DSA Theory Test for Car Drivers
The Official DSA Theory Test Revision Papers for Car Drivers
The Official DSA Guide to Learning to Drive
Helping Learners to Practise - the official DSA guide
The Official DSA Guide to Driving - the essential skills
The Official DSA Guide to Learning to Ride
The Official DSA Guide to Riding - the essential skills
The Official DSA Theory Test for Drivers of Large Vehicles
The Official DSA Guide to Driving Buses and Coaches
The Official DSA Guide to Driving Goods Vehicles
The Official DSA Guide to Tractor and Specialist Vehicle Driving Tests
The Official DSA Theory Test for Car Drivers (CD-Rom)
The Official DSA Theory Test for Motorcyclists (CD-Rom)
The Official DSA Theory Test for Drivers of Large Vehicles (CD-Rom)
The Official DSA Guide to Hazard Perception (DVD) (also available on VHS)
Prepare for your Practical Driving Test (DVD)

Directgov

Directgov is the place to find all government motoring information and services. From logbooks to licensing, from driving tests to road tax, go to:

www.direct.gov.uk/motoring

Theory and practical tests
DSA bookings and enquiries

Online **www.dsa.gov.uk**
Tel **0870 0101 372**
Fax **0870 0104 372**
Minicom **0870 0106 372**
Welsh speakers **0870 0100 372**

DVTA (Northern Ireland)
Theory test **0845 600 6700**
Practical test **0870 247 2471**

Driving Standards Agency
(Headquarters)

www.dsa.gov.uk

Stanley House, 56 Talbot Street, Nottingham NG1 5GU

Tel **0115 901 2500**
Fax **0115 901 2510**

Driver & Vehicle Testing Agency
(Headquarters)

www.dvtani.gov.uk

Balmoral Road, Belfast BT12 6QL

Tel **02890 681 831**
Fax **02890 665 520**

Driver & Vehicle Licensing Agency
(GB Licence Enquiries)

www.dvla.gov.uk

Longview Road, Swansea SA6 7JL

Tel **0870 240 0009**
Fax **01792 783 071**
Minicom **01792 782 787**

Driver & Vehicle Licensing in Northern Ireland

www.dvlni.gov.uk

County Hall, Castlerock Road, Coleraine BT51 3TB

Tel **02870 341 469**
24 hour tel **0345 111 222**
Minicom **02870 341 380**

The Driving Standards Agency (DSA) is an executive agency of the Department for Transport. You'll see the DSA logo at test centres.

DSA aims to promote road safety through the advancement of driving standards by

- establishing and developing high standards and best practice in driving and riding on the road; before people start to drive, as they learn, and after they pass their test
- ensuring high standards of instruction for different types of driver and rider
- conducting the statutory theory and practical tests efficiently, fairly and consistently across the country
- providing a centre of excellence for driver training and driving standards
- developing a range of publications and other publicity material designed to promote safe driving for life.

The Driving Standards Agency recognises and values its customers. We will treat all our customers with respect, and deliver our services in an objective, polite and fair way.

www.dsa.gov.uk

The Driver and Vehicle Testing Agency (DVTA) is an executive agency within the Department of the Environment for Northern Ireland.

Its primary aim is to promote and improve road safety through the advancement of driving standards and implementation of the Government's policies for improving the mechanical standards of vehicles.

www.dvtani.gov.uk

CONTENTS

About the theory test

A message from the Chief Driving Examiner 7
Getting started 8
The theory test 12
After the theory test 19
Using the question and answer sections 21

Section one **alertness** 22
Section two **attitude** 34
Section three **safety and your motorcycle** 46
Section four **safety margins** 80
Section five **hazard awareness** 96
Section six **vulnerable road users** 118
Section seven **other types of vehicle** 146
Section eight **motorcycle handling** 156
Section nine **motorway rules** 178
Section ten **rules of the road** 200
Section eleven **road and traffic signs** 222
Section twelve **documents** 278
Section thirteen **accidents** 294
Section fourteen **motorcycle loading** 314

Annexes

1 List of theory test centres 326
2 Service standards 328

introduction
ABOUT THE THEORY TEST

This section covers:

- getting started
- the theory test
- after the theory test
- using the question and answer sections

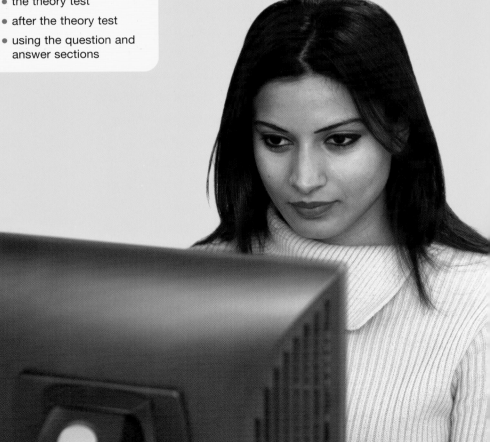

Message from the Chief Driving Examiner

With the ever-increasing volume of traffic on the roads today, it's important to make sure that new drivers have a positive attitude and a broad spread of riding knowledge and ability.

Since July 1996 all new riders have had to pass a separate theory test before obtaining a full licence. In November 2002 the original multiple choice test was extended to include a hazard perception part. The introduction of the separate theory test has been a major step towards improving road safety in the UK.

All aspects of the theory test are continually monitored, and the question bank is regularly updated to take account of changes to legislation and best riding practices. This book contains the whole theory test question bank, set out in an easy-to-read style, with explanations as to why the answers are correct.

However, to prepare properly for the test, you should study the source material; this consists of:

The Highway Code

Know Your Traffic Signs

The Official DSA Guide to Riding - the essential skills

To help you practise for the multiple choice questions, *The Official DSA Theory Test for Motorcyclists (CD-Rom)* contains the full question bank and allows you to take mock multiple choice tests. You can prepare for the hazard perception part of the test by working through *The Official DSA Guide to Hazard Perception (DVD)* which is also available as a VHS video and booklet package.

Using these training aids will give you an extensive knowledge of riding theory, and will help you towards a better understanding of practical riding skills.

You'll never know all the answers. Throughout your riding career there will always be more to learn.

Remember, as a rider you have a responsibility for the safety of your machine, any pillion passenger you carry and other road users. By being reliable, efficient and safe you'll be on your way to becoming a good rider.

Trevor Wedge

Trevor Wedge
Chief Driving Examiner and
Director of Safer Driving

Getting started

Applying for your licence

You must have a valid provisional driving licence before you can ride on the road.

Licences are issued by the Driver and Vehicle Licensing Agency (DVLA). Application forms D1 and D750 can be obtained from any post office. In Northern Ireland the issuing authority is Driver and Vehicle Licensing Northern Ireland and the form is a DL1.

Send these forms to the appropriate office, which is shown on the form. You must enclose the required passport-type photographs, as all provisional licences now issued are photocard licences.

When you receive your provisional licence, check that all details are correct before you ride on the road. If you need to contact DVLA, their telephone number is 0870 240 0009 (DVLNI is 02870 341469).

You will need to show both parts of your provisional licence when you take your theory test.

Residency requirements

You can't take a test or obtain a full licence unless you are normally resident in this country. Normal residence means the place where you reside because of personal or occupational ties. However, if you moved to the United Kingdom (UK) having recently been permanently resident in another state of the EC/EEA (European Economic Area), you must have been normally resident in the UK for 185 days in the 12 months prior to your application for a driving test or full driving licence.

Compulsory Basic Training

Before you take your practical motorcycle test you must attend and successfully complete a Compulsory Basic Training (CBT) course (except in Northern Ireland). CBT courses can be given only by training bodies approved by DSA. Frequent checks are made to ensure a high standard of instruction.

The course will include

- classroom training
- practical skills training.

You can find out about CBT courses from

- DSA (visit www.dsa.gov.uk or call 0115 901 2595)
- your motorcycle dealer
- your local Road Safety Officer (by contacting your local council).

DSA also produces *The Official DSA Guide to Learning to Ride* which will give you details about the course (see p10 for further details).

About the theory test

The theory test is a screen-based test, and consists of two parts.

It has been devised to test your knowledge of riding theory, in particular the rules of the road and best riding practice.

Your knowledge of this information is tested in the first part of the theory test, as a series of multiple choice questions. More information about this part of the test is given on page 15 and the questions are given in the main part of the book, beginning on page 22.

The second part of the theory test is called hazard perception, more information about this is given on page 17.

Don't forget to buy some good quality protective gear. It could save your life

Can I take the practical test first?

No. You have to pass your theory test before you can book a practical test.

Does everyone have to take the theory test?

Most people in the UK who are learning to ride or drive will have to sit a theory test. However, you won't have to take a motorcycle theory test again to upgrade to a motorcycle licence if you have already passed a motorcycle (A) theory test and then a practical moped test.

Any enquiries about whether you have to take a theory test should be addressed to the Customer Services Unit, Driving Standards Agency, Stanley House, 56 Talbot Street, Nottingham, NG1 5GU, telephone 0115 901 2500 (for Northern Ireland address enquiries to DVTA Theory Test Section, Balmoral Road, Belfast BT12, tel 02890 681831).

Foreign licence holders: If you hold a foreign licence issued outside the EC/EEA, first check with the Driver Vehicle Licensing Agency (telephone 0870 240 0009, for Northern Ireland call 02870 341469), to see whether you can exchange your licence. If you cannot exchange your licence, you will need to apply for a provisional licence and take a theory and practical test.

Preparing for your theory test

Although you have to pass your theory test before you can take your practical test, it's recommended that you start studying for your theory test, but don't actually take it until you have some practical experience of riding.

To prepare for the multiple choice part of the theory test, we strongly recommend that you study the books from which the questions are taken as well as the questions themselves. These books are:

The Highway Code - this is essential reading for all road users. It contains the most up-to-date advice on road safety and the laws which apply to all road users.

Know Your Traffic Signs - this contains most of the signs and road markings that you are likely to come across.

The Official DSA Guide to Riding - the essential skills - this is the official reference book, giving practical advice and best practice for all riders.

The Official DSA Guide to Learning to Ride – gives full details of basic machine handling for compulsory basic training and the full practical test syllabus.

These books will help you to answer the questions correctly and will also help you when studying for your practical test. The information in them will be relevant throughout your riding life so make sure you always have an up-to-date copy that you can refer to.

It's important that you study, not just to pass the test, but to become a safer rider

Other study aids

The Official DSA Theory Test for Motorcyclists (CD-Rom) – this is an alternative way of preparing for the multiple choice part of the theory test. It contains all the questions and answers and also allows you to take mock tests.

The Official Guide to Hazard Perception (DVD) - We strongly recommend that you use this, preferably with your trainer, to prepare for the hazard perception part of the test. Alternatively, this is available as a VHS and booklet pack.

The DVD is packed with useful tips, quizzes and expert advice. It also includes interactive hazard perception clips, with feedback on your performance.

Why do the questions keep changing?

To make sure that all candidates are being tested fairly, questions and video clips are under continuous review.

Some of the questions may be changed as a result of customer feedback. They may also be changed to reflect revised legislation, and the publications listed above are updated to reflect such changes.

Can I take a mock test?

You can take mock tests for the multiple choice part of the theory test online at **www.direct.gov.uk/motoring**

All the officail training materials listed are available online at **www.tsoshop.co.uk/dsa** or by mail order from **0870 241 4523**.

They are also available from bookshops and selected computer software retailers.

The theory test

Booking your theory test

The easiest ways to book your test are online or by phone. You can also book by post.

Booking online or by telephone - by using these methods you'll be given the date and time of your test immediately.

Book online at www.direct.gov.uk/motoring (for Northern Ireland use www.dvtani.gov.uk)

To book by telephone, call 0870 0101 372 (0845 600 6700 for Northern Ireland).

If you're deaf and use a minicom machine, call 0870 0106 372 and if you are a Welsh speaker, call 0870 0100 372.

You will need your:

- DVLA or DVLNI driving licence number
- credit or debit card details (the card holder must book the test). We accept Mastercard, Visa, Delta, Switch/Maestro, Visa Electron and Solo.

You'll be given a booking number and should receive an appointment letter within eight days.

How do I cancel or postpone my test?

To cancel or postpone your theory test appointment you must give at least **three clear working days** before your test date, otherwise you'll lose your fee. You can do this online or by telephone. Only in exceptional circumstances, such as documented ill-health or family bereavement, can this rule be waived.

What if I don't receive an acknowledgement?

If you don't receive an acknowledgement within the time specified above, please contact the booking office online or by telephone to check that an appointment has been made. We can't take responsibility for postal delays. If you miss your test appointment you'll lose your fee.

Where can I take the test?

There are over 150 theory test centres throughout England, Scotland and Wales, and six in Northern Ireland. Most people have a test centre within 20 miles of their home, but this will vary depending on the density of population in your area. There is a list of test centres on page 326.

When are test centres open?

Test centres are usually open on weekdays, some evenings and some Saturdays.

Booking by post - If you prefer to book by post, you'll need to fill in an application form. These are available from theory or driving test centres, or your instructor may have one.

You should receive an appointment letter within ten days of posting your application form.

If you require a theory test in a language other than English or provision for special needs please turn to page 14.

Taking your theory test

Arriving at the test centre - You must make sure that when you arrive at the test centre you have all the relevant documents with you, or you won't be able to take your test and you'll lose your fee.

You'll need

- your signed photocard licence and paper counterpart, or
- your signed driving licence and valid passport (your passport doesn't have to be British).

No other form of identification is acceptable.

Other forms of identification may be acceptable in Northern Ireland, please check www.doeni.gov.uk/dvta or refer to your test appointment letter.

All documents must be original. We can't accept photocopies.

The test centre staff will check your documents and make sure that you take the right category of test.

Remember, if you don't bring your documents your test will be cancelled.

Make sure that you arrive in plenty of time so you aren't rushed. If you arrive after the session has started you may not be allowed to take the test.

You'll then be ready to start your test. It's a screen-based test and is made up of a multiple choice part and a hazard perception part.

Languages other than English

You can listen through a headset to the test being read out in one of 20 other languages as well as English. These are: Albanian, Arabic, Bengali, Cantonese, Dari, Farsi, Gujarati, Hindi, Kashmiri, Kurdish, Mirpuri, Polish, Portuguese, Punjabi, Pushto, Spanish, Tamil, Turkish, Urdu and Welsh.

In Wales, and at theory test centres on the Welsh borders, you can take your theory test with Welsh text on screen.

To take your test in a language other than those listed above, you may bring a translator with you to certain theory test centres. The translator must be approved by DSA and you must make arrangements when you book your test. You have to arrange and pay for the services of the translator yourself.

Tests with translators can be taken at the following test centres: Aldershot, Birkenhead, Birmingham, Cardiff, Derby, Edinburgh, Glasgow, Ipswich, Leeds, Milton Keynes, Preston, Southgate and all test centres in Northern Ireland.

Provision for special needs

Every effort is made to ensure that the theory test can be taken by all candidates. It's important that you state your needs when you book your test so that the necessary arrangements can be made.

Reading difficulties - There's an English language voiceover, on a headset, to help you if you have reading difficulties or dyslexia.

You can ask for up to twice the normal time to take the multiple choice part of the test.

If you need extra time you will be asked to provide a letter from a suitable independent person who knows about your reading ability (such as a teacher or employer). Please check with the Special Needs section on the normal booking number (see p12) if you're unsure who to ask.

We can't guarantee to return any original documents, so please send copies only.

Hearing difficulties - If you're deaf or have other hearing difficulties, the multiple choice part and the introduction to the hazard perception part of the test can be delivered in British Sign Language (BSL) by an on-screen signer.

A BSL interpreter or lip speaker can be provided if requested at the time of booking. If you have any other requirements please call the Special Needs section on the normal booking number (see p12).

Physical disabilities - If you have a physical disability which would make it difficult for you to use a mouse button to respond to the clips in the hazard perception part of the test, we may be able to make special arrangements for you to use a different method if you let us know when you book your test.

Multiple choice questions

The first part of the theory test consists of 35 multiple choice questions. You select your answers for this part of the test by simply touching the screen. This 'touch screen' has been carefully designed to make it easy to use.

Before you start you'll be given the chance to work through a practice session for up to 15 minutes to get used to the system. Staff at the test centre will be available to help you if you have any difficulties.

The questions will cover a variety of topics relating to road safety, the environment and documentation. Only one question will appear on the screen at a time.

Most questions will ask you to mark one correct answer from four possible answers given. Some questions may ask for two or more correct answers from a selection, but this is shown clearly on the screen. If you try to move on without marking the correct number of answers you'll be reminded that more answers are needed.

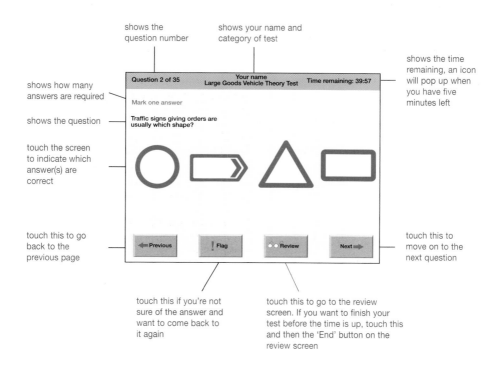

shows the question number

shows your name and category of test

shows the time remaining, an icon will pop up when you have five minutes left

shows how many answers are required

shows the question

touch the screen to indicate which answer(s) are correct

touch this to go back to the previous page

touch this to move on to the next question

touch this if you're not sure of the answer and want to come back to it again

touch this to go to the review screen. If you want to finish your test before the time is up, touch this and then the 'End' button on the review screen

15

To answer, you need to touch the box alongside the answer or answers you think are correct. If you change your mind and don't want that answer to be selected, touch it again. You can then choose another answer.

Take your time and read the questions carefully. You're given 40 minutes for this part of the test, so relax and don't rush. Extra time can be provided if you have special needs and you let us know when you book your test.

Some questions will take longer to answer than others, but there are no trick questions. The time remaining is displayed on screen.

You'll be able to move backwards and forwards through the questions and you can also 'flag' questions that you'd like to look at again. It's easy to change your answer if you want to.

Try to answer all the questions. If you're well prepared you shouldn't find them difficult.

Before you finish this part of the test, if you have time, you can use the 'review' feature to check your answers. If you want to finish your test before the full time, touch the 'review' button and then the 'end' button on the review screen. When you touch the review button you will see the following screen.

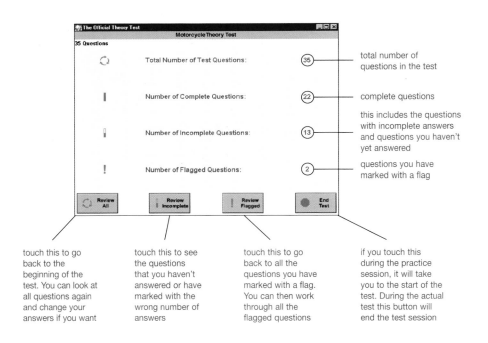

total number of questions in the test

complete questions

this includes the questions with incomplete answers and questions you haven't yet answered

questions you have marked with a flag

touch this to go back to the beginning of the test. You can look at all questions again and change your answers if you want

touch this to see the questions that you haven't answered or have marked with the wrong number of answers

touch this to go back to all the questions you have marked with a flag. You can then work through all the flagged questions

if you touch this during the practice session, it will take you to the start of the test. During the actual test this button will end the test session

16

Hazard perception

After you've finished the multiple choice part, there is a break of up to three minutes before you start the hazard perception part of the test. You cannot leave your seat during this break. This part of the test will consist of a series of film clips, shown from a rider's point of view.

Before you start this part of the test you'll be shown a short tutorial video that explains how the test works and gives you a chance to see a sample film clip. This will help you to understand what you need to do. You can run this video a second time if you want to.

During the hazard perception part of the test you'll be shown 14 film clips. Each clip contains one or more developing hazards. You should respond by pressing the mouse button **as soon as you see** a hazard

developing that may result in you, the rider, having to take some action, such as changing speed or direction. The earlier you notice a developing hazard and make a response, the higher your score. There are 15 scoreable hazards in total.

Your response will not cause the scene in the video to change in any way. However, a red flag will appear on the bottom of the screen to show that your response has been noted.

Before each clip starts, there will be a 10-second pause to allow you to see the new road situation.

The hazard perception part of the test lasts about 20 minutes. For this part of the test there is no extra time available, and you can't repeat any of the clips - you don't get a second chance to see a hazard when you're riding on the road.

Trial questions

We're constantly checking the questions and clips to help us decide whether to use them in future tests. After the hazard perception part of the test you may be asked to try a few trial questions and clips. You don't have to do these if you don't want to, and if you answer them they won't count towards your final score.

Customer satisfaction survey

We want to ensure our customers are completely satisfied with the service they receive. At the end of your test you'll be shown some questions designed to give us information about you and how happy you are with the service you received from us.

Your answers will be treated in the strictest confidence. They are not part of the test and they won't be used in determining your final score or for marketing purposes. You'll be asked if you want to complete the survey, there's no obligation to do so.

The result

You should receive your result at the test centre within 10 minutes of completing the test.

You'll be given a score for each part of the test (the multiple choice part and the hazard perception part). You'll need to pass both parts to pass the theory test. If you fail one of the parts you'll have to take the whole test again.

What's the pass mark?

To pass the multiple choice part of the theory test you must answer at least 30 questions correctly. For learner car drivers and bike riders the pass mark for the hazard perception part is 44 out of 75.

If I don't pass, when can I take the test again?

If you fail your test, you've shown that you're not fully prepared. You'll have to wait at least three clear working days before you take the theory test again.

Good preparation will save you time and money.

Why do I have to retake both parts of the test if I only fail one?

It's really only one test. The theory test has always included questions relating to hazard awareness – the second part simply tests the same skills in a more effective way. The two parts are only presented separately in the theory test because different scoring methods are used.

After the theory test

When you pass your theory test you'll be given a certificate. Keep this carefully, you'll need it when you go for your practical test.

This certificate has a life of two years from the date of your test. This means that you have to take and pass the practical test within this two-year period. If you don't, you'll have to take and pass the theory test again before you can book your practical test.

Your practical test

Your next step is to prepare for and take a practical test. To help you prepare for this *The Official DSA Guide to Learning to Ride* has details of the practical test. As well as giving the full test syllabus, it explains the skills you should show and faults you should avoid when taking your test.

Please refer to the back of this book for information about other publications which will help you prepare for your practical test.

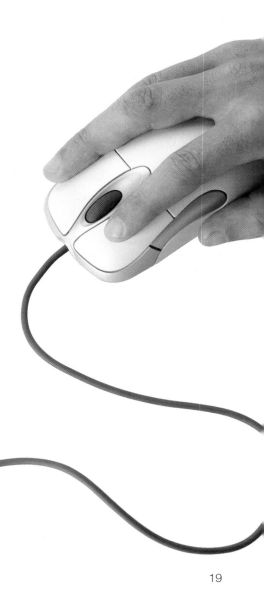

If this is your first full licence and you get six penalty points in the first two years of riding, your licence will be revoked and you'll have to go right back to the beginning and retake your theory test.
Don't risk it, ride safe

Using the question and answer sections

The following part of the book contains all the questions that could be used in the multiple choice part of the theory test.

For easy reference, and to help you to study, the questions have been divided into topics and put into sections. Although this isn't how you'll find them in your test, it's helpful if you want to refer to particular subjects.

The questions are in the left-hand column with a choice of answers beneath. On the right-hand side of the page you'll find the correct answers and a brief explanation of why they are correct. There will also be some advice on correct riding procedures.

Don't just learn the answers. It's important that you know why the answers are correct. This will help you with your practical skills and prepare you to become a safe and confident rider.

Taking exams or tests is rarely a pleasant experience, but you can make your test less stressful by being confident that you have the knowledge to answer the questions correctly.

Make studying more enjoyable by involving friends and relatives. Take part in a question and answer game. Test those 'experienced' riders who've had their licence a while: they might learn something too!

Best wishes for your test. Once you're on the road, don't forget everything you've learnt

Some of the questions in this book will not be used in Northern Ireland theory tests. These questions are marked as follows: *NI EXEMPT*

section one
ALERTNESS

This section covers:

- observation
- anticipation
- concentration
- awareness
- distraction
- boredom

1.1   *Mark **one** answer*

You are about to turn right. What should you do just before you turn?

⊙ Give the correct signal

⊙ Take a 'lifesaver' glance over your shoulder

⊙ Select the correct gear

⊙ Get in position ready for the turn

⊙ **Take a 'lifesaver' glance over your shoulder**

When you are turning right, plan your approach to the junction. Signal and select the correct gear in good time.

Just before you turn, take a 'lifesaver' glance for a final check behind and to the side of you.

1.2   *Mark **one** answer*

What is the 'lifesaver' when riding a motorcycle?

⊙ A certificate every motorcyclist must have

⊙ A final, rearward glance before changing direction

⊙ A part of the motorcycle tool kit

⊙ A mirror fitted to check blind spots

⊙ **A final, rearward glance before changing direction**

This action makes you aware of what's happening behind and alongside you. The 'lifesaver' glance should be timed so that you still have time to react if it isn't safe to perform the manoeuvre.

1.3   *Mark **one** answer*

You see road signs showing a sharp bend ahead. What should you do?

⊙ Continue at the same speed

⊙ Slow down as you go around the bend

⊙ Slow down as you come out of the bend

⊙ Slow down before the bend

⊙ **Slow down before the bend**

Always look for any advance warning of hazards, such as road signs and hazard warning lines. Use this information to plan ahead and to help you avoid the need for late, harsh braking.

Your motorcycle should be upright and moving in a straight line when you brake. This will help you to keep maximum control when dealing with the hazard.

You are riding at night and are dazzled by the headlights of an oncoming car. You should

- ⊙ slow down or stop
- ⊙ close your eyes
- ⊙ flash your headlight
- ⊙ turn your head away

⊙ **slow down or stop**

If you are dazzled by lights when riding, slow down or stop until your eyes have adjusted.

Taking a hand off the handlebars to adjust your visor while riding could lead to loss of control. A dirty or scratched visor could cause dazzle and impair vision further.

When riding, your shoulders obstruct the view in your mirrors. To overcome this you should

- ⊙ indicate earlier than normal
- ⊙ fit smaller mirrors
- ⊙ extend the mirror arms
- ⊙ brake earlier than normal

⊙ **extend the mirror arms**

It's essential that you have a clear view all around. Check that your mirrors are correctly adjusted before you move off.

On a motorcycle you should only use a mobile telephone when you

- ⊙ have a pillion passenger to help
- ⊙ have parked in a safe place
- ⊙ have a motorcycle with automatic gears
- ⊙ are travelling on a quiet road

⊙ **have parked in a safe place**

It's important that you're in full control of your machine at all times. If you need to use a mobile phone you must stop at a safe place before you do so. Even using a hands-free kit would be a distraction for you. Don't take the risk.

1.7 — *Mark **one** answer*

You are riding along a motorway. You see an accident on the other side of the road. Your lane is clear. You should

- assist the emergency services
- stop, and cross the road to help
- concentrate on what is happening ahead
- place a warning triangle in the road

concentrate on what is happening ahead

Always concentrate on the road ahead. If you become distracted you may not see a hazard ahead until it's too late to avoid it.

1.8 — *Mark **one** answer*

You are riding at night. You have your headlight on main beam. Another vehicle is overtaking you. When should you dip your headlight?

- When the other vehicle signals to overtake
- As soon as the other vehicle moves out to overtake
- As soon as the other vehicle passes you
- After the other vehicle pulls in front of you

As soon as the other vehicle passes you

At night you should dip your headlight to avoid dazzling oncoming drivers or those ahead of you. If you're being overtaken, dip your headlight as the other vehicle comes past.

When you switch to dipped beam your view of the road ahead will be reduced, so look ahead for hazards on your side of the road before you do so.

1.9 — *Mark **one** answer*

To move off safely from a parked position you should

- signal if other drivers will need to slow down
- leave your motorcycle on its stand until the road is clear
- give an arm signal as well as using your indicators
- look over your shoulder for a final check

look over your shoulder for a final check

Before you move off from the side of the road on a motorcycle you must take a final look around over your shoulder. There may be another road user who is not visible in your mirrors.

*Mark **one** answer*

Riding a motorcycle when you are cold could cause you to

- be more alert
- be more relaxed
- react more quickly
- lose concentration

⊙ **lose concentration**

It can be difficult to keep warm when riding a motorcycle. Although it isn't cheap, proper motorcycle clothing will keep you warm and is essential in cold weather. It also offers safety benefits in the event of an accident.

*Mark **one** answer*

It is vital to check the 'blind area' before

- changing gear
- giving signals
- slowing down
- changing lanes

⊙ **changing lanes**

Other vehicles may be hidden in the blind spots that are not covered by your mirrors. Always make sure it is safe before changing lanes by taking a 'lifesaver' check.

*Mark **one** answer*

You should always check the 'blind areas' before

- moving off
- slowing down
- changing gear
- giving a signal

⊙ **moving off**

These are the areas behind and to either side of you which are not covered by your mirrors. You should always check these areas before moving off or changing direction.

*Mark **one** answer*

The 'blind area' should be checked before

- giving a signal
- applying the brakes
- changing direction
- giving an arm signal

⊙ **changing direction**

The areas not covered by your mirrors are called blind spots. They should always be checked before changing direction. This check is so important that it is called the 'lifesaver'.

1.14
*Mark **one** answer*

You are riding at night and are dazzled by the lights of an approaching vehicle. What should you do?

⊙ Switch off your headlight

⊙ Switch to main beam

⊙ Slow down and stop

⊙ Flash your headlight

⊙ **Slow down and stop**

If your view of the road ahead is restricted because you are being dazzled by approaching headlights, slow down and if you need to, pull over and stop.

1.15
*Mark **one** answer*

Why can it be helpful to have mirrors fitted on each side of your motorcycle ?

⊙ To judge the gap when filtering in traffic

⊙ To give protection when riding in poor weather

⊙ To make your motorcycle appear larger to other drivers

⊙ To give you the best view of the road behind

⊙ **To give you the best view of the road behind**

When riding on the road you need to know as much about following traffic as you can. A mirror fitted on each side of your motorcycle will help give you the best view of the road behind.

1.16
*Mark **one** answer*

In motorcycling, the term 'lifesaver' refers to

⊙ a final rearward glance

⊙ an approved safety helmet

⊙ a reflective jacket

⊙ the two-second rule

⊙ **a final rearward glance**

Mirrors on motorcycles don't always give a clear view behind. There will be times when you need to look round to see the full picture.

You are about to emerge from a junction. Your pillion passenger tells you it's clear. When should you rely on their judgement?

- ⊙ Never, you should always look for yourself
- ⊙ When the roads are very busy
- ⊙ When the roads are very quiet
- ⊙ Only when they are a qualified rider

⊙ **Never, you should always look for yourself**

Your passenger may

- be inexperienced in judging traffic situations
- have a poor view
- not have seen a potential hazard.

You are responsible for your own safety and that of any passengers you carry. You should always make your own checks to be sure it is safe to pull out.

You are about to emerge from a junction. Your pillion passenger tells you it's safe to go. What should you do?

- ⊙ Go, if you are sure they can see clearly
- ⊙ Check for yourself before pulling out
- ⊙ Take their advice and ride on
- ⊙ Ask them to check again before you go

⊙ **Check for yourself before pulling out**

You must rely on your own judgement when making decisions. Only you know your own capabilities and the performance of your machine.

What must you do before stopping normally?

- ⊙ Put both feet down
- ⊙ Select first gear
- ⊙ Use your mirrors
- ⊙ Move into neutral

⊙ **Use your mirrors**

Check your mirrors before slowing down or stopping as there could be vehicles close behind you. If necessary, look behind before stopping.

1.20
*Mark **two** answers*

You want to change lanes in busy, moving traffic. Why could looking over your shoulder help?

- ⊙ Mirrors may not cover blind spots
- ⊙ To avoid having to give a signal
- ⊙ So traffic ahead will make room for you
- ⊙ So your balance will not be affected
- ⊙ Drivers behind you would be warned

⊙ **Mirrors may not cover blind spots**

⊙ **Drivers behind you would be warned**

Before you change lanes you need to know that there's a safe gap to move into. Looking over your shoulder

- allows you to see into the area not covered by the mirrors, where another vehicle could be hidden from your view
- warns following motorists that you want to change lanes.

1.21
*Mark **one** answer*

You have been waiting for some time to make a right turn into a side road. What should you do just before you make the turn?

- ⊙ Move close to the kerb
- ⊙ Select a higher gear
- ⊙ Make a 'lifesaver' check
- ⊙ Wave to the oncoming traffic

⊙ **Make a 'lifesaver' check**

Remember your 'lifesaver' glance before you start to turn. If you've been waiting for some time and a queue has built up behind you, a vehicle further back may try to overtake.

It is especially important to look out for other motorcycles in this situation which may be approaching at speed.

1.22
*Mark **one** answer*

You are turning right onto a dual carriageway. What should you do before emerging?

- ⊙ Stop, and then select a very low gear
- ⊙ Position in the left gutter of the side road
- ⊙ Check that the central reservation is wide enough
- ⊙ Check there is enough room for vehicles behind you

⊙ **Check that the central reservation is wide enough**

Before emerging right onto a dual carriageway make sure that the central reservation is wide enough to protect your vehicle. If it's not, you should treat it as one road and check that it's clear in both directions before pulling out. Otherwise, you could obstruct part of the carriageway and cause a hazard, both for yourself and other road users.

As you approach this bridge you should

- ⊙ move into the middle of the road to get a better view
- ⊙ slow down
- ⊙ get over the bridge as quickly as possible
- ⊙ consider using your horn
- ⊙ find another route
- ⊙ beware of pedestrians

- ⊙ **slow down**

- ⊙ **consider using your horn**

- ⊙ **beware of pedestrians**

This sign gives you a warning. The brow of the hill prevents you seeing oncoming traffic so you must be cautious.

The bridge is narrow and there may not be enough room for you to pass an oncoming vehicle at this point.

There is no footpath, so pedestrians may be walking in the road.

Consider the hidden hazards and be ready to react if necessary.

Before you make a U-turn in the road, you should

- ⊙ give an arm signal as well as using your indicators
- ⊙ signal so that other drivers can slow down for you
- ⊙ look over your shoulder for a final check
- ⊙ select a higher gear than normal

- ⊙ **look over your shoulder for a final check**

If you want to make a U-turn, slow down and ensure that the road is clear in both directions. Make sure that the road is wide enough to carry out the manoeuvre safely.

In which of these situations should you avoid overtaking?

- ⊙ Just after a bend
- ⊙ In a one-way street
- ⊙ On a 30 mph road
- ⊙ Approaching a dip in the road

- ⊙ **Approaching a dip in the road**

As you begin to think about overtaking, ask yourself if it's really necessary. If you can't see well ahead stay back and wait for a safer place to pull out.

1.26

When riding a different motorcycle
you should

⊙ ask someone to ride with you for the
first time

⊙ ride as soon as possible as all controls
and switches are the same

⊙ leave your gloves behind so switches
can be operated more easily

⊙ be sure you know where all controls
and switches are

⊙ **be sure you know where all
controls and switches are**

Before you ride any motorcycle make
sure you're familiar with the layout of all
the controls and switches. While control
layouts are generally similar, there may
be differences in their feel and method
of operation.

1.27

This road marking warns

⊙ drivers to use the hard shoulder

⊙ overtaking drivers there is a bend to
the left

⊙ overtaking drivers to move back to
the left

⊙ drivers that it is safe to overtake

⊙ **overtaking drivers to move
back to the left**

You should plan your overtaking to take
into account any hazards ahead. In this
picture the marking indicates that you are
approaching a junction. You will not have
time to overtake and move back into the
left safely.

1.28

Which of the following should you do
before stopping?

⊙ Sound the horn

⊙ Use the mirrors

⊙ Select a higher gear

⊙ Flash your headlights

⊙ **Use the mirrors**

Before pulling up check the mirrors to see
what is happening behind you. Also assess
what is ahead and make sure you give the
correct signal if it helps other road users.

Your mobile phone rings while you are travelling. You should

- ⊙ stop immediately
- ⊙ answer it immediately
- ⊙ pull up in a suitable place
- ⊙ pull up at the nearest kerb

⊙ **pull up in a suitable place**

Always use the safe option. It is not worth taking the risk of endangering other road users. If you need to use a mobile phone, make sure that you pull up in a place that does not obstruct other road users. Using a message service will enable you to complete your journey without interruptions and you can catch up with your calls when you take your rest breaks.

Why are these yellow lines painted across the road?

- ⊙ To help you choose the correct lane
- ⊙ To help you keep the correct separation distance
- ⊙ To make you aware of your speed
- ⊙ To tell you the distance to the roundabout

⊙ **To make you aware of your speed**

These lines are often found on the approach to a roundabout or a dangerous junction. They give you extra warning to adjust your speed. Look well ahead and do this in good time.

You are approaching traffic lights that have been on green for some time. You should

- ⊙ accelerate hard
- ⊙ maintain your speed
- ⊙ be ready to stop
- ⊙ brake hard

⊙ **be ready to stop**

The longer traffic lights have been on green, the greater the chance of them changing. Always allow for this on approach and be prepared to stop.

1.32
Mark **one** answer

When following a large vehicle you should keep well back because this

- ◉ allows you to corner more quickly
- ◉ helps the large vehicle to stop more easily
- ◉ allows the driver to see you in the mirrors
- ◉ helps you to keep out of the wind

◉ **allows the driver to see you in the mirrors**

If you're following a large vehicle but are so close to it that you can't see the exterior mirrors, the driver can't see you.

Keeping well back will also allow you to see the road ahead by looking past either side of the large vehicle.

1.33
Mark **one** answer

When you see a hazard ahead you should use the mirrors. Why is this?

- ◉ Because you will need to accelerate out of danger
- ◉ To assess how your actions will affect following traffic
- ◉ Because you will need to brake sharply to a stop
- ◉ To check what is happening on the road ahead

◉ **To assess how your actions will affect following traffic**

You should be constantly scanning the road for clues about what is going to happen next. Check your mirrors regularly, particularly as soon as you spot a hazard. What is happening behind may affect your response to hazards ahead.

1.34
Mark **one** answer

You are waiting to turn right at the end of a road. Your view is obstructed by parked vehicles. What should you do?

- ◉ Stop and then move forward slowly and carefully for a proper view
- ◉ Move quickly to where you can see so you only block traffic from one direction
- ◉ Wait for a pedestrian to let you know when it is safe for you to emerge
- ◉ Turn your vehicle around immediately and find another junction to use

◉ **Stop and then move forward slowly and carefully for a proper view**

At junctions your view is often restricted by buildings, trees or parked cars. You need to be able to see in order to judge a safe gap. Edge forward slowly and keep looking all the time. Don't cause other road users to change speed or direction as you emerge.

section two
ATTITUDE

This section covers:

- consideration
- close following
- courtesy
- priority

2.1
*Mark **one** answer*

You are riding towards a zebra crossing. Pedestrians are waiting to cross. You should

⊙ give way to the elderly and infirm only

⊙ slow down and prepare to stop

⊙ use your headlight to indicate they can cross

⊙ wave at them to cross the road

⊙ **slow down and prepare to stop**

Look for people waiting to cross and be ready to slow down or stop. Some pedestrians may be hesitant. Children can be unpredictable and may hesitate or run out unexpectedly.

2.2
*Mark **one** answer*

You are riding a motorcycle and following a large vehicle at 40 mph. You should position yourself

⊙ close behind to make it easier to overtake the vehicle

⊙ to the left of the road to make it easier to be seen

⊙ close behind the vehicle to keep out of the wind

⊙ well back so that you can see past the vehicle

⊙ **well back so that you can see past the vehicle**

You need to be able to see well down the road and be ready for any hazards. Staying too close to the vehicle will reduce your view of the road ahead and the driver of the vehicle in front may not be able to see you either.

Without a safe separation gap you do not have the time and space necessary to react to any hazards.

2.3
*Mark **one** answer*

You are riding on a country road. Two horses with riders are in the distance. You should

⊙ continue at your normal speed

⊙ change down the gears quickly

⊙ slow down and be ready to stop

⊙ flash your headlight to warn them

⊙ **slow down and be ready to stop**

Animals are easily frightened by moving motor vehicles. If you're approaching horses keep your speed down and watch to see if the rider has any difficulty keeping control. Always be ready to stop if necessary.

You are approaching a red light at a puffin crossing. Pedestrians are on the crossing. The red light will stay on until

- ⊙ you start to edge forward on to the crossing
- ⊙ the pedestrians have reached a safe position
- ⊙ the pedestrians are clear of the front of your motorcycle
- ⊙ a driver from the opposite direction reaches the crossing

⊙ **the pedestrians have reached a safe position**

The electronic device will automatically detect when the pedestrians have reached a safe position. Don't proceed until the green light shows it is safe to do so.

You are riding a slow-moving scooter on a narrow winding road. You should

- ⊙ keep well out to stop vehicles overtaking dangerously
- ⊙ wave vehicles behind you to pass, if you think they can overtake quickly
- ⊙ pull in safely when you can, to let vehicles behind you overtake
- ⊙ give a left signal when it is safe for vehicles to overtake you

⊙ **pull in safely when you can, to let vehicles behind you overtake**

Try not to hold up a queue of traffic. This might lead to other road users becoming impatient and attempting dangerous manoeuvres.

If you're riding a slow-moving scooter or small motorcycle on a narrow road and a queue of traffic has built up behind you, look out for a safe place to pull in.

At a pelican crossing the flashing amber light means you MUST

- ⊙ stop and wait for the green light
- ⊙ stop and wait for the red light
- ⊙ give way to pedestrians waiting to cross
- ⊙ give way to pedestrians already on the crossing

⊙ **give way to pedestrians already on the crossing**

Pelican crossings are signal-controlled crossings operated by pedestrians. Push-button controls change the signals. Pelican crossings have no red-and-amber stage before green. Instead, they have a flashing amber light, which means you must give way to pedestrians already on the crossing, but if it is clear, you may continue.

2.7
*Mark **two** answers*

When riding a motorcycle your normal road position should allow

- other vehicles to overtake on your left
- the driver ahead to see you in their mirrors
- you to prevent vehicles behind from overtaking
- you to be seen by traffic that is emerging from junctions ahead
- you to ride within half a metre (1 foot 8 ins) of the kerb

- **the driver ahead to see you in their mirrors**

- **you to be seen by traffic that is emerging from junctions ahead**

Aim to ride in the middle of your lane. Avoid riding in the gutter or in the centre of the road, where you might obstruct overtaking traffic or put yourself in danger from oncoming traffic. Riding in this position could also encourage other traffic to overtake you on the left.

2.8
*Mark **one** answer*

You should never wave people across at pedestrian crossings because

- there may be another vehicle coming
- they may not be looking
- it is safer for you to carry on
- they may not be ready to cross

- **there may be another vehicle coming**

If people are waiting to use a pedestrian crossing, slow down and be prepared to stop. Don't wave them across the road since another driver may not

- have seen them
- have seen your signal
- be able to stop safely.

2.9
*Mark **one** answer*

'Tailgating' means

- using the rear door of a hatchback car
- reversing into a parking space
- following another vehicle too closely
- driving with rear fog lights on

- **following another vehicle too closely**

'Tailgating' is used to describe this dangerous practice, often seen in fast-moving traffic and on motorways. Following the vehicle in front too closely is dangerous because it

- restricts your view of the road ahead
- leaves you no safety margin if the vehicle in front slows down or stops suddenly.

Following this vehicle too closely is unwise because

- your brakes will overheat
- your view ahead is increased
- your engine will overheat
- your view ahead is reduced

⊙ **your view ahead is reduced**

Staying back will increase your view of the road ahead. This will help you to see any hazards that might occur and allow you more time to react.

You are following a vehicle on a wet road. You should leave a time gap of at least

- one second
- two seconds
- three seconds
- four seconds

⊙ **four seconds**

Wet roads will reduce your tyres' grip on the road. The safe separation gap of at least two seconds in dry conditions should be doubled in wet weather.

A long, heavily-laden lorry is taking a long time to overtake you. What should you do?

- Speed up
- Slow down
- Hold your speed
- Change direction

⊙ **Slow down**

A long lorry with a heavy load will need more time to pass you than a car, especially on an uphill stretch of road. Slow down and allow the lorry to pass.

2.13 *Mark **three** answers*

Which of the following vehicles will use blue flashing beacons?

⊙ Motorway maintenance

⊙ Bomb disposal

⊙ Blood transfusion

⊙ Police patrol

⊙ Breakdown recovery

⊙ **Bomb disposal**

⊙ **Blood transfusion**

⊙ **Police patrol**

When you see emergency vehicles with blue flashing beacons move out of the way as soon as it is safe to do so.

2.14 *Mark **three** answers*

Which THREE of these emergency services might have blue flashing beacons?

⊙ Coastguard

⊙ Bomb disposal

⊙ Gritting lorries

⊙ Animal ambulances

⊙ Mountain rescue

⊙ Doctors' cars

⊙ **Coastguard**

⊙ **Bomb disposal**

⊙ **Mountain rescue**

When attending an emergency these vehicles will be travelling at speed. You should help their progress by pulling over and allowing them to pass. Do so safely. Don't stop suddenly or in a dangerous position.

2.15 *Mark **one** answer*

When being followed by an ambulance showing a flashing blue beacon you should

⊙ pull over as soon as safely possible to let it pass

⊙ accelerate hard to get away from it

⊙ maintain your speed and course

⊙ brake harshly and immediately stop in the road

⊙ **pull over as soon as safely possible to let it pass**

Pull over in a place where the ambulance can pass safely. Check that there are no bollards or obstructions in the road that will prevent it from doing so.

2.16 — Mark **one** answer

What type of emergency vehicle is fitted with a green flashing beacon?

- ⊙ Fire engine
- ⊙ Road gritter
- ⊙ Ambulance
- ⊙ Doctor's car

⊙ **Doctor's car**

A green flashing beacon on a vehicle means the driver or passenger is a doctor on an emergency call. Give way to them if it's safe to do so. Be aware that the vehicle may be travelling quickly or may stop in a hurry.

2.17 — Mark **one** answer

A flashing green beacon on a vehicle means

- ⊙ police on non-urgent duties
- ⊙ doctor on an emergency call
- ⊙ road safety patrol operating
- ⊙ gritting in progress

⊙ **doctor on an emergency call**

If you see a vehicle with a flashing green beacon approaching, allow it to pass when you can do so safely. Be aware that someone's life could depend on the driver making good progress through traffic.

2.18 — Mark **one** answer

Diamond-shaped signs give instructions to

- ⊙ tram drivers
- ⊙ bus drivers
- ⊙ lorry drivers
- ⊙ taxi drivers

⊙ **tram drivers**

These signs only apply to trams. They are directed at tram drivers but you should know their meaning so that you're aware of the priorities and are able to anticipate the actions of the driver.

2.19
*Mark **one** answer*

On a road where trams operate, which of these vehicles will be most at risk from the tram rails?

⊙ Cars

⊙ Cycles

⊙ Buses

⊙ Lorries

⊙ **Cycles**

The narrow wheels of a bicycle can become stuck in the tram rails, causing the cyclist to stop suddenly, wobble or even lose balance altogether.

The tram lines are also slippery which could cause a cyclist to slide or fall off.

2.20
*Mark **one** answer*

What should you use your horn for?

⊙ To alert others to your presence

⊙ To allow you right of way

⊙ To greet other road users

⊙ To signal your annoyance

⊙ **To alert others to your presence**

Your horn must not be used between 11.30 pm and 7 am in a built-up area or when you are stationary, unless a moving vehicle poses a danger. Its function is to alert other road users to your presence.

2.21
*Mark **one** answer*

You are in a one-way street and want to turn right. You should position yourself

⊙ in the right-hand lane

⊙ in the left-hand lane

⊙ in either lane, depending on the traffic

⊙ just left of the centre line

⊙ **in the right-hand lane**

If you're travelling in a one-way street and wish to turn right you should take up a position in the right-hand lane. This will enable other road users not wishing to turn to proceed on the left. Indicate your intention and take up your position in good time.

You wish to turn right ahead. Why should you take up the correct position in good time?

- ⊙ To allow other drivers to pull out in front of you
- ⊙ To give a better view into the road that you're joining
- ⊙ To help other road users know what you intend to do
- ⊙ To allow drivers to pass you on the right

⊙ **To help other road users know what you intend to do**

If you wish to turn right into a side road take up your position in good time. Move to the centre of the road when it's safe to do so. This will allow vehicles to pass you on the left. Early planning will show other traffic what you intend to do.

At which type of crossing are cyclists allowed to ride across with pedestrians?

- ⊙ Toucan
- ⊙ Puffin
- ⊙ Pelican
- ⊙ Zebra

⊙ **Toucan**

A toucan crossing is designed to allow pedestrians and cyclists to cross at the same time. Look out for cyclists approaching the crossing at speed.

You are travelling at the legal speed limit. A vehicle comes up quickly behind, flashing its headlights. You should

- ⊙ accelerate to make a gap behind you
- ⊙ touch the brakes sharply to show your brake lights
- ⊙ maintain your speed to prevent the vehicle from overtaking
- ⊙ allow the vehicle to overtake

⊙ **allow the vehicle to overtake**

Don't enforce the speed limit by blocking another vehicle's progress. This will only lead to the other driver becoming more frustrated. Allow the other vehicle to pass when you can do so safely.

2.25 *Mark **one** answer*

You should ONLY flash your headlights to other road users

⊙ to show that you are giving way

⊙ to show that you are about to turn

⊙ to tell them that you have right of way

⊙ to let them know that you are there

⊙ **to let them know that you are there**

You should only flash your headlights to warn others of your presence. Don't use them to

• greet others

• show impatience

• give up your priority.

Other road users could misunderstand your signal.

2.26 *Mark **one** answer*

You are approaching unmarked crossroads. How should you deal with this type of junction?

⊙ Accelerate and keep to the middle

⊙ Slow down and keep to the right

⊙ Accelerate looking to the left

⊙ Slow down and look both ways

⊙ **Slow down and look both ways**

Be extra-cautious, especially when your view is restricted by hedges, bushes, walls and large vehicles etc. In the summer months these junctions can become more difficult to deal with when growing foliage may obscure your view.

2.27 *Mark **one** answer*

You are approaching a pelican crossing. The amber light is flashing. You must

⊙ give way to pedestrians who are crossing

⊙ encourage pedestrians to cross

⊙ not move until the green light appears

⊙ stop even if the crossing is clear

⊙ **give way to pedestrians who are crossing**

While the pedestrians are crossing don't encourage them to cross by waving or flashing your headlights: other road users may misunderstand your signal.

Don't harass them by creeping forward or revving your engine.

2.28

*Mark **one** answer*

The conditions are good and dry.
You could use the 'two-second rule'

⊙ before restarting the engine after it has stalled

⊙ to keep a safe gap from the vehicle in front

⊙ before using the 'Mirror-Signal-Manoeuvre' routine

⊙ when emerging on wet roads

⊙ **to keep a safe gap from the vehicle in front**

To measure this, choose a fixed reference point such as a bridge, sign or tree. When the vehicle ahead passes the object, say to yourself 'Only a fool breaks the two-second rule.' If you reach the object before you finish saying this, you're TOO CLOSE.

2.29

*Mark **one** answer*

At a puffin crossing, which colour follows the green signal?

⊙ Steady red

⊙ Flashing amber

⊙ Steady amber

⊙ Flashing green

⊙ **Steady amber**

Puffin crossings have infra-red sensors which detect when pedestrians are crossing and hold the red traffic signal until the crossing is clear. The use of a sensor means there is no flashing amber phase as there is with a pelican crossing.

2.30

*Mark **one** answer*

You are in a line of traffic. The driver behind you is following very closely. What action should you take?

⊙ Ignore the following driver and continue to travel within the speed limit

⊙ Slow down, gradually increasing the gap between you and the vehicle in front

⊙ Signal left and wave the following driver past

⊙ Move over to a position just left of the centre line of the road

⊙ **Slow down, gradually increasing the gap between you and the vehicle in front**

It can be worrying to see that the car behind is following you too closely. Give yourself a greater safety margin by easing back from the vehicle in front.

2.31   *Mark **one** answer*

A vehicle has a flashing green beacon. What does this mean?

⊙ A doctor is answering an emergency call

⊙ The vehicle is slow-moving

⊙ It is a motorway police patrol vehicle

⊙ The vehicle is carrying hazardous chemicals

⊙ **A doctor is answering an emergency call**

A doctor attending an emergency may show a green flashing beacon on their vehicle. Give way to them when you can do so safely as they will need to reach their destination quickly. Be aware that they might pull over suddenly.

2.32   *Mark **one** answer*

A bus has stopped at a bus stop ahead of you. Its right-hand indicator is flashing. You should

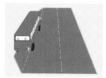

⊙ flash your headlights and slow down

⊙ slow down and give way if it is safe to do so

⊙ sound your horn and keep going

⊙ slow down and then sound your horn

⊙ **slow down and give way if it is safe to do so**

Give way to buses whenever you can do so safely, especially when they signal to pull away from bus stops. Look out for people leaving the bus and crossing the road.

section three
SAFETY AND YOUR MOTORCYCLE

This section covers:

- fault detection
- defects
- safety equipment
- emissions
- noise

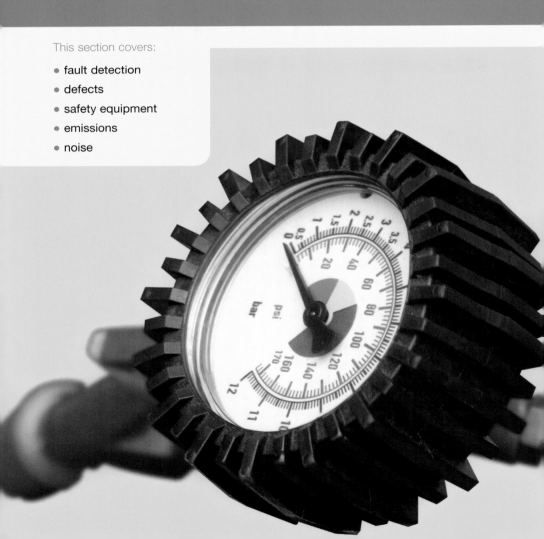

3.1

*Mark **one** answer*

A loose drive chain on a motorcycle could cause

- ⊙ the front wheel to wobble
- ⊙ the ignition to cut out
- ⊙ the brakes to fail
- ⊙ the rear wheel to lock

⊙ **the rear wheel to lock**

Drive chains are subject to wear and require frequent adjustment to maintain the correct tension. Allowing the drive chain to run dry will greatly increase the rate of wear, so it is important to keep it lubricated. If the chain becomes worn or slack it can jump off the sprocket and lock the rear wheel.

3.2

*Mark **one** answer*

What is the most important reason why you should keep your motorcycle regularly maintained?

- ⊙ To accelerate faster than other traffic
- ⊙ So the motorcycle can carry panniers
- ⊙ To keep the machine roadworthy
- ⊙ So the motorcycle can carry a passenger

⊙ **To keep the machine roadworthy**

Whenever you use any motorcycle on the road it must be in a roadworthy condition. Regular maintenance should identify any faults at an early stage and help prevent more serious problems.

3.3

*Mark **one** answer*

Your motorcycle has tubed tyres fitted as standard. When replacing a tyre you should

- ⊙ replace the tube if it is 6 months old
- ⊙ replace the tube if it has covered 6,000 miles
- ⊙ replace the tube only if replacing the rear tyre
- ⊙ replace the tube with each change of tyre

⊙ **replace the tube with each change of tyre**

It isn't worth taking risks to save money. Your life could depend on the condition of your motorcycle, so make sure it is properly maintained.

*Mark **one** answer*

How should you ride a motorcycle when NEW tyres have just been fitted?

⊙ Carefully, until the shiny surface is worn off

⊙ By braking hard especially into bends

⊙ Through normal riding with higher air pressures

⊙ By riding at faster than normal speeds

⊙ **Carefully, until the shiny surface is worn off**

New tyres have a shiny finish which needs to wear off before the tyre will give the best grip. Take extra care if the road surface is wet or slippery.

*Mark **one** answer*

When riding and wearing brightly coloured clothing you will

⊙ dazzle other motorists on the road

⊙ be seen more easily by other motorists

⊙ create a hazard by distracting other drivers

⊙ be able to ride on unlit roads at night with sidelights

⊙ **be seen more easily by other motorists**

For your own safety you need other road users to see you easily. Wearing brightly coloured or fluorescent clothing will help you to achieve this during daylight.

At night, wearing clothing that includes reflective material is the best way of helping others to see you.

*Mark **one** answer*

You are riding a motorcycle in very hot weather. You should

⊙ ride with your visor fully open

⊙ continue to wear protective clothing

⊙ wear trainers instead of boots

⊙ slacken your helmet strap

⊙ **continue to wear protective clothing**

Always wear your protective clothing, whatever the weather.

In very hot weather it's tempting to ride in light summer clothes. Don't take the risk. If you fall from your motorcycle you'll have no protection from the hard road surface.

3.7

*Mark **one** answer*

Why should you wear fluorescent clothing when riding in daylight?

- It reduces wind resistance
- It prevents injury if you come off the machine
- It helps other road users to see you
- It keeps you cool in hot weather

⊙ **It helps other road users to see you**

Motorcycles are smaller and therefore harder to see than other vehicles on the road, so you need to make yourself as visible as possible to other road users. Fluorescent clothing will help achieve this, reducing the risk of an accident. You must be visible from all sides.

3.8

*Mark **one** answer*

Why should riders wear reflective clothing?

- To protect them from the cold
- To protect them from direct sunlight
- To be seen better in daylight
- To be seen better at night

⊙ **To be seen better at night**

Fluorescent clothing will help others to see you during the day. At night, however, you should wear clothing that reflects the light. This allows other road users to see you more easily in their headlights. Ask your local motorcycle dealer about fluorescent and reflective clothing.

3.9

*Mark **one** answer*

Which of the following fairings would give you the best weather protection?

- Handlebar
- Sports
- Touring
- Windscreen

⊙ **Touring**

Fairings give protection to the hands, legs and feet. They also make riding more comfortable by keeping you out of the wind.

3.10 *Mark **one** answer*

Your visor becomes badly scratched. You should

- polish it with a fine abrasive
- replace it
- wash it in soapy water
- clean it with petrol

⊙ **replace it**

Your visor protects your eyes from wind, rain, insects and road dirt. It's therefore important to keep it clean and in good repair. A badly scratched visor might

- obscure your view
- cause dazzle from lights of oncoming vehicles.

3.11 *Mark **one** answer*

The legal minimum depth of tread for motorcycle tyres is

- 1 mm
- 1.6 mm
- 2.5 mm
- 4 mm

⊙ **1 mm**

The entire original tread should be continuous. Don't ride a motorcycle with worn tyres. Your tyres are your only contact with the road so it's very important that you ensure they are in good condition.

3.12 *Mark **three** answers*

Which of the following makes it easier for motorcyclists to be seen?

- Using a dipped headlight
- Wearing a fluorescent jacket
- Wearing a white helmet
- Wearing a grey helmet
- Wearing black leathers
- Using a tinted visor

⊙ **Using a dipped headlight**

⊙ **Wearing a fluorescent jacket**

⊙ **Wearing a white helmet**

Many road accidents involving motorcyclists occur because another road user didn't see them. Do what you can to make yourself more visible to others.

Be aware that you're vulnerable and ride defensively.

3.13

*Mark **one** answer*

Your oil light comes on as you are riding. You should

- go to a dealer for an oil change
- go to the nearest garage for their advice
- ride slowly for a few miles to see if the light goes out
- stop as quickly as possible and try to find the cause

- **stop as quickly as possible and try to find the cause**

If the oil pressure warning light comes on when the engine is running you may have a serious problem. Pull over as soon as you can, stop the engine and investigate the cause.

3.14

*Mark **two** answers*

Motorcycle tyres MUST

- have the same tread pattern
- be correctly inflated
- be the same size, front and rear
- both be the same make
- have sufficient tread depth

- **be correctly inflated**
- **have sufficient tread depth**

Your safety and that of others may depend on the condition of your tyres. Before you ride you must check they are correctly inflated and have sufficient tread depth.

Make sure these checks become part of a routine.

3.15

*Mark **one** answer*

Riding your motorcycle with a slack or worn drive chain may cause

- an engine misfire
- early tyre wear
- increased emissions
- a locked wheel

- **a locked wheel**

Check your drive chain regularly; adjust and lubricate it if necessary. It needs to be adjusted until the free play is as specified in the vehicle handbook.

51

You forget to switch the choke off after the engine warms up. This could

⊙ flatten the battery

⊙ reduce braking distances

⊙ use less fuel

⊙ cause much more engine wear

⊙ **cause much more engine wear**

Leaving the choke on for too long will cause unnecessary engine wear and waste fuel.

When riding your motorcycle a tyre bursts. What should you do?

⊙ Slow gently to a stop

⊙ Brake firmly to a stop

⊙ Change to a high gear

⊙ Lower the side stand

⊙ **Slow gently to a stop**

If a tyre bursts, close the throttle smoothly and slow gently to a stop, holding the handlebars firmly to help you keep a straight course.

A motorcycle engine that is properly maintained will

⊙ use much more fuel

⊙ have lower exhaust emissions

⊙ increase your insurance premiums

⊙ not need to have an MOT

⊙ **have lower exhaust emissions**

A badly maintained engine can emit more exhaust fumes than one that is correctly serviced. This can be damaging to the environment and also cost you more in fuel.

3.19   *Mark **one** answer*

What should you clean visors and goggles with?

⊙ Petrol

⊙ White spirit

⊙ Antifreeze

⊙ Soapy water

⊙ **Soapy water**

It is very important to keep your visor or goggles clean. Clean them using warm soapy water. Do not use solvents or petrol.

3.20   *Mark **one** answer*

You are riding on a quiet road. Your visor fogs up. What should you do?

⊙ Continue at a reduced speed

⊙ Stop as soon as possible and wipe it

⊙ Build up speed to increase air flow

⊙ Close the helmet air vents

⊙ **Stop as soon as possible and wipe it**

In cold and wet weather your visor may fog up. If this happens when you are riding choose somewhere safe to stop, and wipe it clean with a damp cloth. Special anti-fog products are available at motorcycle dealers.

3.21   *Mark **one** answer*

You are riding in hot weather. What is the safest type of footwear?

⊙ Sandals

⊙ Trainers

⊙ Shoes

⊙ Boots

⊙ **Boots**

It is important to wear good boots when you ride a motorcycle. Boots protect your feet and shins from knocks, and give some protection in an accident. They also help keep you warm and dry in cold or wet weather.

3.22
*Mark **one** answer*

Which of the following should not be used to fasten your safety helmet?

- ⊙ Double D ring fastening
- ⊙ Velcro tab
- ⊙ Quick release fastening
- ⊙ Bar and buckle

⊙ **Velcro tab**

Some helmet straps have a velcro tab in addition to the main fastening, which is intended to secure the strap so that it does not flap in the wind. It should NOT be used on its own to fasten the helmet.

3.23
*Mark **one** answer*

After warming up the engine you leave the choke ON. What will this do?

- ⊙ Discharge the battery
- ⊙ Use more fuel
- ⊙ Improve handling
- ⊙ Use less fuel

⊙ **Use more fuel**

Leaving the choke on for too long could waste fuel and cause unnecessary pollution.

3.24
*Mark **two** answers*

You want to ride your motorcycle in the dark. What could you wear to be seen more easily?

- ⊙ A black leather jacket
- ⊙ Reflective clothing
- ⊙ A white helmet
- ⊙ A red helmet

⊙ **Reflective clothing**

⊙ **A white helmet**

When riding in the dark you will be easier to see if you wear reflective clothing and a white helmet. A light-coloured helmet contrasts starkly with the surrounding darkness, while reflective clothing reflects the light from other vehicles and makes the rider much more visible.

3.25
*Mark **one** answer*

Your motorcycle has a catalytic converter. Its purpose is to reduce

⊙ exhaust noise

⊙ fuel consumption

⊙ exhaust emissions

⊙ engine noise

⊙ **exhaust emissions**

Catalytic converters reduce the toxic and polluting gases given out by the engine.

Never use leaded or lead replacement petrol in a vehicle with a catalytic converter, as even one tankful can permanently damage the system.

3.26
*Mark **one** answer*

Refitting which of the following will disturb your wheel alignment?

⊙ front wheel

⊙ front brakes

⊙ rear brakes

⊙ rear wheel

⊙ **rear wheel**

When refitting the rear wheel or adjusting the drive chain it is possible to disturb the wheel alignment. Incorrect alignment can cause instability, especially when cornering, and increased tyre wear.

3.27
*Mark **one** answer*

After refitting your rear wheel what should you check?

⊙ Your steering damper

⊙ Your side stand

⊙ Your wheel alignment

⊙ Your suspension preload

⊙ **Your wheel alignment**

After refitting the rear wheel or adjusting the drive chain you should check your wheel alignment. Incorrect alignment will result in excessive tyre wear and poor road holding.

3.28

Mark **one** answer

You are checking your direction indicators. How often per second must they flash?

- ⊙ Between 1 and 2 times
- ⊙ Between 3 and 4 times
- ⊙ Between 5 and 6 times
- ⊙ Between 7 and 8 times

⊙ **Between 1 and 2 times**

You should check that all your lights work properly before every journey. Make sure that any signals you give can be clearly seen.

If you're not sure whether your signals can be seen you can use arm signals as well to make your intentions clear. Only do this if you're going slowly.

3.29

Mark **one** answer

After adjusting the final drive chain what should you check?

- ⊙ The rear wheel alignment
- ⊙ The suspension adjustment
- ⊙ The rear shock absorber
- ⊙ The front suspension forks

⊙ **The rear wheel alignment**

Always check the rear wheel alignment after adjusting the chain tension. Marks on the chain adjuster may be provided to make this easy. Incorrect alignment can cause instability and increased tyre wear.

3.30

Mark **one** answer

Your steering feels wobbly. Which of these is a likely cause?

- ⊙ Tyre pressure is too high
- ⊙ Incorrectly adjusted brakes
- ⊙ Worn steering head bearings
- ⊙ A broken clutch cable

⊙ **Worn steering head bearings**

Worn bearings in the steering head can make your motorcycle very difficult to control. They should be checked for wear and correct adjustment.

3.31
*Mark **one** answer*

You see oil on your front forks. Should you be concerned about this?

- ⊙ No, unless the amount of oil increases
- ⊙ No, lubrication here is perfectly normal
- ⊙ Yes, it is illegal to ride with an oil leak
- ⊙ Yes, oil could drip onto your tyre

⊙ **Yes, oil could drip onto your tyre**

Oil leaking from your forks could get on to your tyre or brake disc. This could result in your tyre losing grip, or your brakes being less effective. A loss of front fork oil will also affect handling and stability.

3.32
*Mark **one** answer*

You have a faulty oil seal on a shock absorber. Why is this a serious problem?

- ⊙ It will cause excessive chain wear
- ⊙ Dripping oil could reduce the grip of your tyre
- ⊙ Your motorcycle will be harder to ride uphill
- ⊙ Your motorcycle will not accelerate so quickly

⊙ **Dripping oil could reduce the grip of your tyre**

Leaking oil could affect the grip of your tyres and also the effectiveness of your brakes. This could result in a loss of control, putting you and other road users in danger.

3.33
*Mark **one** answer*

Oil is leaking from your forks. Why should you NOT ride a motorcycle in this condition?

- ⊙ Your brakes could be affected by dripping oil
- ⊙ Your steering is likely to seize up
- ⊙ The forks will quickly begin to rust
- ⊙ The motorcycle will become too noisy

⊙ **Your brakes could be affected by dripping oil**

Oil dripping from forks and shock absorbers is dangerous if it gets onto brakes and tyres. Replace faulty oil seals immediately.

*Mark **one** answer*

You have adjusted your drive chain. If this is not done properly, what problem could it cause?

⊙ Inaccurate speedometer reading

⊙ Loss of braking power

⊙ Incorrect rear wheel alignment

⊙ Excessive fuel consumption

⊙ **Incorrect rear wheel alignment**

After carrying out drive chain adjustment, you should always check the rear wheel alignment. Many motorcycles have alignment guides stamped onto the frame to help you do this correctly.

3.35 *Mark **one** answer*

You have adjusted your drive chain. Why is it also important to check rear wheel alignment?

⊙ Your tyre may be more likely to puncture

⊙ Fuel consumption could be greatly increased

⊙ You may not be able to reach top speed

⊙ Your motorcycle could be unstable on bends

⊙ **Your motorcycle could be unstable on bends**

Rear wheel alignment can be disturbed by adjustments to the drive chain. It's very important to make sure that the wheel is still properly aligned after doing this.

3.36 *Mark **one** answer*

There is a cut in the sidewall of one of your tyres. What should you do about this?

⊙ Replace the tyre before riding the motorcycle

⊙ Check regularly to see if it gets any worse

⊙ Repair the puncture before riding the motorcycle

⊙ Reduce pressure in the tyre before you ride

⊙ **Replace the tyre before riding the motorcycle**

A cut in the sidewall can be very dangerous. The tyre is in danger of blowing out if you ride the motorcycle in this condition.

3.37   *Mark **one** answer*

You need to put air into your tyres. How would you find out the correct pressure to use?

⊙ It will be shown on the tyre wall

⊙ It will be stamped on the wheel

⊙ By checking the vehicle owner's manual

⊙ By checking the registration document

⊙ **By checking the vehicle owner's manual**

Tyre pressures should be checked regularly. Use your vehicle manual to find advice on the correct pressures to use.

3.38   *Mark **one** answer*

You can prevent a cable operated clutch from becoming stiff by keeping the cable

⊙ tight

⊙ dry

⊙ slack

⊙ oiled

⊙ **oiled**

Keeping the cable oiled will help it to move smoothly through its outer casing. This will extend the life of the cable and assist your control of the motorcycle.

3.39   *Mark **one** answer*

When adusting your chain it is important for the wheels to be aligned accurately. Incorrect wheel alignment can cause

⊙ a serious loss of power

⊙ reduced braking performance

⊙ increased tyre wear

⊙ reduced ground clearance

⊙ **increased tyre wear**

If a motorcycle's wheels are incorrectly aligned tyres may wear unevenly and the motorcycle can become unstable, especially when cornering.

What problem can incorrectly aligned wheels cause?

- ⊙ Faulty headlight adjustment
- ⊙ Reduced braking performance
- ⊙ Better ground clearance
- ⊙ Instability when cornering

⊙ **Instability when cornering**

Wheels should be aligned accurately after refitting your rear wheel. Incorrect wheel alignment can cause uneven tyre wear and poor handling.

Most motorcycles have wheel alignment guides stamped onto the swinging arm.

What is most likely to be affected by incorrect wheel alignment?

- ⊙ Braking performance
- ⊙ Stability
- ⊙ Acceleration
- ⊙ Suspension preload

⊙ **Stability**

It is important that your wheels are aligned accurately. It will be necessary to do this after removing your rear wheel or adjusting the chain.

Incorrect alignment can cause instability, especially when cornering. It can also increase tyre wear.

Why should you wear specialist motorcycle clothing when riding?

- ⊙ Because the law requires you to do so
- ⊙ Because it looks better than ordinary clothing
- ⊙ Because it gives best protection from the weather
- ⊙ Because it will reduce your insurance

⊙ **Because it gives best protection from the weather**

If you become cold and wet when riding, this can have a serious effect on your concentration and control of your motorcycle.

Proper riding gear can help shield you from the weather, as well as giving protection in the event of an accident.

3.43
*Mark **one** answer*

When leaving your motorcycle parked, you should always

⊙ remove the battery lead
⊙ pull it onto the kerb
⊙ use the steering lock
⊙ leave the parking light on.

⊙ **use the steering lock**

When leaving your motorcycle you should always use the steering lock. You should also consider using additional locking devices such as a U-lock, disc lock or chain. If possible fasten it to an immovable post or another motorcycle.

3.44
*Mark **one** answer*

You are parking your motorcycle. Chaining it to an immovable object will

⊙ be against the law
⊙ give extra security
⊙ be likely to cause damage
⊙ leave the motorcycle unstable

⊙ **give extra security**

Theft of motorcycles is a very common crime. If you can, secure your vehicle to a lamp post or other such object, to help reduce the chances of it being stolen.

3.45
*Mark **one** answer*

You are parking your motorcycle and sidecar on a hill. What is the best way to stop it rolling away?

⊙ Leave it in neutral
⊙ Put the rear wheel on the pavement
⊙ Leave it in a low gear
⊙ Park very close to another vehicle

⊙ **Leave it in a low gear**

To make sure a sidecar outfit doesn't roll away when parking you should leave it in a low gear, and wedge it against the kerb or place a block behind the wheel.

61

An engine cut-out switch should be used to

⊙ reduce speed in an emergency

⊙ prevent the motorcycle being stolen

⊙ stop the engine normally

⊙ stop the engine in an emergency

⊙ **stop the engine in an emergency**

If you are involved in an accident, using the engine cut-out switch will help to reduce any fire hazard.

You enter a road where there are road humps. What should you do?

⊙ Maintain a reduced speed throughout

⊙ Accelerate quickly between each one

⊙ Always keep to the maximum legal speed

⊙ Ride slowly at school times only

⊙ **Maintain a reduced speed throughout**

The humps are there for a reason; to reduce the speed of the traffic. Don't accelerate harshly between them, as this means you will only have to brake sharply to negotiate the next hump.

Harsh braking and acceleration uses more fuel as well as causing wear and tear to your vehicle.

When should you especially check the engine oil level?

⊙ Before a long journey

⊙ When the engine is hot

⊙ Early in the morning

⊙ Every 6000 miles

⊙ **Before a long journey**

Also make checks on

• fuel

• water

• tyres.

3.49

Mark one answer

You service your own motorcycle. How should you get rid of the old engine oil?

⊙ Take it to a local authority site

⊙ Pour it down a drain

⊙ Tip it into a hole in the ground

⊙ Put it into your dustbin

⊙ **Take it to a local authority site**

Never pour the oil down any drain. The oil is highly pollutant and could harm wildlife. Confine it in a container and dispose of it properly at an authorised site.

3.50

Mark one answer

You are leaving your motorcycle parked on a road. When may you leave the engine running?

⊙ If you will be parked for less than five minutes

⊙ If the battery is flat

⊙ When in a 20 mph zone

⊙ Not on any occasion

⊙ **Not on any occasion**

When you leave your motorcycle parked on a road

• switch off the engine

• use the steering lock and remove the ignition key

• take any tank bags, panniers or loose luggage with you

• set the alarm if it has one

• use an additional lock and chain or cable lock.

3.51

Mark one answer

What safeguard could you take against fire risk to your motorcycle?

⊙ Keep water levels above maximum

⊙ Check out any strong smell of petrol

⊙ Avoid riding with a full tank of petrol

⊙ Use unleaded petrol

⊙ **Check out any strong smell of petrol**

The fuel in your motorcycle can be a dangerous fire hazard. Don't

• use a naked flame if you can smell fuel

• smoke when refuelling your vehicle.

3.52

Which of the following would NOT make you more visible in daylight?

- ⊙ Wearing a black helmet
- ⊙ Wearing a white helmet
- ⊙ Switching on your dipped headlight
- ⊙ Wearing a fluorescent jacket

⊙ **Wearing a black helmet**

Wearing bright or fluorescent clothes will help other road users to see you. Wearing a white or brightly coloured helmet can also make you more visible.

3.53

It would be illegal to ride with a helmet on when

- ⊙ the helmet is not fastened correctly
- ⊙ the helmet is more than four years old
- ⊙ you have borrowed someone else's helmet
- ⊙ the helmet does not have chin protection

⊙ **the helmet is not fastened correctly**

A motorcycle helmet that is incorrectly fastened is liable to come off in an accident and provides little or no protection. By law, whenever you ride on the road your helmet must be correctly fastened.

3.54

When may you have to increase the tyre pressures on your motorcycle?

- ⊙ When carrying a passenger
- ⊙ After a long journey
- ⊙ When carrying a load
- ⊙ When riding at high speeds
- ⊙ When riding in hot weather

⊙ **When carrying a passenger**

⊙ **When carrying a load**

⊙ **When riding at high speeds**

Read the manufacturer's handbook to see if they recommend increasing tyre pressures under certain conditions.

3.55 *Mark **two** answers*

Which TWO of these items on a motorcycle MUST be kept clean?

- Number plate
- Wheels
- Engine
- Fairing
- Headlight

- ⊙ **Number plate**
- ⊙ **Headlight**

Maintenance is a vital part of road safety. Lights, indicators, reflectors and number plates MUST be kept clean and clear.

3.56 *Mark **one** answer*

You should use the engine cut-out switch on your motorcycle to

- save wear and tear on the battery
- stop the engine for a short time
- stop the engine in an emergency
- save wear and tear on the ignition

- ⊙ **stop the engine in an emergency**

Only use the engine cut-out switch in an emergency. When stopping the engine normally, use the ignition switch. This will help you

- remember to take your keys with you when leaving your motorcycle
- prevent starting problems caused by the cut-out switch being left in the 'off' position.

3.57 *Mark **one** answer*

You have adjusted the tension on your drive chain. You should check the

- rear wheel alignment
- tyre pressures
- valve clearances
- sidelights

- ⊙ **rear wheel alignment**

Drive chains wear and need frequent adjustment and lubrication. If the drive chain is worn or slack it can jump off the sprocket and lock the rear wheel.

When you have adjusted the chain tension, you need to check the rear wheel alignment. Marks by the chain adjusters may be provided to make this easier.

A friend offers you a second-hand safety helmet for you to use. Why may this be a bad idea?

⊙ It may be damaged

⊙ You will be breaking the law

⊙ You will affect your insurance cover

⊙ It may be a full-face type

⊙ **It may be damaged**

A second hand helmet may look in good condition but it may have received damage that is not visible to the naked eye. A damaged helmet could be unreliable in an accident. Don't take the risk.

A properly serviced motorcycle will give

⊙ lower insurance premiums

⊙ a refund on your road tax

⊙ better fuel economy

⊙ cleaner exhaust emissions

⊙ **better fuel economy**

⊙ **cleaner exhaust emissions**

When you purchase your motorcycle, check at what intervals you should have it serviced. This can vary depending on model or manufacturer. Use the service manual and keep it up to date.

A loosely adjusted drive chain could

⊙ lock the rear wheel

⊙ make wheels wobble

⊙ cause a braking fault

⊙ affect your headlight beam

⊙ **lock the rear wheel**

A motorcycle chain will stretch as it wears and needs adjusting to keep the tension correct. In extreme cases a loose chain can jump the sprocket and become wedged in the rear wheel. This could cause serious loss of control and result in an accident.

3.61
*Mark **four** answers*

You are riding a motorcycle of more than 50 cc. Which FOUR would make a tyre illegal?

⊙ Tread less than 1.6 mm deep
⊙ Tread less than 1 mm deep
⊙ A large bulge in the wall
⊙ A recut tread
⊙ Exposed ply or cord
⊙ A stone wedged in the tread

⊙ **Tread less than 1 mm deep**

⊙ **A large bulge in the wall**

⊙ **A recut tread**

⊙ **Exposed ply or cord**

When checking tyres make sure there are no bulges or cuts in the side walls. Always buy your tyres from a reputable dealer to ensure quality and value for money.

3.62
*Mark **two** answers*

You should maintain cable operated brakes

⊙ by regular adjustment when necessary
⊙ at normal service times only
⊙ yearly, before taking the motorcycle for its MOT
⊙ by oiling cables and pivots regularly

⊙ **by regular adjustment when necessary**

⊙ **by oiling cables and pivots regularly**

Keeping your brakes in good working order is vital for road safety. With cable operated brakes the cables need

• adjustment because they will stretch with use

• lubrication to prevent friction and wear of the cables and pivots.

3.63
*Mark **one** answer*

Your motorcycle is NOT fitted with daytime running lights. When MUST you use a dipped headlight during the day?

⊙ On country roads
⊙ In poor visibility
⊙ Along narrow streets
⊙ When parking

⊙ **In poor visibility**

It's important that other road users can see you clearly at all times. It will help other road users to see you if you use a dipped headlight during the day. You MUST use a dipped headlight during the day if visibility is seriously reduced, that is, when you can't see for more than 100 metres (328 feet).

Tyre pressures should usually be increased on your motorcycle when

⊙ riding on a wet road

⊙ carrying a pillion passenger

⊙ travelling on an uneven surface

⊙ riding on twisty roads

⊙ **carrying a pillion passenger**

Sometimes manufacturers advise you to increase your tyre pressures for high-speed riding and when carrying extra weight. This information can be found in the handbook.

Which TWO are badly affected if the tyres are under-inflated?

⊙ Braking

⊙ Steering

⊙ Changing gear

⊙ Parking

⊙ **Braking**

⊙ **Steering**

Your tyres are your only contact with the road so it is very important to ensure that they are free from defects, have sufficient tread depth and are correctly inflated. Correct tyre pressures help reduce the risk of skidding and provide a safer and more comfortable drive or ride.

You must NOT sound your horn

⊙ between 10 pm and 6 am in a built-up area

⊙ at any time in a built-up area

⊙ between 11.30 pm and 7 am in a built-up area

⊙ between 11.30 pm and 6 am on any road

⊙ **between 11.30 pm and 7 am in a built-up area**

Vehicles can be noisy. Every effort must be made to prevent excessive noise, especially in built-up areas at night. Don't

• rev the engine

• sound the horn

unnecessarily.

It is illegal to sound your horn in a built-up area between 11.30 pm and 7 am, except when another vehicle poses a danger.

3.67
*Mark **three** answers*

The pictured vehicle is 'environmentally friendly' because it

- reduces noise pollution
- uses diesel fuel
- uses electricity
- uses unleaded fuel
- reduces parking spaces
- reduces town traffic

⊙ **reduces noise pollution**

⊙ **uses electricity**

⊙ **reduces town traffic**

Trams are powered by electricity and therefore do not emit exhaust fumes. They are also much quieter than petrol or diesel engines and can carry a large number of passengers.

3.68
*Mark **one** answer*

Supertrams or Light Rapid Transit (LRT) systems are environmentally friendly because

- they use diesel power
- they use quieter roads
- they use electric power
- they do not operate during rush hour

⊙ **they use electric power**

This means that they do not emit toxic fumes, which add to city pollution problems. They are also a lot quieter and smoother to ride on.

3.69
*Mark **one** answer*

'Red routes' in major cities have been introduced to

- raise the speed limits
- help the traffic flow
- provide better parking
- allow lorries to load more freely

⊙ **help the traffic flow**

Traffic jams today are often caused by the volume of traffic. However, inconsiderate parking can lead to the closure of an inside lane or traffic having to wait for oncoming vehicles. Driving slowly in traffic increases fuel consumption and causes a build-up of exhaust fumes.

69

Road humps, chicanes, and narrowings are

- ⊙ always at major road works
- ⊙ used to increase traffic speed
- ⊙ at toll-bridge approaches only
- ⊙ traffic calming measures

⊙ **traffic calming measures**

Traffic calming measures help keep vehicle speeds low in sensitive areas.

A pedestrian is much more likely to survive an accident with a motor vehicle travelling at 20 mph than at 40 mph.

The purpose of a catalytic converter is to reduce

- ⊙ fuel consumption
- ⊙ the risk of fire
- ⊙ toxic exhaust gases
- ⊙ engine wear

⊙ **toxic exhaust gases**

Catalytic converters are designed to reduce toxic emissions by up to 90%. They work more efficiently when the engine has reached its normal working temperature.

Catalytic converters are fitted to make the

- ⊙ engine produce more power
- ⊙ exhaust system easier to replace
- ⊙ engine run quietly
- ⊙ exhaust fumes cleaner

⊙ **exhaust fumes cleaner**

Harmful gases in the exhaust system pollute the atmosphere. These gases are reduced by up to 90% if a catalytic converter is fitted. Cleaner air benefits everyone, especially people who live or work near congested roads.

It is essential that tyre pressures are checked regularly. When should this be done?

- ⊙ After any lengthy journey
- ⊙ After travelling at high speed
- ⊙ When tyres are hot
- ⊙ When tyres are cold

⊙ **When tyres are cold**

When you check the tyre pressures do so when the tyres are cold. This will give you a more accurate reading. The heat generated from a long journey will raise the pressure inside the tyre.

3.74
*Mark **one** answer*

When should you NOT use your horn in a built-up area?

⊙ Between 8 pm and 8 am

⊙ Between 9 pm and dawn

⊙ Between dusk and 8 am

⊙ Between 11.30 pm and 7 am

⊙ **Between 11.30 pm and 7 am**

Only sound your horn to prevent an accident. If you need to let someone know you are there, you could flash your headlights instead.

3.75
*Mark **one** answer*

You will use more fuel if your tyres are

⊙ under-inflated

⊙ of different makes

⊙ over-inflated

⊙ new and hardly used

⊙ **under-inflated**

Check your tyre pressures frequently – normally once a week. If pressures are lower than those recommended by the manufacturer, there will be more 'rolling resistance'. The engine will have to work harder to overcome this, leading to increased fuel consumption.

3.76
*Mark **two** answers*

How should you dispose of a used battery?

⊙ Take it to a local authority site

⊙ Put it in the dustbin

⊙ Break it up into pieces

⊙ Leave it on waste land

⊙ Take it to a garage

⊙ Burn it on a fire

⊙ **Take it to a local authority site**

⊙ **Take it to a garage**

Batteries contain acid which is hazardous and must be disposed of safely.

3.77   *Mark **one** answer*

What is most likely to cause high fuel consumption?

⊙ Poor steering control

⊙ Accelerating around bends

⊙ Staying in high gears

⊙ Harsh braking and accelerating

⊙ **Harsh braking and accelerating**

Accelerating and braking gently and smoothly will help to save fuel, reduce wear on your vehicle and is better for the environment.

3.78   *Mark **one** answer*

The fluid level in your battery is low. What should you top it up with?

⊙ Battery acid

⊙ Distilled water

⊙ Engine oil

⊙ Engine coolant

⊙ **Distilled water**

Some modern batteries are maintenance-free. Check your vehicle handbook and, if necessary, make sure that the plates in each battery cell are covered.

3.79   *Mark **one** answer*

You have too much oil in your engine. What could this cause?

⊙ Low oil pressure

⊙ Engine overheating

⊙ Chain wear

⊙ Oil leaks

⊙ **Oil leaks**

Too much oil in the engine will create excess pressure and could damage engine seals and cause oil leaks. Any excess oil should be drained off.

3.80
*Mark **one** answer*

You are parked on the road at night. Where must you use parking lights?

⊙ Where there are continuous white lines in the middle of the road

⊙ Where the speed limit exceeds 30 mph

⊙ Where you are facing oncoming traffic

⊙ Where you are near a bus stop

⊙ **Where the speed limit exceeds 30 mph**

When parking at night, park in the direction of the traffic. This will enable other road users to see the reflectors on the rear of your vehicle. Use your parking lights if the speed limit is over 30 mph.

3.81
*Mark **one** answer*

Which of these, if allowed to get low, could cause an accident?

⊙ Anti-freeze level

⊙ Brake fluid level

⊙ Battery water level

⊙ Radiator coolant level

⊙ **Brake fluid level**

You should carry out frequent checks on all fluid levels but particularly brake fluid. As the friction material on your brake shoes or pads wears down, the brake fluid level will fall. If it falls below the minimum mark on the fluid reservoir, air could enter the hydraulic system and this would lead to loss of braking efficiency.

3.82
*Mark **three** answers*

Motor vehicles can harm the environment. This has resulted in

⊙ air pollution

⊙ damage to buildings

⊙ less risk to health

⊙ improved public transport

⊙ less use of electrical vehicles

⊙ using up of natural resources

⊙ **air pollution**

⊙ **damage to buildings**

⊙ **using up of natural resources**

Exhaust emissions are harmful to health. Together with vibration from heavy traffic this can result in damage to buildings. Most petrol and diesel fuels come from a finite and non-renewable source. Anything you can do to reduce your use of these fuels will help the environment.

3.83

Excessive or uneven tyre wear can be caused by faults in which THREE of the following?

⊙ The gearbox
⊙ The braking system
⊙ The accelerator
⊙ The exhaust system
⊙ Wheel alignment
⊙ The suspension

⊙ **The braking system**

⊙ **Wheel alignment**

⊙ **The suspension**

Regular servicing will help to detect faults at an early stage and this will avoid the risk of minor faults becoming serious or even dangerous.

3.84

You need to top up your battery. What level should you fill to?

⊙ The top of the battery
⊙ Half-way up the battery
⊙ Just below the cell plates
⊙ Just above the cell plates

⊙ **Just above the cell plates**

Top up the battery with distilled water and make sure each cell plate is covered.

3.85

You are parking on a two-way road at night. The speed limit is 40 mph. You should park on the

⊙ left with parking lights on
⊙ left with no lights on
⊙ right with parking lights on
⊙ right with dipped headlights on

⊙ **left with parking lights on**

On a two-way road you may only park at night, without leaving the vehicle's lights on, if you're facing in the direction of the traffic flow, the road has a speed limit of 30 mph or less and you're at least 10 metres (32 feet) away from any junction.

3.86 — Mark **one** answer

Before starting a journey it is wise to plan your route. How can you do this?

- ⊙ Look at a map
- ⊙ Contact your local garage
- ⊙ Look in your vehicle handbook
- ⊙ Check your vehicle registration document

⊙ **Look at a map**

Planning your journey before you set out can help to make it much easier, more pleasant and ease traffic congestion. Look at a map to help you to do this. You may need different scale maps depending on where and how far you're going. Printing or writing out the route can also help.

3.87 — NI EXEMPT — Mark **one** answer

It can help to plan your route before starting a journey. You can do this by contacting

- ⊙ your local filling station
- ⊙ a motoring organisation
- ⊙ the Driver Vehicle Licensing Agency
- ⊙ your vehicle manufacturer

⊙ **a motoring organisation**

Most motoring organisations will give you a detailed plan of your trip showing directions and distance. Some will also include advice on rest and fuel stops. The Highways Agency website will also give you information on roadworks and accidents and gives expected delay times.

3.88 — Mark **one** answer

How can you plan your route before starting a long journey?

- ⊙ Check your vehicle's workshop manual
- ⊙ Ask your local garage
- ⊙ Use a route planner on the internet
- ⊙ Consult your travel agents

⊙ **Use a route planner on the internet**

Various route planners are available on the internet. Most of them give you various options allowing you to choose the most direct, quickest or scenic route. They can also include rest and fuel stops and distances. Print them off and take them with you.

Planning your route before setting out can be helpful. How can you do this?

- ⊙ Look in a motoring magazine
- ⊙ Only visit places you know
- ⊙ Try to travel at busy times
- ⊙ Print or write down the route

⊙ **Print or write down the route**

Print or write down your route before setting out. Some places are not well signed so using place names and road numbers may help you avoid problems en route. Try to get an idea of how far you're going before you leave. You can also use it to re-check the next stage at each rest stop.

Why is it a good idea to plan your journey to avoid busy times?

- ⊙ You will have an easier journey
- ⊙ You will have a more stressful journey
- ⊙ Your journey time will be longer
- ⊙ It will cause more traffic congestion

⊙ **You will have an easier journey**

No one likes to spend time in traffic queues. Try to avoid busy times related to school or work travel. As well as moving vehicles you should also consider congestion caused by parked cars, buses and coaches around schools.

Planning your journey to avoid busy times has a number of advantages. One of these is

- ⊙ your journey will take longer
- ⊙ you will have a more pleasant journey
- ⊙ you will cause more pollution
- ⊙ your stress level will be greater

⊙ **you will have a more pleasant journey**

Having a pleasant journey can have safety benefits. You will be less tired and stressed and this will allow you to concentrate more on your driving or riding.

3.92 — Mark **one** answer

It is a good idea to plan your journey to avoid busy times. This is because

- your vehicle will use more fuel
- you will see less road works
- it will help to ease congestion
- you will travel a much shorter distance

- **it will help to ease congestion**

Avoiding busy times means that you are not adding needlessly to traffic congestion. Other advantages are that you will use less fuel and feel less stressed.

3.93 — Mark **one** answer

By avoiding busy times when travelling

- you are more likely to be held up
- your journey time will be longer
- you will travel a much shorter distance
- you are less likely to be delayed

- **you are less likely to be delayed**

If possible, avoid the early morning and late afternoon and early evening 'rush hour'. Doing this should allow you to travel in a more relaxed frame of mind, concentrate solely on what you're doing and arrive at your destination feeling less stressed.

3.94 — Mark **one** answer

It can help to plan your route before starting a journey. Why should you also plan an alternative route?

- Your original route may be blocked
- Your maps may have different scales
- You may find you have to pay a congestion charge
- Because you may get held up by a tractor

- **Your original route may be blocked**

It can be frustrating and worrying to find your planned route is blocked by roadworks or diversions. If you have planned an alternative you will feel less stressed and able to concentrate fully on your driving or riding. If your original route is mostly on motorways it's a good idea to plan an alternative using non-motorway roads. Always carry a map with you just in case you need to refer to it.

*Mark **one** answer*

As well as planning your route before starting a journey, you should also plan an alternative route. Why is this?

- ⊙ To let another driver overtake
- ⊙ Your first route may be blocked
- ⊙ To avoid a railway level crossing
- ⊙ In case you have to avoid emergency vehicles

⊙ **Your first route may be blocked**

It's a good idea to plan an alternative route in case your original route is blocked for any reason. You're less likely to feel worried and stressed if you've got an alternative in mind. This will enable you to concentrate fully on your driving or riding. Always carry a map that covers the area you will travel in.

---

*Mark **one** answer*

Who of these will not have to pay Congestion Charges in London?

- ⊙ A van driver making deliveries
- ⊙ A rider of a two-wheeled vehicle
- ⊙ A car driver whose vehicle is more than 1000 cc
- ⊙ A driver who just wants to park in the area

⊙ **A rider of a two-wheeled vehicle**

Congestion charging schemes have been introduced in the London area. Some road users are exempt from the charges. These include two-wheeled vehicle users, residents living within the zone and disabled people who hold a blue badge. So they are not unfairly penalised, NHS staff, firefighters and patients too ill to use public transport, may be able to claim reimbursement.

---

*Mark **one** answer*

You are making an appointment and will have to travel a long distance. You should

- ⊙ allow plenty of time for your journey
- ⊙ plan to go at busy times
- ⊙ avoid all national speed limit roads
- ⊙ prevent other drivers from overtaking

⊙ **allow plenty of time for your journey**

Always allow plenty of time for your journey in case of unforseen problems. Anything can happen, punctures, breakdowns, road closures, diversions etc. You will feel less stressed and less inclined to take risks if you are not 'pushed for time'.

3.98   *Mark one answer*

Rapid acceleration and heavy braking can lead to

⊙ reduced pollution

⊙ increased fuel consumption

⊙ reduced exhaust emissions

⊙ increased road safety

⊙ **increased fuel consumption**

Using the controls smoothly can reduce fuel consumption by about 15% as well as reducing wear and tear on your vehicle. Plan ahead and anticipate changes of speed well in advance. This will reduce the need to accelerate rapidly or brake sharply.

3.99   *Mark one answer*

What percentage of all emissions does road transport account for?

⊙ 10%

⊙ 20%

⊙ 30%

⊙ 40%

⊙ **20%**

Transport is an essential part of modern life but it does have environmental effects. In heavily populated areas traffic is the biggest source of air pollution. Eco-safe driving and riding will reduce emissions and can make a surprising difference to local air quality.

section four
SAFETY
MARGINS

This section covers:

- stopping distances
- road surfaces
- skidding
- weather conditions

4.1   *Mark **one** answer*

Your overall stopping distance will be longer when riding

- at night
- in the fog
- with a passenger
- up a hill

⊙ **with a passenger**

When carrying a passenger on a motorcycle the overall weight will be much more than when riding alone. This additional weight will make it harder for you to stop quickly in an emergency.

4.2   *Mark **one** answer*

On a wet road what is the safest way to stop?

- Change gear without braking
- Use the back brake only
- Use the front brake only
- Use both brakes

⊙ **Use both brakes**

Motorcyclists need to take extra care when stopping on wet road surfaces. Plan well ahead so that you're able to brake in good time. You should

- ensure your motorcycle is upright
- brake when travelling in a straight line.

4.3   *Mark **one** answer*

You are riding in heavy rain when your rear wheel skids as you accelerate. To get control again you must

- change down to a lower gear
- ease off the throttle
- brake to reduce speed
- put your feet down

⊙ **ease off the throttle**

If you feel your back wheel beginning to skid as you pull away, ease off the throttle. This will give your rear tyre the chance to grip the road and stop the skid.

4.4   *Mark **one** answer*

It is snowing. Before starting your journey you should

- think if you need to ride at all
- try to avoid taking a passenger
- plan a route avoiding towns
- take a hot drink before setting out

⊙ **think if you need to ride at all**

Do not ride in snowy or icy conditions unless your journey is essential. If you must go out, try and keep to main roads which are more likely to be clear and well gritted.

Why should you ride with a dipped headlight on in the daytime?

⊙ It helps other road users to see you

⊙ It means that you can ride faster

⊙ Other vehicles will get out of the way

⊙ So that it is already on when it gets dark

⊙ **It helps other road users to see you**

Make yourself as visible as possible, from the side as well as from the front and rear. Having your headlight on, even in good daylight, can help make you more conspicuous.

Motorcyclists are only allowed to use high-intensity rear fog lights when

⊙ a pillion passenger is being carried

⊙ they ride a large touring machine

⊙ visibility is 100 metres (328 feet) or less

⊙ they are riding on the road for the first time

⊙ **visibility is 100 metres (328 feet) or less**

If your motorcycle is fitted with high-intensity rear fog lights you must only use them when visibility is seriously reduced, that is, when you can see no further than 100 metres (328 feet). This rule also applies to all other motor vehicles using these lights.

When riding at night you should

⊙ ride with your headlight on dipped beam

⊙ wear reflective clothing

⊙ wear a tinted visor

⊙ ride in the centre of the road

⊙ give arm signals

⊙ **ride with your headlight on dipped beam**

⊙ **wear reflective clothing**

At night you should wear clothing that includes reflective material to help other road users to see you. This could be a tabard or reflective body strap.

4.8
*Mark **three** answers*

You MUST use your headlight

- ⊙ when riding in a group
- ⊙ at night when street lighting is poor
- ⊙ when carrying a passenger
- ⊙ on motorways during darkness
- ⊙ at times of poor visibility
- ⊙ when parked on an unlit road

- ⊙ **at night when street lighting is poor**
- ⊙ **on motorways during darkness**
- ⊙ **at times of poor visibility**

Your headlight helps you to see in the dark and helps other road users to see you.

You must use your headlight

- when visibility is seriously reduced
- at night, except on restricted roads where street lighting is not more than 185 metres (600 feet) apart.

4.9
*Mark **one** answer*

You are riding in town at night. The roads are wet after rain. The reflections from wet surfaces will

- ⊙ affect your stopping distance
- ⊙ affect your road holding
- ⊙ make it easy to see unlit objects
- ⊙ make it hard to see unlit objects

- ⊙ **make it hard to see unlit objects**

If you can't see clearly, slow down and stop. Make sure that your visor or goggles are clean. Be extra-cautious in these conditions and allow twice the normal separation distance.

4.10

*Mark **two** answers*

You are riding through a flood. Which TWO should you do?

- ⊙ Keep in a high gear and stand up on the footrests
- ⊙ Keep the engine running fast to keep water out of the exhaust
- ⊙ Ride slowly and test your brakes when you are out of the water
- ⊙ Turn your headlight off to avoid any electrical damage

- ⊙ **Keep the engine running fast to keep water out of the exhaust**
- ⊙ **Ride slowly and test your brakes when you are out of the water**

Take extra care when riding through flood water or fords. Ride through with high engine revs while partly slipping the clutch to prevent water entering the exhaust system.

Try your brakes as soon as you are clear.

You have just ridden through a flood. When clear of the water you should test your

- ⊙ starter motor
- ⊙ headlight
- ⊙ steering
- ⊙ brakes

⊙ **brakes**

If you have ridden through deep water your brakes may be less effective. If they have been affected, ride slowly while gently applying both brakes until normal braking is restored.

When going through flood water you should ride

- ⊙ quickly in a high gear
- ⊙ slowly in a high gear
- ⊙ quickly in a low gear
- ⊙ slowly in a low gear

⊙ **slowly in a low gear**

If you have to go through a flood, ride slowly in a low gear. Keep the engine running fast enough to keep water out of the exhaust. You may need to slip the clutch to do this.

When riding at night you should NOT

- ⊙ switch on full beam headlights
- ⊙ overtake slower vehicles in front
- ⊙ use dipped beam headlights
- ⊙ use tinted glasses, lenses or visors

⊙ **use tinted glasses, lenses or visors**

Do not use tinted glasses, lenses or visors at night because they reduce the amount of available light reaching your eyes. It's also important to keep your visor or goggles clean to give a clear view of the road at all times.

4.14　*Mark **two** answers*

Which of the following should you do when riding in fog?

- ⊙ Keep close to the vehicle in front
- ⊙ Use your dipped headlight
- ⊙ Ride close to the centre of the road
- ⊙ Keep your visor or goggles clear
- ⊙ Keep the vehicle in front in view

⊙ **Use your dipped headlight**

⊙ **Keep your visor or goggles clear**

You must use your dipped headlight when visibility is seriously reduced. In fog a film of mist can form over the outside of your visor or goggles. This can further reduce your ability to see. Be aware of this hazard and keep your visor or goggles clear.

4.15　*Mark **one** answer*

You are riding in heavy rain. Why should you try to avoid this marked area?

- ⊙ It is illegal to ride over bus stops
- ⊙ The painted lines may be slippery
- ⊙ Cyclists may be using the bus stop
- ⊙ Only emergency vehicles may drive over bus stops

⊙ **The painted lines may be slippery**

Painted lines and road markings can be very slippery, especially for motorcyclists. Try to avoid them if you can do so safely.

4.16　*Mark **one** answer*

When riding at night you should

- ⊙ wear reflective clothing
- ⊙ wear a tinted visor
- ⊙ ride in the middle of the road
- ⊙ always give arm signals

⊙ **wear reflective clothing**

You need to make yourself as visible as possible, from the front and rear and also from the side. Don't just rely on your headlight and tail light. Wear clothing that uses reflective material as this stands out in other vehicles' headlights.

*Mark **one** answer*

When riding in extremely cold conditions what can you do to keep warm?

- ⊙ Stay close to the vehicles in front
- ⊙ Wear suitable clothing
- ⊙ Lie flat on the tank
- ⊙ Put one hand on the exhaust pipe

⊙ **Wear suitable clothing**

Motorcyclists are exposed to the elements and can become very cold when riding in wintry conditions. It's important to keep warm or your concentration could be affected.

The only way to stay warm is to wear suitable clothing. If you do find yourself getting cold then stop at a suitable place to warm up.

*Mark **two** answers*

You are riding at night. To be seen more easily you should

- ⊙ ride with your headlight on dipped beam
- ⊙ wear reflective clothing
- ⊙ keep the motorcycle clean
- ⊙ stay well out to the right
- ⊙ wear waterproof clothing

⊙ **ride with your headlight on dipped beam**

⊙ **wear reflective clothing**

Reflective clothing works by reflecting light from the headlights of the other vehicles. This will make it easier for you to be seen.

Fluorescent clothing, although effective during the day, won't show up as well as reflective clothing at night.

*Mark **one** answer*

Your overall stopping distance will be much longer when riding

- ⊙ in the rain
- ⊙ in fog
- ⊙ at night
- ⊙ in strong winds

⊙ **in the rain**

Extra care should be taken in wet weather. Wet roads will affect the time it takes you to stop. Your stopping distance could be at least doubled.

4.20 *Mark **four** answers*

The road surface is very important to motorcyclists. Which FOUR of these are more likely to reduce the stability of your motorcycle?

⊙ Potholes
⊙ Drain covers
⊙ Concrete
⊙ Oil patches
⊙ Tarmac
⊙ Loose gravel

⊙ **Potholes**

⊙ **Drain covers**

⊙ **Oil patches**

⊙ **Loose gravel**

Apart from the weather conditions, the road surface and any changes in it can affect the stability of your motorcycle. Be on the lookout for poor road surfaces and be aware of any traffic around you, in case you need to take avoiding action.

4.21 *Mark **two** answers*

You are riding in very hot weather. What are TWO effects that melting tar has on the control of your motorcycle?

⊙ It can make the surface slippery
⊙ It can reduce tyre grip
⊙ It can reduce stopping distances
⊙ It can improve braking efficiency

⊙ **It can make the surface slippery**

⊙ **It can reduce tyre grip**

If the tarmac road surface has softened in the heat, take extra care when braking and cornering.

You should also look out for loose chippings where roads have been resurfaced. These will reduce your tyres' grip and can fly up, causing injury and damage.

4.22 *Mark **one** answer*

What can cause your tyres to skid and lose their grip on the road surface?

⊙ Giving hand signals
⊙ Riding one handed
⊙ Looking over your shoulder
⊙ Heavy braking

⊙ **Heavy braking**

You can cause your motorcycle to skid by heavy or uncoordinated braking, as well as excessive acceleration, swerving or changing direction too sharply, and leaning over too far.

You are riding past queuing traffic. Why should you be more cautious when approaching this road marking?

⊙ Lorries will be unloading here

⊙ School children will be crossing here

⊙ Pedestrians will be standing in the road

⊙ Traffic could be emerging and may not see you

⊙ **Traffic could be emerging and may not see you**

When riding past queuing traffic look out for 'keep clear' road markings that will indicate a side road or entrance on the left. Vehicles may emerge between gaps in the traffic.

It has rained after a long dry spell. You should be very careful because the road surface will be unusually

⊙ loose

⊙ dry

⊙ sticky

⊙ slippery

⊙ **slippery**

The road surface can become unusually slippery when it rains after a long dry spell. Take extra care, particularly at junctions, bends and roundabouts, and allow double the usual stopping distance.

When riding in heavy rain a film of water can build up between your tyres and the road surface. This may result in loss of control. What can you do to avoid this happening?

⊙ Keep your speed down

⊙ Increase your tyre pressures

⊙ Decrease your tyre pressures

⊙ Keep trying your brakes

⊙ **Keep your speed down**

There is a greater risk of aquaplaning when riding at speed. Keeping your speed down will help prevent aquaplaning.

If you can do so safely, try to avoid pools of water on the road.

4.26
*Mark **one** answer*

When riding in heavy rain a film of water can build up between your tyres and the road. This is known as aquaplaning. What should you do to keep control?

⊙ Use your rear brakes gently
⊙ Steer to the crown of the road
⊙ Ease off the throttle smoothly
⊙ Change up into a higher gear.

⊙ **Ease off the throttle smoothly**

If your vehicle starts to aquaplane ease off the throttle smoothly. Do not brake or turn the steering until tyre grip has been restored.

4.27

*Mark **one** answer*

You are on a good, dry road surface and your motorcycle has good brakes and tyres. What is the typical overall stopping distance at 40 mph?

⊙ 23 metres (75 feet)
⊙ 36 metres (120 feet)
⊙ 53 metres (175 feet)
⊙ 96 metres (315 feet)

⊙ **36 metres (120 feet)**

Factors that affect how long it takes you to stop include

• how fast you're going
• whether you're travelling on the level, uphill or downhill
• the weather and road conditions
• the condition of your tyres, brakes and suspension
• your reaction times.

4.28
*Mark **one** answer*

After riding through deep water you notice your scooter brakes do not work properly. What would be the best way to dry them out?

⊙ Ride slowly, braking lightly
⊙ Ride quickly, braking harshly
⊙ Stop and dry them with a cloth
⊙ Stop and wait for a few minutes

⊙ **Ride slowly, braking lightly**

You can help to dry out brakes by riding slowly and applying light pressure to the brake pedal/lever. DO NOT ride at normal speeds until they are working normally again.

4.29 Mark **two** answers

You have to ride in foggy weather. You should

- stay close to the centre of the road
- switch only your sidelights on
- switch on your dipped headlights
- be aware of others not using their headlights
- always ride in the gutter to see the kerb

- **switch on your dipped headlights**

- **be aware of others not using their headlights**

Only travel in fog if your journey is absolutely necessary. Fog is often patchy and visibility can suddenly reduce without warning.

4.30 Mark **one** answer

Only a fool breaks the two-second rule refers to

- the time recommended when using the choke
- the separation distance when riding in good conditions
- restarting a stalled engine in busy traffic
- the time you should keep your foot down at a junction

- **the separation distance when riding in good conditions**

It is very important that you always leave a safe gap between yourself and any vehicle you're following. In good conditions you need to leave at least one metre for every mile per hour of your speed or a two-second time interval.

4.31 Mark **two** answers

You are riding on a motorway in a crosswind. You should take extra care when

- approaching service areas
- overtaking a large vehicle
- riding in slow-moving traffic
- approaching an exit
- riding in exposed places

- **overtaking a large vehicle**

- **riding in exposed places**

Take extra care when overtaking large vehicles as they can cause air turbulence and buffeting. Beware of crosswinds when riding on exposed stretches of road, which can suddenly blow you off course.

Bear in mind that strong winds can also affect the stability of other road users.

4.32
*Mark **one** answer*

At a mini roundabout it is important that a motorcyclist should avoid

⊙ turning right

⊙ using signals

⊙ taking 'lifesavers'

⊙ the painted area

⊙ **the painted area**

Avoid riding over the painted area as these can become very slippery, especially when wet. Even on dry roads only a small part of the motorcycle's tyre makes contact with the road. Any reduction in grip can therefore affect the stability of your machine.

4.33
*Mark **one** answer*

Why should you try to avoid riding over this marked area?

⊙ It is illegal to ride over bus stops

⊙ It will alter your machine's centre of gravity

⊙ Pedestrians may be waiting at the bus stop

⊙ A bus may have left patches of oil

⊙ **A bus may have left patches of oil**

Try to anticipate slippery road surfaces. Watch out for oil patches at places where vehicles stop for some time, such as bus stops, lay-bys and busy junctions.

4.34
*Mark **one** answer*

Your overall stopping distance comprises thinking and braking distance. You are on a good, dry road surface with good brakes and tyres. What is the typical BRAKING distance at 50 mph?

⊙ 14 metres (46 feet)

⊙ 24 metres (79 feet)

⊙ 38 metres (125 feet)

⊙ 55 metres (180 feet)

⊙ **38 metres (125 feet)**

Different factors can affect how long it takes you to stop, such as weather and road conditions, vehicle condition and loading. You also need to add reaction time to this. The overall stopping distance at 50 mph includes 15 metres thinking distance (the reaction time before braking starts) plus your braking distance of 38 metres', giving a typical overall stopping distance of 53 metres (175 feet) in good conditions.

You are riding at speed through surface water. A thin film of water has built up between your tyres and the road surface. To keep control what should you do?

- ⊙ Turn the steering quickly
- ⊙ Use the rear brake gently
- ⊙ Use both brakes gently
- ⊙ Ease off the throttle

⊙ **Ease off the throttle**

Riding at speed in places where surface water has collected can cause a film of water to build up between your tyres and the road. This is known as aquaplaning: it results in serious loss of steering and braking control and can cause you to crash. The faster you are going, the more likely it is to happen.

If you start to aquaplane, reduce speed by easing off the throttle smoothly.

Braking distances on ice can be

- ⊙ twice the normal distance
- ⊙ five times the normal distance
- ⊙ seven times the normal distance
- ⊙ ten times the normal distance

⊙ **ten times the normal distance**

In icy and snowy weather, your stopping distance will increase by up to ten times compared to good, dry conditions.

Take extra care when braking, accelerating and steering, to cut down the risk of skidding.

Freezing conditions will affect the distance it takes you to come to a stop. You should expect stopping distances to increase by up to

- ⊙ two times
- ⊙ three times
- ⊙ five times
- ⊙ ten times

⊙ **ten times**

Your tyre grip is greatly reduced on icy roads and you need to allow up to ten times the normal stopping distance.

4.38   *Mark **one** answer*

In windy conditions you need to take
extra care when

⊙ using the brakes

⊙ making a hill start

⊙ turning into a narrow road

⊙ passing pedal cyclists

⊙ **passing pedal cyclists**

You should always give cyclists plenty of
room when overtaking. When it's windy, a
sudden gust could blow them off course.

4.39   *Mark **one** answer*

When approaching a right-hand bend you
should keep well to the left. Why is this?

⊙ To improve your view of the road

⊙ To overcome the effect of the road's
slope

⊙ To let faster traffic from behind overtake

⊙ To be positioned safely if you skid

⊙ **To improve your view
of the road**

Doing this will give you an earlier view
around the bend and enable you to see
any hazards sooner.

It also reduces the risk of collision with an
oncoming vehicle that may have drifted
over the centre line while taking the bend.

4.40   *Mark **three** answers*

You should not overtake when

⊙ intending to turn left shortly afterwards

⊙ in a one-way street

⊙ approaching a junction

⊙ going up a long hill

⊙ the view ahead is blocked

⊙ **intending to turn left
shortly afterwards**

⊙ **approaching a junction**

⊙ **the view ahead is blocked**

Before you overtake you should ask
yourself if it's really necessary. Arriving
safely is more important than taking
unnecessary risks.

4.41
*Mark **one** answer*

You have just gone through deep water. To dry off the brakes you should

- ⊙ accelerate and keep to a high speed for a short time
- ⊙ go slowly while gently applying the brakes
- ⊙ avoid using the brakes at all for a few miles
- ⊙ stop for at least an hour to allow them time to dry

⊙ **go slowly while gently applying the brakes**

Water on the brakes will act as a lubricant, causing them to work less efficiently. Using the brakes lightly as you go along will dry them out.

4.42
*Mark **two** answers*

In very hot weather the road surface can become soft. Which TWO of the following will be most affected?

- ⊙ The suspension
- ⊙ The grip of the tyres
- ⊙ The braking
- ⊙ The exhaust

⊙ **The grip of the tyres**

⊙ **The braking**

Only a small part of your tyres is in contact with the road. This is why you must consider the surface you're travelling on, and alter your speed to suit the road conditions.

4.43
*Mark **one** answer*

Where are you most likely to be affected by a side wind?

- ⊙ On a narrow country lane
- ⊙ On an open stretch of road
- ⊙ On a busy stretch of road
- ⊙ On a long, straight road

⊙ **On an open stretch of road**

In windy conditions, care must be taken on exposed roads. A strong gust of wind can blow you off course. Watch out for other road users who are particularly likely to be affected, such as

- cyclists
- motorcyclists
- high-sided lorries
- vehicles towing trailers.

4.44   *Mark **one** answer*

In good conditions, what is the typical stopping distance at 70 mph?

- ⊙ 53 metres (175 feet)
- ⊙ 60 metres (197 feet)
- ⊙ 73 metres (240 feet)
- ⊙ 96 metres (315 feet)

⊙ **96 metres (315 feet)**

Note that this is the typical stopping distance. It will take at least this distance to think, brake and stop in good conditions. In poor conditions it will take much longer.

4.45   *Mark **one** answer*

What is the shortest overall stopping distance on a dry road at 60 mph?

- ⊙ 53 metres (175 feet)
- ⊙ 58 metres (190 feet)
- ⊙ 73 metres (240 feet)
- ⊙ 96 metres (315 feet)

⊙ **73 metres (240 feet)**

This distance is the equivalent of 18 car lengths. Try pacing out 73 metres and then look back. It's probably further than you think.

4.46   *Mark **one** answer*

You are following a vehicle at a safe distance on a wet road. Another driver overtakes you and pulls into the gap you have left. What should you do?

- ⊙ Flash your headlights as a warning
- ⊙ Try to overtake safely as soon as you can
- ⊙ Drop back to regain a safe distance
- ⊙ Stay close to the other vehicle until it moves on

⊙ **Drop back to regain a safe distance**

Wet weather will affect the time it takes for you to stop and can affect your control.

Your speed should allow you to stop safely and in good time. If another vehicle pulls into the gap you've left, ease back until you've regained your stopping distance.

section five
HAZARD AWARENESS

This section covers:

- anticipation
- attention
- speed and distance
- reaction time
- alcohol and drugs
- tiredness

5.1
*Mark **two** answers*

You get cold and wet when riding. Which TWO are likely to happen?

- You may lose concentration
- You may slide off the seat
- Your visor may freeze up
- Your reaction times may be slower
- Your helmet may loosen

⊙ **You may lose concentration**

⊙ **Your reaction times may be slower**

When you're riding a motorcycle make sure you're wearing suitable clothing. If you become cold and uncomfortable this could cause you to lose concentration and could slow down your reaction time.

5.2
*Mark **one** answer*

You are riding up to a zebra crossing. You intend to stop for waiting pedestrians. How could you let them know you are stopping?

- By signalling with your left arm
- By waving them across
- By flashing your headlight
- By signalling with your right arm

⊙ **By signalling with your right arm**

Giving the correct arm signal would indicate to approaching vehicles, as well as pedestrians, that you are stopping at the pedestrian crossing.

5.3
*Mark **one** answer*

You are about to ride home. You cannot find the glasses you need to wear. You should

- ride home slowly, keeping to quiet roads
- borrow a friend's glasses and use those
- ride home at night, so that the lights will help you
- find a way of getting home without riding

⊙ **find a way of getting home without riding**

Don't be tempted to ride if you've lost or forgotten your glasses. You must be able to see clearly when riding. If you can't you will be endangering yourself and other road users.

5.4 *Mark **three** answers*

Which THREE of these are likely effects of drinking alcohol?

- ⊙ Reduced co-ordination
- ⊙ Increased confidence
- ⊙ Poor judgement
- ⊙ Increased concentration
- ⊙ Faster reactions
- ⊙ Colour blindness

⊙ **Reduced co-ordination**

⊙ **Increased confidence**

⊙ **Poor judgement**

Alcohol can increase confidence to a point where a rider's behaviour might become 'out of character'. Someone who normally behaves sensibly suddenly takes risks and could endanger themselves and others.

Never drink and ride, or accept a ride from anyone who's been drinking.

5.5 *Mark **one** answer*

You find that you need glasses to read vehicle number plates at the required distance. When MUST you wear them?

- ⊙ Only in bad weather conditions
- ⊙ At all times when riding
- ⊙ Only when you think it necessary
- ⊙ Only in bad light or at night time

⊙ **At all times when riding**

Have your eyesight tested before you start your practical training. Then, throughout your riding life, have periodical checks to ensure that your eyesight hasn't deteriorated.

5.6 *Mark **three** answers*

Drinking any amount of alcohol is likely to

- ⊙ slow down your reactions to hazards
- ⊙ increase the speed of your reactions
- ⊙ worsen your judgement of speed
- ⊙ improve your awareness of danger
- ⊙ give a false sense of confidence

⊙ **slow down your reactions to hazards**

⊙ **worsen your judgement of speed**

⊙ **give a false sense of confidence**

Never drink if you are going to ride. It's always the safest option not to drink at all. Don't take risks – it's not worth it.

5.7   *Mark **one** answer*

Which of the following types of glasses should NOT be worn when riding at night?

⊙ Half-moon

⊙ Round

⊙ Bi-focal

⊙ Tinted

⊙ **Tinted**

If you are riding at night or in poor visibility, tinted lenses or a tinted visor will reduce the amount of available light reaching your eyes, making you less able to see clearly.

5.8   *Mark **one** answer*

For which of these may you use hazard warning lights?

⊙ When riding on a motorway to warn traffic behind of a hazard ahead

⊙ When you are double parked on a two way road

⊙ When your direction indicators are not working

⊙ When warning oncoming traffic that you intend to stop

⊙ **When riding on a motorway to warn traffic behind of a hazard ahead**

Hazard warning lights are an important safety feature. Use them when riding on a motorway to warn following traffic of danger ahead. You should also use them if your motorcycle has broken down and is causing an obstruction.

5.9   *Mark **two** answers*

Where would you expect to see these markers?

⊙ On a motorway sign

⊙ At the entrance to a narrow bridge

⊙ On a large goods vehicle

⊙ On a builder's skip placed on the road

⊙ **On a large goods vehicle**

⊙ **On a builder's skip placed on the road**

These markers must be fitted to vehicles over 13 metres long, large goods vehicles, and rubbish skips placed in the road. They are reflective to make them easier to see in the dark.

5.10
*Mark **one** answer*

When riding long distances at speed, noise can cause fatigue. What can you do to help reduce this?

- ☉ Vary your speed
- ☉ Wear ear plugs
- ☉ Use an open-face helmet
- ☉ Ride in an upright position

☉ **Wear ear plugs**

Wearing ear plugs can help prevent hearing damage and also fatigue caused by noise.

5.11
*Mark **one** answer*

Why should you wear ear plugs when riding a motorcycle?

- ☉ To help to prevent ear damage
- ☉ To make you less aware of traffic
- ☉ To help to keep you warm
- ☉ To make your helmet fit better

☉ **To help to prevent ear damage**

The use of ear plugs is recommended to reduce the effect of noise levels and protect your hearing.

5.12
*Mark **two** answers*

Why should you be especially cautious when going past this stationary bus?

- ☉ There is traffic approaching in the distance
- ☉ The driver may open the door
- ☉ It may suddenly move off
- ☉ People may cross the road in front of it
- ☉ There are bicycles parked on the pavement

☉ **It may suddenly move off**

☉ **People may cross the road in front of it**

A stationary bus at a bus stop can hide pedestrians just in front of it who might be about to cross the road. Only go past at a speed that will enable you to stop safely if you need to.

5.13
*Mark **one** answer*

You are convicted of riding after drinking too much alcohol. How could this affect your insurance?

⊙ Your insurance may become invalid

⊙ The amount of excess you pay will be reduced

⊙ You will only be able to get third party cover

⊙ Cover will only be given for riding smaller motorcycles

⊙ **Your insurance may become invalid**

Riding while under the influence of drink or drugs can invalidate your insurance. This also endangers yourself and others. It's not a risk worth taking.

5.14
*Mark **one** answer*

Why should you check over your shoulder before turning right into a side road?

⊙ To make sure the side road is clear

⊙ To check for emerging traffic

⊙ To check for overtaking vehicles

⊙ To confirm your intention to turn

⊙ **To check for overtaking vehicles**

Take a last check over your shoulder before committing yourself to a manoeuvre. This is especially important when turning right, as other road users may not have seen your signal or may not understand your intentions.

5.15
*Mark **two** answers*

You are not sure if your cough medicine will affect you. What TWO things should you do?

⊙ Ask your doctor

⊙ Check the medicine label

⊙ Ride if you feel alright

⊙ Ask a friend or relative for advice

⊙ **Ask your doctor**

⊙ **Check the medicine label**

If you're taking medicine or drugs prescribed by your doctor, check to ensure that they won't make you drowsy. If you forget to ask when you're at the surgery, check with your pharmacist.

*Mark **one** answer*

When should you use hazard warning lights?

⊙ When you are double-parked on a two-way road

⊙ When your direction indicators are not working

⊙ When warning oncoming traffic that you intend to stop

⊙ When your motorcycle has broken down and is causing an obstruction

⊙ **When your motorcycle has broken down and is causing an obstruction**

Hazard warning lights are an important safety feature and should be used if you have broken down and are causing an obstruction. Don't use them as an excuse to park illegally, such as when using a cash machine or post box. You may also use them on motorways to warn following traffic of danger ahead.

*Mark **one** answer*

It is a very hot day. What would you expect to find?

⊙ Mud on the road

⊙ A soft road surface

⊙ Roadworks ahead

⊙ Banks of fog

⊙ **A soft road surface**

In very hot weather the road surface can become soft and melt. Take care when braking and cornering on the softer tarmac, as this can lead to reduced grip and skidding.

*Mark **one** answer*

You see this road marking in between queuing traffic. What should you look out for?

⊙ Overhanging trees

⊙ Roadworks

⊙ Traffic wardens

⊙ Traffic emerging

⊙ **Traffic emerging**

'Keep clear' markings should not be obstructed. They can be found in congested areas to help traffic waiting to emerge onto a busy road.

5.19

*Mark **one** answer*

When riding how can you help to reduce the risk of hearing damage?

⊙ Wearing goggles

⊙ Using ear plugs

⊙ Wearing a scarf

⊙ Keeping the visor up

⊙ **Using ear plugs**

Using ear plugs can help prevent hearing damage and fatigue caused by noise.

5.20

*Mark **one** answer*

What is the main hazard shown in this picture?

⊙ Vehicles turning right

⊙ Vehicles doing U-turns

⊙ The cyclist crossing the road

⊙ Parked cars around the corner

⊙ **The cyclist crossing the road**

Look at the picture carefully and try to imagine you're there. The cyclist in this picture appears to be trying to cross the road. You must be able to deal with the unexpected, especially when you're approaching a hazardous junction. Look well ahead to give yourself time to deal with any hazards.

5.21

*Mark **one** answer*

Which road user has caused a hazard?

⊙ The parked car (arrowed A)

⊙ The pedestrian waiting to cross (arrowed B)

⊙ The moving car (arrowed C)

⊙ The car turning (arrowed D)

⊙ **The parked car (arrowed A)**

The car arrowed A is parked within the area marked by zigzag lines at the pedestrian crossing. Parking here is illegal. It also

• blocks the view for pedestrians wishing to cross the road

• restricts the view of the crossing for approaching traffic.

What should the driver of the car approaching the crossing do?

- Continue at the same speed
- Sound the horn
- Drive through quickly
- Slow down and get ready to stop

⊙ Slow down and get ready to stop

Look well ahead to see if any hazards are developing. This will give you more time to deal with them in the correct way. The man in the picture is clearly intending to cross the road. You should be travelling at a speed that allows you to check your mirror, slow down and stop in good time. You shouldn't have to brake harshly.

You are on a dual carriageway. Ahead you see a vehicle with an amber flashing light. What could this be?

- An ambulance
- A fire engine
- A doctor on call
- A disabled person's vehicle

⊙ A disabled person's vehicle

An amber flashing light on a vehicle indicates that it is slow-moving.

Battery powered vehicles used by disabled people are limited to 8 mph. On dual carriageways they must display an amber flashing light.

You are going out to a social event and alcohol will be available. You will be riding your motorcycle shortly afterwards. What is the safest thing to do?

- Stay just below the legal limit
- Have soft drinks and alcohol in turn
- Don't go beyond the legal limit
- Stick to non-alcoholic drinks

⊙ Stick to non-alcoholic drinks

The legal limit of alcohol is 80 milligrams per 100 millilitres of blood. However, drinking even the smallest amount of alcohol can affect your judgement and reactions. The safest and best option is to avoid any alcohol at all when riding or driving.

5.25
*Mark **three** answers*

What THREE things should the driver of the grey car (arrowed) be especially aware of?

- Pedestrians stepping out between cars
- Other cars behind the grey car
- Doors opening on parked cars
- The bumpy road surface
- Cars leaving parking spaces
- Empty parking spaces

- **Pedestrians stepping out between cars**
- **Doors opening on parked cars**
- **Cars leaving parking spaces**

You need to be aware that other road users may not have seen you. Always be on the lookout for hazards that may develop suddenly and need you to take avoiding action.

5.26
*Mark **one** answer*

In heavy motorway traffic you are being followed closely by the vehicle behind. How can you lower the risk of an accident?

- Increase your distance from the vehicle in front
- Tap your foot on the brake pedal sharply
- Switch on your hazard lights
- Move onto the hard shoulder and stop

- **Increase your distance from the vehicle in front**

On a busy motorway, traffic may still travel at high speeds despite the vehicles being close together. Don't follow too close to the vehicle in front. If a driver behind seems to be 'pushing' you, increase your distance from the vehicle in front by slowing down gently. This will lessen the risk of an accident involving several vehicles.

You see this sign ahead. You should expect the road to

- ⊙ go steeply uphill
- ⊙ go steeply downhill
- ⊙ bend sharply to the left
- ⊙ bend sharply to the right

⊙ **bend sharply to the left**

Adjust your speed in good time and select the correct gear for your speed. Going too fast into the bend could cause you to lose control.

Braking late and harshly while changing direction reduces your vehicle's grip on the road, and is likely to cause a skid.

You are approaching this cyclist. You should

- ⊙ overtake before the cyclist gets to the junction
- ⊙ flash your headlights at the cyclist
- ⊙ slow down and allow the cyclist to turn
- ⊙ overtake the cyclist on the left-hand side

⊙ **slow down and allow the cyclist to turn**

Keep well back and allow the cyclist room to take up the correct position for the turn. Don't get too close behind or try to squeeze past.

5.29   *Mark **one** answer*

Why must you take extra care when turning right at this junction?

⊙ Road surface is poor

⊙ Footpaths are narrow

⊙ Road markings are faint

⊙ There is reduced visibility

⊙ **There is reduced visibility**

You may have to pull forward slowly until you can see up and down the road. Be aware that the traffic approaching the junction can't see you either. If you don't know that it's clear, don't go.

5.30   *Mark **one** answer*

When approaching this bridge you should give way to

⊙ bicycles

⊙ buses

⊙ motorcycles

⊙ cars

⊙ **buses**

A double-deck bus or high-sided lorry will have to take up a position in the centre of the road so that it can clear the bridge. There is normally a sign to indicate this.

Look well down the road, through the bridge and be aware you may have to stop and give way to an oncoming large vehicle.

*Mark **one** answer*

What type of vehicle could you expect to meet in the middle of the road?

- ⊙ Lorry
- ⊙ Bicycle
- ⊙ Car
- ⊙ Motorcycle

⊙ **Lorry**

The highest point of the bridge is in the centre so a large vehicle might have to move to the centre of the road to allow it enough room to pass under the bridge.

*Mark **one** answer*

At this blind junction you must stop

- ⊙ behind the line, then edge forward to see clearly
- ⊙ beyond the line at a point where you can see clearly
- ⊙ only if there is traffic on the main road
- ⊙ only if you are turning to the right

⊙ **behind the line, then edge forward to see clearly**

The 'stop' sign has been put here because there is a poor view into the main road. You must stop because it will not be possible to assess the situation on the move, however slowly you are travelling.

5.33
*Mark **one** answer*

A driver pulls out of a side road in front of you. You have to brake hard. You should

- ignore the error and stay calm
- flash your lights to show your annoyance
- sound your horn to show your annoyance
- overtake as soon as possible

⊙ **ignore the error and stay calm**

Where there are a number of side roads, be alert. Be especially careful if there are a lot of parked vehicles because they can make it more difficult for drivers emerging to see you.

Try to be tolerant if a vehicle does emerge and you have to brake quickly. Don't react aggressively.

5.34
*Mark **one** answer*

An elderly person's driving ability could be affected because they may be unable to

- obtain car insurance
- understand road signs
- react very quickly
- give signals correctly

⊙ **react very quickly**

Be tolerant of older drivers. Poor eyesight and hearing could affect the speed with which they react to a hazard and may cause them to be hesitant.

5.35
*Mark **one** answer*

You have just passed these warning lights. What hazard would you expect to see next?

- A level crossing with no barrier
- An ambulance station
- A school crossing patrol
- An opening bridge

⊙ **A school crossing patrol**

These lights warn that children may be crossing the road to a nearby school. Slow down so that you're ready to stop if necessary.

You are planning a long journey. Do you need to plan rest stops?

⊙ Yes, you should plan to stop every half an hour

⊙ Yes, regular stops help concentration

⊙ No, you will be less tired if you get there as soon as possible

⊙ No, only fuel stops will be needed

⊙ **Yes, regular stops help concentration**

Try to plan your journey so that you can take rest stops. It's recommended that you take a break of at least 15 minutes after every two hours of driving. This should help to maintain your concentration.

A driver does something that upsets you. You should

⊙ try not to react

⊙ let them know how you feel

⊙ flash your headlights several times

⊙ sound your horn

⊙ **try not to react**

There are occasions when other road users make a misjudgement or a mistake. If this happens try not to let it annoy you. Don't react by showing anger. Sounding your horn, flashing your headlights or shouting won't help the situation. Good anticipation will help to prevent these incidents becoming accidents.

The red lights are flashing. What should you do when approaching this level crossing?

⊙ Go through quickly

⊙ Go through carefully

⊙ Stop before the barrier

⊙ Switch on hazard warning lights

⊙ **Stop before the barrier**

At level crossings the red lights flash when the barrier is down or is about to come down. You must stop, even if the barriers are not yet down.

In this picture there's a junction on the left just before the crossing, you should keep this junction clear.

When you are able to cross don't

• go onto the crossing unless the road is clear on the other side

• follow other vehicles nose to tail over it

• stop on or just past the crossing.

5.39
*Mark **one** answer*

You are approaching crossroads. The traffic lights have failed. What should you do?

- Brake and stop only for large vehicles
- Brake sharply to a stop before looking
- Be prepared to brake sharply to a stop
- Be prepared to stop for any traffic

◉ **Be prepared to stop for any traffic**

When approaching a junction where the traffic lights have failed you should proceed with caution. Treat the situation as an unmarked junction and be prepared to stop.

5.40
*Mark **one** answer*

What should the driver of the red car (arrowed) do?

- Wave the pedestrians who are waiting to cross
- Wait for the pedestrian in the road to cross
- Quickly drive behind the pedestrian in the road
- Tell the pedestrian in the road she should not have crossed

◉ **Wait for the pedestrian in the road to cross**

Some people might take longer to cross the road. They may be elderly or have a disability.

Be patient and don't hurry them by showing your impatience. They might have poor eyesight or not be able to hear traffic approaching.

If pedestrians are standing at the side of the road, don't signal or wave them to cross. Other road users may not have seen your signal and this could lead the pedestrians into a hazardous situation.

5.41
*Mark **one** answer*

Why are mirrors often slightly curved (convex)?

- They give a wider field of vision
- They totally cover blind spots
- They make it easier to judge the speed of following traffic
- They make following traffic look bigger

◉ **They give a wider field of vision**

Although a convex mirror gives a wide view of the scene behind, you should be aware that it will not show you everything behind or to the side of the vehicle. Before you move off you will need to check over your shoulder to look for anything not visible in the mirrors.

*Mark **one** answer*

You are following a slower-moving vehicle on a narrow country road. There is a junction just ahead on the right. What should you do?

⊙ Overtake after checking your mirrors and signalling

⊙ Stay behind until you are past the junction

⊙ Accelerate quickly to pass before the junction

⊙ Slow down and prepare to overtake on the left

⊙ **Stay behind until you are past the junction**

You should never overtake as you approach a junction. If a vehicle emerged from the junction while you were overtaking, a dangerous situation could develop very quickly.

*Mark **one** answer*

What should you do as you approach this overhead bridge?

⊙ Move out to the centre of the road before going through

⊙ Find another route, this is only for high vehicles

⊙ Be prepared to give way to large vehicles in the middle of the road

⊙ Move across to the right hand side before going through

⊙ **Be prepared to give way to large vehicles in the middle of the road**

Oncoming large vehicles may need to move to the middle of the road so that they can pass safely under the bridge. There will not be enough room for you to continue and you should be ready to stop and wait.

5.44   *Mark **one** answer*

What does this signal from a police officer mean to oncoming traffic?

⊙ Go ahead

⊙ Stop

⊙ Turn left

⊙ Turn right

⊙ **Stop**

Police officers may need to direct traffic, for example, at a junction where the traffic lights have broken down. Check your copy of The Highway Code for the signals that they use.

5.45   *Mark **one** answer*

You see this sign on the rear of a slow-moving lorry that you want to pass. It is travelling in the middle lane of a three-lane motorway. You should

⊙ cautiously approach the lorry then pass on either side

⊙ follow the lorry until you can leave the motorway

⊙ wait on the hard shoulder until the lorry has stopped

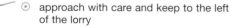 ⊙ approach with care and keep to the left of the lorry

⊙ **approach with care and keep to the left of the lorry**

This sign is found on slow-moving or stationary works vehicles. If you wish to overtake, do so on the left, as indicated. Be aware that there might be workmen in the area.

You think the driver of the vehicle in front has forgotten to cancel their right indicator. You should

- ⊙ flash your lights to alert the driver
- ⊙ sound your horn before overtaking
- ⊙ overtake on the left if there is room
- ⊙ stay behind and not overtake

⊙ **stay behind and not overtake**

The driver may be unsure of the location of a junction and turn suddenly. Be cautious and don't attempt to overtake.

What is the main hazard the driver of the red car (arrowed) should be aware of?

- ⊙ Glare from the sun may affect the driver's vision
- ⊙ The black car may stop suddenly
- ⊙ The bus may move out into the road
- ⊙ Oncoming vehicles will assume the driver is turning right

⊙ **The bus may move out into the road**

If you can do so safely give way to buses signalling to move off at bus stops. Try to anticipate the actions of other road users around you. The driver of the red car should be prepared for the bus pulling out. As you approach a bus stop look to see how many passengers are waiting to board. If the last one has just got on, the bus is likely to move off.

This yellow sign on a vehicle indicates this is

- ⊙ a broken-down vehicle
- ⊙ a school bus
- ⊙ an ice cream van
- ⊙ a private ambulance

⊙ **a school bus**

Buses which carry children to and from school may stop at places other than scheduled bus stops. Be aware that they might pull over at any time to allow children to get on or off. This will normally be when traffic is heavy during rush hour.

5.49   *Mark **two** answers*

What TWO main hazards should you be aware of when going along this street?

- Glare from the sun
- Car doors opening suddenly
- Lack of road markings
- The headlights on parked cars being switched on
- Large goods vehicles
- Children running out from between vehicles

⊙ **Car doors opening suddenly**

⊙ **Children running out from between vehicles**

On roads where there are many parked vehicles you should take extra care. You might not be able to see children between parked cars and they may run out into the road without looking.

People may open car doors without realising the hazard this can create. You will also need to look well down the road for oncoming traffic.

5.50   *Mark **one** answer*

What is the main hazard you should be aware of when following this cyclist?

- The cyclist may move to the left and dismount
- The cyclist may swerve out into the road
- The contents of the cyclist's carrier may fall onto the road
- The cyclist may wish to turn right at the end of the road

⊙ **The cyclist may swerve out into the road**

When following a cyclist be aware that they also have to deal with the hazards around them. They may

- wobble or swerve to avoid a pothole in the road
- see a potential hazard and change direction suddenly.

Don't follow them too closely or rev your engine impatiently.

A driver's behaviour has upset you.
It may help if you

◉ stop and take a break

◉ shout abusive language

◉ gesture to them with your hand

◉ follow their car, flashing your headlights

◉ **stop and take a break**

Tiredness may make you more irritable than you would be normally. You might react differently to situations because of it. If you feel yourself becoming tense, take a break.

In areas where there are 'traffic calming' measures you should

◉ travel at a reduced speed

◉ always travel at the speed limit

◉ position in the centre of the road

◉ only slow down if pedestrians are near

◉ **travel at a reduced speed**

Traffic calming measures such as road humps, chicanes and narrowings are intended to slow you down. Maintain a reduced speed until you reach the end of these features. They are there to protect pedestrians. Kill your speed!

When approaching this hazard why should you slow down?

◉ Because of the bend

◉ Because it's hard to see to the right

◉ Because of approaching traffic

◉ Because of animals crossing

◉ Because of the level crossing

◉ **Because of the bend**

◉ **Because of the level crossing**

There are two hazards clearly signed in this picture. You should be preparing for the bend by slowing down and selecting the correct gear. You might also have to stop at the level crossing, so be alert and be prepared to stop if necessary.

5.54
Mark one answer

Why are place names painted on the road surface?

⊙ To restrict the flow of traffic

⊙ To warn you of oncoming traffic

⊙ To enable you to change lanes early

⊙ To prevent you changing lanes

⊙ **To enable you to change lanes early**

The names of towns and cities may be painted on the road at busy junctions and complex road systems. Their purpose is to let you move into the correct lane in good time, allowing traffic to flow more freely.

5.55
Mark one answer

Some two-way roads are divided into three lanes. Why are these particularly dangerous?

⊙ Traffic in both directions can use the middle lane to overtake

⊙ Traffic can travel faster in poor weather conditions

⊙ Traffic can overtake on the left

⊙ Traffic uses the middle lane for emergencies only

⊙ **Traffic in both directions can use the middle lane to overtake**

If you intend to overtake you must consider that approaching traffic could be planning the same manoeuvre. When you have considered the situation and have decided it is safe, indicate your intentions early. This will show the approaching traffic that you intend to pull out.

5.56
Mark three answers

To avoid an accident when entering a contraflow system, you should

⊙ reduce speed in good time

⊙ switch lanes any time to make progress

⊙ choose an appropriate lane early

⊙ keep the correct separation distance

⊙ increase speed to pass through quickly

⊙ follow other motorists closely to avoid long queues

⊙ **reduce speed in good time**

⊙ **choose an appropriate lane early**

⊙ **keep the correct separation distance**

In a contraflow system you will be travelling close to oncoming traffic and sometimes in narrow lanes. You should

• obey the temporary signs governing speed limits

• get into the correct lane in good time

• keep a safe separation distance from the vehicle ahead.

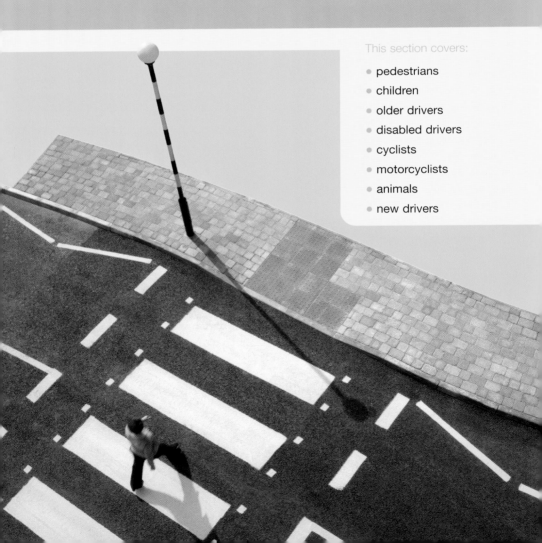

section six
VULNERABLE ROAD USERS

This section covers:

- pedestrians
- children
- older drivers
- disabled drivers
- cyclists
- motorcyclists
- animals
- new drivers

6.1
*Mark **one** answer*

You should not ride too closely behind a lorry because

- ⊙ you will breathe in the lorry's exhaust fumes
- ⊙ wind from the lorry will slow you down
- ⊙ drivers behind you may not be able to see you
- ⊙ it will reduce your view ahead

⊙ **it will reduce your view ahead**

If you're following too close behind a large vehicle your view beyond it will be restricted. Drop back. This will help you to see more of the road ahead.

It will also help the driver of the large vehicle to see you in the mirror and gives you a safe separation distance in which to take avoiding action if a hazardous situation arises.

6.2
*Mark **one** answer*

You are riding along a main road with many side roads. Why should you be particularly careful?

- ⊙ Gusts of wind from the side roads may push you off course
- ⊙ Drivers coming out from side roads may not see you
- ⊙ The road will be more slippery where cars have been turning
- ⊙ Drivers will be travelling slowly when they approach a junction

⊙ **Drivers coming out from side roads may not see you**

If you're riding along a main road with a lot of side roads, be alert. Drivers approaching or emerging from side roads may not be able to see you. Be especially careful if there are parked vehicles. Always ride at a speed that will enable you to slow down and stop in good time.

If you look well ahead and anticipate the actions of other road users you'll avoid having to brake suddenly.

6.3
*Mark **three** answers*

You are riding on a country lane. You see cattle on the road. You should

- ⊙ slow down
- ⊙ stop if necessary
- ⊙ give plenty of room
- ⊙ rev your engine
- ⊙ sound your horn
- ⊙ ride up close behind them

⊙ **slow down**

⊙ **stop if necessary**

⊙ **give plenty of room**

Try not to startle the animals. They can be easily frightened by noise or by traffic passing too closely.

A learner driver has begun to emerge into your path from a side road on the left. You should

- ⊙ be ready to slow down and stop
- ⊙ let them emerge then ride close behind
- ⊙ turn into the side road
- ⊙ brake hard, then wave them out

⊙ **be ready to slow down and stop**

If you see another vehicle begin to emerge into your path you should ride defensively. Always be ready to slow down or stop if necessary.

The vehicle ahead is being driven by a learner. You should

- ⊙ keep calm and be patient
- ⊙ ride up close behind
- ⊙ put your headlight on full beam
- ⊙ sound your horn and overtake

⊙ **keep calm and be patient**

Learners might take longer to react to traffic situations. Don't unnerve them by riding up close behind or showing signs of impatience.

You are riding in fast-flowing traffic. The vehicle behind is following too closely. You should

- ⊙ slow down gradually to increase the gap in front of you
- ⊙ slow down as quickly as possible by braking
- ⊙ accelerate to get away from the vehicle behind you
- ⊙ apply the brakes sharply to warn the driver behind

⊙ **slow down gradually to increase the gap in front of you**

It is dangerous for vehicles to travel too close together. Visibility is reduced and there is a higher risk of collision if a vehicle brakes suddenly to avoid a hazard.

By increasing the separation distance between you and the vehicle in front, you have a greater safety margin. It also gives space for the vehicles behind to overtake you if they wish.

6.7

Mark one answer

You are riding towards a zebra crossing. Waiting to cross is a person in a wheelchair. You should

⊙ continue on your way

⊙ wave to the person to cross

⊙ wave to the person to wait

⊙ be prepared to stop

⊙ **be prepared to stop**

As you would with an able-bodied person, you should prepare to slow down and stop. Don't wave them across, as other traffic may not stop.

6.8

Mark one answer

Why should you allow extra room when overtaking another motorcyclist on a windy day?

⊙ The rider may turn off suddenly to get out of the wind

⊙ The rider may be blown across in front of you

⊙ The rider may stop suddenly

⊙ The rider may be travelling faster than normal

⊙ **The rider may be blown across in front of you**

On a windy day, be aware that the blustery conditions might blow you or other motorcyclists out of position. Think about this before deciding to overtake.

6.9

Mark two answers

You have stopped at a pelican crossing. A disabled person is crossing slowly in front of you. The lights have now changed to green. You should

⊙ allow the person to cross

⊙ ride in front of the person

⊙ ride behind the person

⊙ sound your horn

⊙ be patient

⊙ edge forward slowly

⊙ **allow the person to cross**

⊙ **be patient**

At a pelican crossing the green light means you may proceed as long as the crossing is clear. If someone hasn't finished crossing, be patient and wait for them.

121

Where should you take particular care to look out for other motorcyclists and cyclists?

- On dual carriageways
- At junctions
- At zebra crossings
- On one-way streets

⊙ **At junctions**

Other motorcyclists and cyclists may be difficult to see on the road, particularly at junctions. If your view is blocked by other traffic you may not be able to see them approaching.

What is a main cause of accidents among young and new motorcyclists?

- Using borrowed equipment
- Lack of experience and judgement
- Riding in bad weather conditions
- Riding on country roads

⊙ **Lack of experience and judgement**

Young and inexperienced riders are far more likely to be involved in accidents than more experienced ones. Don't overestimate your abilities and never ride too fast for the conditions. You must always be able to pull up safely within the distance you can see to be clear. Your life could depend on it.

Which of the following is applicable to young motorcyclists?

- They are normally better than experienced riders
- They are usually less likely to have accidents
- They are often over-confident of their own ability
- They are more likely to get cheaper insurance

⊙ **They are often over-confident of their own ability**

Younger motorcyclists can often have more confidence than ability. It takes time to gain experience and become a good rider. Make sure you have the right attitude and put safety first.

6.13
*Mark **one** answer*

Young motorcyclists can often be the cause of accidents due to

- being too cautious at junctions
- riding in the middle of their lane
- showing off and being competitive
- riding when the weather is poor

⊙ **showing off and being competitive**

Over-confidence, lack of experience and poor judgement can lead to disaster. No matter what anyone says, don't do anything that could endanger lives. It's not worth the risk.

6.14
*Mark **one** answer*

Why is it vital for a rider to make a 'lifesaver' check before turning right?

- To check for any overtaking traffic
- To confirm that they are about to turn
- To make sure the side road is clear
- To check that the rear indicator is flashing

⊙ **To check for any overtaking traffic**

The 'lifesaver' glance makes you aware of what is happening behind and alongside you before altering your course. This glance must be timed so that you still have time to react if it isn't safe to carry out your manoeuvre.

6.15
*Mark **two** answers*

You are about to overtake horse riders. Which TWO of the following could scare the horses?

- Sounding your horn
- Giving arm signals
- Riding slowly
- Revving your engine

⊙ **Sounding your horn**

⊙ **Revving your engine**

When passing horses allow them plenty of space and slow down. Animals can be frightened by sudden or loud noises, so don't sound your horn or rev the engine.

The road outside this school is marked with yellow zigzag lines. What do these lines mean?

- ⊙ You may park on the lines when dropping off school children
- ⊙ You may park on the lines when picking up school children
- ⊙ You must not wait or park your motorcycle here
- ⊙ You must stay with your motorcycle if you park here

⊙ **You must not wait or park your motorcycle here**

Parking here will block the view of the school gates, endangering the lives of children on their way to and from school.

Which sign means that there may be people walking along the road?

⊙

Always check the road signs. Triangular signs are warning signs and they'll keep you informed of hazards ahead and help you to anticipate any problems. There are a number of different signs showing pedestrians. Learn the meaning of each one.

6.18

*Mark **one** answer*

You are turning left at a junction. Pedestrians have started to cross the road. You should

⊙ go on, giving them plenty of room

⊙ stop and wave at them to cross

⊙ blow your horn and proceed

⊙ give way to them

⊙ **give way to them**

If you're turning into a side road, pedestrians already crossing the road have priority and you should give way to them. Don't

• wave them across the road

• sound your horn

• flash your lights

• give any other misleading signal – other road users may misinterpret your signal and you might lead the pedestrian into a dangerous situation.

If a pedestrian is slow or indecisive be patient and wait. Don't hurry them across by revving your engine.

6.19

*Mark **one** answer*

You are turning left from a main road into a side road. People are already crossing the road into which you are turning. You should

⊙ continue, as it is your right of way

⊙ signal to them to continue crossing

⊙ wait and allow them to cross

⊙ sound your horn to warn them of your presence

⊙ **wait and allow them to cross**

Always check the road you're turning into. Approaching at the correct speed will allow you enough time to observe and react.

Give way to any pedestrians already crossing the road.

You are at a road junction, turning into a minor road. There are pedestrians crossing the minor road. You should

⊙ stop and wave the pedestrians across

⊙ sound your horn to let the pedestrians know that you are there

⊙ give way to the pedestrians who are already crossing

⊙ carry on; the pedestrians should give way to you

⊙ **give way to the pedestrians who are already crossing**

Always look into the road you're turning into. If there are pedestrians crossing, give way to them, but don't wave or signal to them to cross.

Signal your intention to turn as you approach.

You are turning left into a side road. What hazards should you be especially aware of?

⊙ One way street

⊙ Pedestrians

⊙ Traffic congestion

⊙ Parked vehicles

⊙ **Pedestrians**

Make sure that you have reduced your speed and are in the correct gear for the turn. Look into the road before you turn and always give way to any pedestrians who are crossing.

You intend to turn right into a side road. Just before turning you should check for motorcyclists who might be

⊙ overtaking on your left

⊙ following you closely

⊙ emerging from the side road

⊙ overtaking on your right

⊙ **overtaking on your right**

Never attempt to change direction to the right without first checking your right-hand mirror. A motorcyclist might not have seen your signal and could be hidden by the car behind you. This action should become a matter of routine.

6.23

*Mark **one** answer*

A toucan crossing is different from other crossings because

- ⊙ moped riders can use it
- ⊙ it is controlled by a traffic warden
- ⊙ it is controlled by two flashing lights
- ⊙ cyclists can use it

⊙ **cyclists can use it**

Toucan crossings are shared by pedestrians and cyclists and they are shown the green light together. Cyclists are permitted to cycle across.

The signals are push-button operated and there is no flashing amber phase.

6.24

*Mark **two** answers*

At toucan crossings

- ⊙ there is no flashing amber light
- ⊙ cyclists are not permitted
- ⊙ there is a continuously flashing amber beacon
- ⊙ pedestrians and cyclists may cross
- ⊙ you only stop if someone is waiting to cross

⊙ **there is no flashing amber light**

⊙ **pedestrians and cyclists may cross**

There are some crossings where cycle routes lead the cyclists to cross at the same place as pedestrians. These are called toucan crossings. Always look out for cyclists, as they're likely to be approaching faster than pedestrians.

6.25

*Mark **one** answer*

How will a school crossing patrol signal you to stop?

- ⊙ By pointing to children on the opposite pavement
- ⊙ By displaying a red light
- ⊙ By displaying a stop sign
- ⊙ By giving you an arm signal

⊙ **By displaying a stop sign**

If a school crossing patrol steps out into the road with a stop sign you must stop. Don't

- • wave anyone across the road
- • get impatient or rev your engine.

Where would you see this sign?

⊙ In the window of a car taking children to school

⊙ At the side of the road

⊙ At playground areas

⊙ On the rear of a school bus or coach

⊙ **On the rear of a school bus or coach**

Vehicles that are used to carry children to and from school will be travelling at busy times of the day. If you're following a vehicle with this sign be prepared for it to make frequent stops. It might pick up or set down passengers in places other than normal bus stops.

Which sign tells you that pedestrians may be walking in the road as there is no pavement?

⊙

Give pedestrians who are walking at the side of the road plenty of room when you pass them. They may turn around when they hear your engine and accidentally step into the road.

You see a pedestrian with a white stick and red band. This means that the person is

⊙ physically disabled

⊙ deaf only

⊙ blind only

⊙ deaf and blind

⊙ **deaf and blind**

If someone is deaf as well as blind, they may be carrying a white stick with a red reflective band.

You can't see if a pedestrian is deaf. Don't assume everyone can hear you approaching.

6.29   *Mark **one** answer*

What does this sign mean?

⊙ No route for pedestrians and cyclists

⊙ A route for pedestrians only

⊙ A route for cyclists only

⊙ A route for pedestrians and cyclists

⊙ **A route for pedestrians
and cyclists**

This sign shows a shared route for
pedestrians and cyclists: when it ends, the
cyclists will be rejoining the main road.

6.30   *Mark **one** answer*

What action would you take when elderly
people are crossing the road?

⊙ Wave them across so they know that
you have seen them

⊙ Be patient and allow them to cross in
their own time

⊙ Rev the engine to let them know that
you are waiting

⊙ Tap the horn in case they are hard
of hearing

⊙ **Be patient and allow them
to cross in their own time**

Be aware that elderly people might take a
long time to cross the road. They might
also be hard of hearing and not hear you
approaching. Don't hurry elderly people
across the road by getting too close to
them or revving your engine.

You see two elderly pedestrians about to cross the road ahead. You should

- ⊙ expect them to wait for you to pass
- ⊙ speed up to get past them quickly
- ⊙ stop and wave them across the road
- ⊙ be careful, they may misjudge your speed

⊙ **be careful, they may misjudge your speed**

Elderly people may have impaired

- hearing
- vision
- concentration
- judgement.

They may also walk slowly and so could take a long time to cross the road.

You are coming up to a roundabout. A cyclist is signalling to turn right. What should you do?

- ⊙ Overtake on the right
- ⊙ Give a horn warning
- ⊙ Signal the cyclist to move across
- ⊙ Give the cyclist plenty of room

⊙ **Give the cyclist plenty of room**

If you're following a cyclist who's signalling to turn right at a roundabout leave plenty of room. Give them space and time to get into the correct lane.

When you are overtaking a cyclist you should leave as much room as you would give to a car. What is the main reason for this?

- ⊙ The cyclist might change lanes
- ⊙ The cyclist might get off the bike
- ⊙ The cyclist might swerve
- ⊙ The cyclist might have to make a right turn

⊙ **The cyclist might swerve**

Look at the road ahead if you intend to overtake a cyclist. Check if the cyclist is likely to need to change direction for a parked vehicle or an uneven road surface. When you have a safe place to overtake leave as much room as you would for a car. Don't cut in sharply or pass too closely.

6.34
*Mark **two** answers*

Which TWO should you allow extra room when overtaking?

- Motorcycles
- Tractors
- Bicycles
- Road-sweeping vehicles

- **Motorcycles**
- **Bicycles**

Don't pass riders too closely as this may cause them to lose balance. Always leave as much room as you would for a car, and don't cut in.

6.35
*Mark **one** answer*

Why should you look particularly for motorcyclists and cyclists at junctions?

- They may want to turn into the side road
- They may slow down to let you turn
- They are harder to see
- They might not see you turn

- **They are harder to see**

Cyclists and motorcyclists are smaller than other vehicles and so are more difficult to see. They can easily become hidden from your view by cars parked near a junction.

6.36
*Mark **one** answer*

You are waiting to come out of a side road. Why should you watch carefully for motorcycles?

- Motorcycles are usually faster than cars
- Police patrols often use motorcycles
- Motorcycles are small and hard to see
- Motorcycles have right of way

- **Motorcycles are small and hard to see**

If you're waiting to emerge from a side road watch out for motorcycles: they're small and can be difficult to see. Be especially careful if there are parked vehicles restricting your view, there might be a motorcycle approaching.

IF YOU DON'T KNOW, DON'T GO.

6.37
Mark **one** answer

In daylight, an approaching motorcyclist is using a dipped headlight. Why?

- So that the rider can be seen more easily
- To stop the battery overcharging
- To improve the rider's vision
- The rider is inviting you to proceed

So that the rider can be seen more easily

A motorcycle can be lost from sight behind another vehicle. The use of the headlight helps to make it more conspicuous and therefore more easily seen.

6.38
Mark **one** answer

Motorcyclists should wear bright clothing mainly because

- they must do so by law
- it helps keep them cool in summer
- the colours are popular
- drivers often do not see them

drivers often do not see them

Motorcycles are small vehicles and can be difficult to see. If the rider wears bright clothing it can make it easier for other road users to see them approaching, especially at junctions.

6.39
Mark **one** answer

There is a slow-moving motorcyclist ahead of you. You are unsure what the rider is going to do. You should

- pass on the left
- pass on the right
- stay behind
- move closer

stay behind

If a motorcyclist is travelling slowly it may be that they are looking for a turning or entrance. Be patient and stay behind them in case they need to make a sudden change of direction.

6.40
Mark one answer

Motorcyclists will often look round over their right shoulder just before turning right. This is because

- they need to listen for following traffic
- motorcycles do not have mirrors
- looking around helps them balance as they turn
- they need to check for traffic in their blind area

- **they need to check for traffic in their blind area**

If you see a motorcyclist take a quick glance over their shoulder, this could mean they are about to change direction. Recognising a clue like this helps you to be prepared and take appropriate action, making you safer on the road.

6.41
Mark three answers

At road junctions which of the following are most vulnerable?

- Cyclists
- Motorcyclists
- Pedestrians
- Car drivers
- Lorry drivers

- **Cyclists**
- **Motorcyclists**
- **Pedestrians**

Pedestrians and riders on two wheels can be harder to see than other road users. Make sure you keep a look-out for them, especially at junctions. Good effective observation, coupled with appropriate action, can save lives.

6.42
Mark one answer

Motorcyclists are particularly vulnerable

- when moving off
- on dual carriageways
- when approaching junctions
- on motorways

- **when approaching junctions**

Another road user failing to see a motorcyclist is a major cause of collisions at junctions. Wherever streams of traffic join or cross there's the potential for this type of accident to occur.

6.43
*Mark **one** answer*

An injured motorcyclist is lying unconscious in the road. You should

⊙ remove the safety helmet
⊙ seek medical assistance
⊙ move the person off the road
⊙ remove the leather jacket

⊙ **seek medical assistance**

If someone has been injured, the sooner proper medical attention is given the better. Either send someone to phone for help or go yourself. Only move an injured person if there is a risk of further danger. Do not remove an injured motorcyclist's safety helmet unless it is essential.

6.44
*Mark **one** answer*

As you approach a pelican crossing the lights change to green. Elderly people are halfway across. You should

⊙ wave them to cross as quickly as they can
⊙ rev your engine to make them hurry
⊙ flash your lights in case they have not heard you
⊙ wait because they will take longer to cross

⊙ **wait because they will take longer to cross**

Even if the lights turn to green, wait for them to clear the crossing. Allow them to cross the road in their own time, and don't try to hurry them by revving your engine.

6.45
*Mark **three** answers*

Which THREE should you do when passing sheep on a road?

⊙ Allow plenty of room
⊙ Go very slowly
⊙ Pass quickly but quietly
⊙ Be ready to stop
⊙ Briefly sound your horn

⊙ **Allow plenty of room**

⊙ **Go very slowly**

⊙ **Be ready to stop**

Slow down and be ready to stop if you see animals in the road ahead. Animals are easily frightened by

• noise

• vehicles passing too close to them.

Stop if signalled to do so by the person in charge.

6.46
*Mark **two** answers*

You are approaching a roundabout. There are horses just ahead of you. You should

⊙ be prepared to stop

⊙ treat them like any other vehicle

⊙ give them plenty of room

⊙ accelerate past as quickly as possible

⊙ sound your horn as a warning

⊙ **be prepared to stop**

⊙ **give them plenty of room**

Horse riders often keep to the outside of the roundabout even if they are turning right. Give them plenty of room and remember that they may have to cross lanes of traffic.

6.47
*Mark **one** answer*

There are flashing amber lights under a school warning sign. What action should you take?

⊙ Reduce speed until you are clear of the area

⊙ Keep up your speed and sound the horn

⊙ Increase your speed to clear the area quickly

⊙ Wait at the lights until they change to green

⊙ **Reduce speed until you are clear of the area**

The flashing amber lights are switched on to warn you that children may be crossing near a school. Slow down and take extra care as you may have to stop.

6.48
*Mark **one** answer*

These road markings must be kept clear to allow

⊙ school children to be dropped off

⊙ for teachers to park

⊙ school children to be picked up

⊙ a clear view of the crossing area

⊙ **a clear view of the crossing area**

The markings are there to show that the area must be kept clear to allow an unrestricted view for

• approaching drivers and riders

• children wanting to cross the road.

Where would you see this sign?

⊙ Near a school crossing

⊙ At a playground entrance

⊙ On a school bus

⊙ At a 'pedestrians only' area

⊙ **On a school bus**

Watch out for children crossing the road from the other side of the bus.

You are following two cyclists. They approach a roundabout in the left-hand lane. In which direction should you expect the cyclists to go?

⊙ Left

⊙ Right

⊙ Any direction

⊙ Straight ahead

⊙ **Any direction**

Cyclists approaching a roundabout in the left-hand lane may be turning right but may not have been able to get into the correct lane due to the heavy traffic. They may also feel safer keeping to the left all the way round the roundabout. Be aware of them and give them plenty of room.

You are travelling behind a moped. You want to turn left just ahead. You should

⊙ overtake the moped before the junction

⊙ pull alongside the moped and stay level until just before the junction

⊙ sound your horn as a warning and pull in front of the moped

⊙ stay behind until the moped has passed the junction

⊙ **stay behind until the moped has passed the junction**

Passing the moped and turning into the junction could mean that you cut across the front of the rider. This might force them to slow down, stop or even lose control. Slow down and stay behind the moped until it has passed the junction and you can then turn safely.

6.52 *Mark **three** answers*

Which THREE of the following are hazards motorcyclists present in queues of traffic?

- ☉ Cutting in just in front of you
- ☉ Riding in single file
- ☉ Passing very close to you
- ☉ Riding with their headlight on dipped beam
- ☉ Filtering between the lanes

⊙ **Cutting in just in front of you**

⊙ **Passing very close to you**

⊙ **Filtering between the lanes**

Where there's more than one lane of queuing traffic, motorcyclists may use the opportunity to make progress by riding between the lanes. Be aware that they may be passing on either side. Check your mirrors before you move off.

6.53 *Mark **one** answer*

You see a horse rider as you approach a roundabout. They are signalling right but keeping well to the left. You should

- ☉ proceed as normal
- ☉ keep close to them
- ☉ cut in front of them
- ☉ stay well back

⊙ **stay well back**

Allow the horse rider to enter and exit the roundabout in their own time. They may feel safer keeping to the left all the way around the roundabout. Don't get up close behind or alongside them. This is very likely to upset the horse and create a dangerous situation.

*Mark **one** answer*

How would you react to drivers who appear to be inexperienced?

- ⊙ Sound your horn to warn them of your presence
- ⊙ Be patient and prepare for them to react more slowly
- ⊙ Flash your headlights to indicate that it is safe for them to proceed
- ⊙ Overtake them as soon as possible

⊙ **Be patient and prepare for them to react more slowly**

Learners might not have confidence when they first start to drive. Allow them plenty of room and don't react adversely to their hesitation. We all learn from experience, but new drivers will have had less practice in dealing with all the situations that might occur.

*Mark **one** answer*

You are following a learner driver who stalls at a junction. You should

- ⊙ be patient as you expect them to make mistakes
- ⊙ stay very close behind and flash your headlights
- ⊙ start to rev your engine if they take too long to restart
- ⊙ immediately steer around them and drive on

⊙ **be patient as you expect them to make mistakes**

Learning is a process of practice and experience. Try to understand this and tolerate those who are at the beginning of this process.

*Mark **one** answer*

You are on a country road. What should you expect to see coming towards you on YOUR side of the road?

- ⊙ Motorcycles
- ⊙ Bicycles
- ⊙ Pedestrians
- ⊙ Horse riders

⊙ **Pedestrians**

On a quiet country road always be aware that there may be a hazard just around the next bend, such as a slow-moving vehicle or pedestrians. Pedestrians are advised to walk on the right-hand side of the road if there is no pavement, so they may be walking towards you on your side of the road.

6.57

*Mark **one** answer*

You are turning left into a side road. Pedestrians are crossing the road near the junction. You must

⊙ wave them on

⊙ sound your horn

⊙ switch on your hazard lights

⊙ wait for them to cross

⊙ **wait for them to cross**

Check that it's clear before you turn into a junction. If there are pedestrians crossing, let them cross in their own time.

6.58

*Mark **one** answer*

You are following a car driven by an elderly driver. You should

⊙ expect the driver to drive badly

⊙ flash your lights and overtake

⊙ be aware that the driver's reactions may not be as fast as yours

⊙ stay very close behind but be careful

⊙ **be aware that the driver's reactions may not be as fast as yours**

You must show consideration to other road users. The reactions of elderly drivers may be slower and they might need more time to deal with a situation. Be tolerant and don't lose patience or show your annoyance.

6.59

*Mark **one** answer*

You should never attempt to overtake a cyclist

⊙ just before you turn left

⊙ on a left hand bend

⊙ on a one-way street

⊙ on a dual carriageway

⊙ **just before you turn left**

If you want to turn left and there's a cyclist in front of you, hold back. Wait until the cyclist has passed the junction and then turn left behind them.

A horse rider is in the left-hand lane approaching a roundabout. You should expect the rider to

⊙ go in any direction

⊙ turn right

⊙ turn left

⊙ go ahead

⊙ **go in any direction**

Horses and their riders will move more slowly than other road users. They might not have time to cut across heavy traffic to take up positions in the offside lane. For this reason a horse and rider may approach a roundabout in the left-hand lane, even though they're turning right.

Powered vehicles used by disabled people are small and hard to see. How do they give early warning when on a dual carriageway?

⊙ They will have a flashing red light

⊙ They will have a flashing green light

⊙ They will have a flashing blue light

⊙ They will have a flashing amber light

⊙ **They will have a flashing amber light**

Powered vehicles used by disabled people are small, low, hard to see and travel very slowly. On a dual carriageway they will have a flashing amber light to warn other road users.

You notice horse riders in front. What should you do FIRST?

⊙ Pull out to the middle of the road

⊙ Slow down and be ready to stop

⊙ Accelerate around them

⊙ Signal right

⊙ **Slow down and be ready to stop**

Be particularly careful when approaching horse riders – slow down and be prepared to stop. Always pass wide and slowly and look out for signals given by horse riders.

Horses are unpredictable: always treat them as potential hazards and take great care when passing them.

6.63   *Mark **one** answer*

Ahead of you there is a moving vehicle with a flashing amber beacon. This means it is

- ⊙ slow moving
- ⊙ broken down
- ⊙ a doctor's car
- ⊙ a school crossing patrol

⊙ **slow moving**

As you approach the vehicle, assess the situation. Due to its slow progress you will need to judge whether it is safe to overtake.

6.64   *Mark **one** answer*

What does this sign mean?

- ⊙ Contraflow pedal cycle lane
- ⊙ With-flow pedal cycle lane
- ⊙ Pedal cycles and buses only
- ⊙ No pedal cycles or buses

⊙ **With-flow pedal cycle lane**

The picture of a cycle will also usually be painted on the road, sometimes with a different colour surface. Leave these clear for cyclists and don't pass too closely when you overtake.

6.65   *Mark **one** answer*

You are following a cyclist. You wish to turn left just ahead. You should

- ⊙ overtake the cyclist before the junction
- ⊙ pull alongside the cyclist and stay level until after the junction
- ⊙ hold back until the cyclist has passed the junction
- ⊙ go around the cyclist on the junction

⊙ **hold back until the cyclist has passed the junction**

Make allowances for cyclists. Allow them plenty of room. Don't try to overtake and then turn left as you would have to cut in across the path of the cyclist. Be patient and stay behind them until they have passed the junction.

6.66

*Mark **one** answer*

At night you see a pedestrian wearing reflective clothing and carrying a bright red light. What does this mean?

- ⊙ You are approaching roadworks
- ⊙ You are approaching an organised walk
- ⊙ You are approaching a slow-moving vehicle
- ⊙ You are approaching an accident blackspot

⊙ **You are approaching an organised walk**

The people involved in the walk should be keeping to the left, but this can't be assumed. Pass slowly, ensuring that you have the time to do so safely. Be aware that the pedestrians have their backs to you and might not know that you're there.

6.67

*Mark **one** answer*

You must not stop on these road markings because you may obstruct

- ⊙ children's view of the crossing area
- ⊙ teachers' access to the school
- ⊙ delivery vehicles' access to the school
- ⊙ emergency vehicles' access to the school

⊙ **children's view of the crossing area**

These markings are found on the road outside schools. DO NOT stop (even to set down or pick up children) or park on them. The markings are to make sure that drivers, riders, children and other pedestrians have a clear view.

6.68

*Mark **one** answer*

The left-hand pavement is closed due to street repairs. What should you do?

- ⊙ Watch out for pedestrians walking in the road
- ⊙ Use your right-hand mirror more often
- ⊙ Speed up to get past the roadworks quicker
- ⊙ Position close to the left-hand kerb

⊙ **Watch out for pedestrians walking in the road**

Where street repairs have closed off pavements, proceed carefully and slowly as pedestrians might have to walk in the road.

6.69 *Mark **one** answer*

You are following a motorcyclist on an uneven road. You should

- allow less room so you can be seen in their mirrors
- overtake immediately
- allow extra room in case they swerve to avoid potholes
- allow the same room as normal because road surfaces do not affect motorcyclists

⊙ **allow extra room in case they swerve to avoid potholes**

Potholes and bumps in the road can unbalance a motorcyclist. For this reason the rider might swerve to avoid an uneven road surface. Watch out at places where this is likely to occur.

6.70 *Mark **one** answer*

You have just passed your test. How can you decrease your risk of accidents on the motorway?

- By keeping up with the car in front
- By never going over 40 mph
- By staying only in the left-hand lane
- By taking further training

⊙ **By taking further training**

You're more likely to have an accident in the first year after taking your test. Lack of experience means that you might not react to hazards as quickly as a more experienced person. Further training will help you to become safer on the roads.

6.71 *Mark **one** answer*

What does this sign tell you?

- No cycling
- Cycle route ahead
- Cycle parking only
- End of cycle route

⊙ **Cycle route ahead**

With people's concern today for the environment, cycle routes are being created in our towns and cities. These are usually defined by road markings and signs.

Respect the presence of cyclists on the road and give them plenty of room if you need to pass.

You are approaching this roundabout and see the cyclist signal right. Why is the cyclist keeping to the left?

- ⊙ It is a quicker route for the cyclist
- ⊙ The cyclist is going to turn left instead
- ⊙ The cyclist thinks The Highway Code does not apply to bicycles
- ⊙ The cyclist is slower and more vulnerable

⊙ **The cyclist is slower and more vulnerable**

Cycling in today's heavy traffic can be hazardous. Some cyclists may not feel happy about crossing the path of traffic to take up a position in an outside lane. Be aware of this and understand that, although in the left-hand lane, the cyclist might be turning right.

You are approaching this crossing. You should

- ⊙ prepare to slow down and stop
- ⊙ stop and wave the pedestrians across
- ⊙ speed up and pass by quickly
- ⊙ continue unless the pedestrians step out

⊙ **prepare to slow down and stop**

Be courteous and prepare to stop. Do not wave people across as this could be dangerous if another vehicle is approaching the crossing.

6.74

You see a pedestrian with a dog. The dog has a yellow or burgundy coat. This especially warns you that the pedestrian is

- ⊙ elderly
- ⊙ dog training
- ⊙ colour blind
- ⊙ deaf

⊙ **deaf**

Take extra care as the pedestrian may not be aware of vehicles approaching.

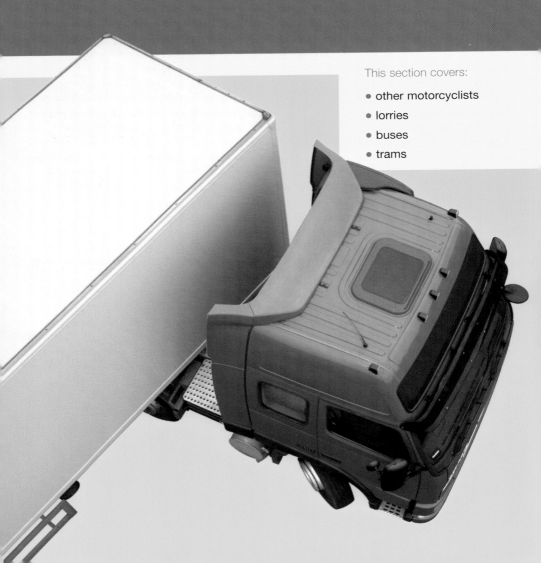

section seven
OTHER TYPES OF VEHICLE

This section covers:
- other motorcyclists
- lorries
- buses
- trams

7.1

You are riding behind a long vehicle. There is a mini-roundabout ahead. The vehicle is signalling left, but positioned to the right. You should

- ⊙ sound your horn
- ⊙ overtake on the left
- ⊙ keep well back
- ⊙ flash your headlights

⊙ **keep well back**

The long vehicle needs more room than other vehicles in order to make the left turn.

Don't overtake on the left – the driver will not expect you to be there and may not see you. Staying well back will also give you a better view around the vehicle.

7.2

Why should you be careful when riding on roads where electric trams operate?

- ⊙ They cannot steer to avoid you
- ⊙ They move quickly and quietly
- ⊙ They are noisy and slow
- ⊙ They can steer to avoid you
- ⊙ They give off harmful exhaust fumes

⊙ **They cannot steer to avoid you**

⊙ **They move quickly and quietly**

Electric trams run on rails and cannot steer to avoid you. Keep a lookout for trams as they move very quietly and can appear suddenly.

7.3

You are about to overtake a slow-moving motorcyclist. Which one of these signs would make you take special care?

⊙   ⊙

⊙   ⊙

⊙

In windy weather, watch out for motorcyclists and also cyclists as they can be blown sideways into your path. When you pass them, leave plenty of room and check their position in your mirror before pulling back in.

You are waiting to emerge left from a minor road. A large vehicle is approaching from the right. You have time to turn, but you should wait. Why?

⊙ The large vehicle can easily hide an overtaking vehicle

⊙ The large vehicle can turn suddenly

⊙ The large vehicle is difficult to steer in a straight line

⊙ The large vehicle can easily hide vehicles from the left

⊙ **The large vehicle can easily hide an overtaking vehicle**

Large vehicles can hide other vehicles that are overtaking, especially motorcycles which may be filtering past queuing traffic. You need to be aware of the possibility of hidden vehicles and not assume that it is safe to emerge.

You are following a long vehicle. It approaches a crossroads and signals left, but moves out to the right. You should

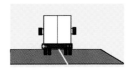

⊙ get closer in order to pass it quickly

⊙ stay well back and give it room

⊙ assume the signal is wrong and it is really turning right

⊙ overtake as it starts to slow down

⊙ **stay well back and give it room**

A lorry may swing out to the right as it approaches a left turn. This is to allow the rear wheels to clear the kerb as it turns. Don't try to filter through if you see a gap on the nearside.

7.6

*Mark **one** answer*

You are following a long vehicle approaching a crossroads. The driver signals right but moves close to the left-hand kerb. What should you do?

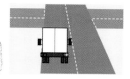

⊙ Warn the driver of the wrong signal

⊙ Wait behind the long vehicle

⊙ Report the driver to the police

⊙ Overtake on the right-hand side

⊙ **Wait behind the long vehicle**

When a long vehicle is going to turn right it may need to keep close to the left-hand kerb. This is to prevent the rear end of the trailer cutting the corner. You need to be aware of how long vehicles behave in such situations. Don't overtake the lorry because it could turn as you're alongside. Stay behind and wait for it to turn.

7.7

*Mark **one** answer*

You are approaching a mini-roundabout. The long vehicle in front is signalling left but positioned over to the right. You should

⊙ sound your horn

⊙ overtake on the left

⊙ follow the same course as the lorry

⊙ keep well back

⊙ **keep well back**

At mini-roundabouts there isn't much room for a long vehicle to manoeuvre. It will have to swing out wide so that it can complete the turn safely. Keep well back and don't try to move up alongside it.

Before overtaking a large vehicle you should keep well back. Why is this?

⊙ To give acceleration space to overtake quickly on blind bends

⊙ To get the best view of the road ahead

⊙ To leave a gap in case the vehicle stops and rolls back

⊙ To offer other drivers a safe gap if they want to overtake you

⊙ **To get the best view of the road ahead**

When following a large vehicle keep well back. If you're too close you won't be able to see the road ahead and the driver of the long vehicle might not be able to see you in their mirrors.

Why is passing a lorry more risky than passing a car?

⊙ Lorries are longer than cars

⊙ Lorries may suddenly pull up

⊙ The brakes of lorries are not as good

⊙ Lorries climb hills more slowly

⊙ **Lorries are longer than cars**

Hazards to watch for include

• oncoming traffic

• junctions

• bends or dips, which could restrict your view

• any signs or road markings prohibiting overtaking.

Never begin to overtake unless you can see that it's safe to complete the manoeuvre.

You keep well back while waiting to overtake a large vehicle. A car fills the gap. You should

⊙ sound your horn

⊙ drop back further

⊙ flash your headlights

⊙ start to overtake

⊙ **drop back further**

It's very frustrating when your separation distance is shortened by another vehicle. React positively, stay calm and drop further back.

7.11   *Mark **one** answer*

You are following a large lorry on a wet road. Spray makes it difficult to see. You should

⊙ drop back until you can see better

⊙ put your headlights on full beam

⊙ keep close to the lorry, away from the spray

⊙ speed up and overtake quickly

⊙ **drop back until you can see better**

Large vehicles may throw up a lot of spray when the roads are wet. This will make it difficult for you to see ahead. Dropping back further will

• move you out of the spray and allow you to see further

• increase your separation distance. It takes longer to stop when the roads are wet and you need to allow more room.

Don't

• follow the vehicle in front too closely

• overtake, unless you can see and are sure that the way ahead is clear.

7.12   *Mark **one** answer*

You are following a large articulated vehicle. It is going to turn left into a narrow road. What action should you take?

⊙ Move out and overtake on the right

⊙ Pass on the left as the vehicle moves out

⊙ Be prepared to stop behind

⊙ Overtake quickly before the lorry moves out

⊙ **Be prepared to stop behind**

Lorries are larger and longer than other vehicles and this can affect their position when approaching junctions. When turning left they may move out to the right so that they don't cut in and mount the kerb with the rear wheels.

*Mark **two** answers*

You are travelling behind a bus that pulls up at a bus stop. What should you do?

- ⊙ Accelerate past the bus sounding your horn
- ⊙ Watch carefully for pedestrians
- ⊙ Be ready to give way to the bus
- ⊙ Pull in closely behind the bus

- ⊙ **Watch carefully for pedestrians**

- ⊙ **Be ready to give way to the bus**

There might be pedestrians crossing from in front of the bus. Look out for them if you intend to pass. Consider staying back and waiting.

How many people are waiting to get on the bus? Check the queue if you can. The bus might move off straight away if there is no one waiting to get on.

If a bus is signalling to pull out, give it priority as long as it is safe to do so.

*Mark **one** answer*

You are following a long lorry. The driver signals to turn left into a narrow road. What should you do?

- ⊙ Overtake on the left before the lorry reaches the junction
- ⊙ Overtake on the right as soon as the lorry slows down
- ⊙ Do not overtake unless you can see there is no oncoming traffic
- ⊙ Do not overtake, stay well back and be prepared to stop

- ⊙ **Do not overtake, stay well back and be prepared to stop**

When turning into narrow roads articulated and long vehicles will need more room. Initially they will need to swing out in the opposite direction to which they intend to turn. They could mask another vehicle turning out of the same junction. DON'T be tempted to overtake them or pass on the inside.

7.15

When you approach a bus signalling to move off from a bus stop you should

⊙ get past before it moves

⊙ allow it to pull away, if it is safe to do so

⊙ flash your headlights as you approach

⊙ signal left and wave the bus on

⊙ **allow it to pull away, if it is safe to do so**

Give way to buses whenever you can do so safely, especially when they signal to pull away from bus stops. Look out for people who've got off the bus and may try to cross the road. Don't

• try to accelerate past before it moves away

• flash your lights – other road users may be misled by this signal.

7.16

You wish to overtake a long, slow-moving vehicle on a busy road. You should

⊙ follow it closely and keep moving out to see the road ahead

⊙ flash your headlights for the oncoming traffic to give way

⊙ stay behind until the driver waves you past

⊙ keep well back until you can see that it is clear

⊙ **keep well back until you can see that it is clear**

If you wish to overtake a long vehicle, stay well back so that you can see the road ahead. DON'T

• get up close to the vehicle – this will restrict your view of the road ahead

• get impatient – overtaking on a busy road calls for sound judgement

• take a gamble – only overtake when you can see that you can safely complete the manoeuvre.

7.17

Which of these is LEAST likely to be affected by crosswinds?

⊙ Cyclists

⊙ Motorcyclists

⊙ High-sided vehicles

⊙ Cars

⊙ **Cars**

Although cars are the least likely to be affected, crosswinds can take anyone by surprise, especially

• after overtaking a large vehicle

• when passing gaps between hedges or buildings

• on exposed sections of road.

What should you do as you approach this lorry?

⊙ Slow down and be prepared to wait

⊙ Make the lorry wait for you

⊙ Flash your lights at the lorry

⊙ Move to the right-hand side of the road

⊙ **Slow down and be prepared to wait**

When turning, long vehicles need much more room on the road than other vehicles. At junctions they may take up the whole of the road space, so be patient and allow them the room they need.

You are following a large vehicle approaching crossroads. The driver signals to turn left. What should you do?

⊙ Overtake if you can leave plenty of room

⊙ Overtake only if there are no oncoming vehicles

⊙ Do not overtake until the vehicle begins to turn

⊙ Do not overtake when at or approaching a junction

⊙ **Do not overtake when at or approaching a junction**

Hold back and wait until the vehicle has turned before proceeding. Do not overtake because the vehicle turning left could hide a vehicle emerging from the same junction.

7.20   *Mark **one** answer*

Powered vehicles, such as wheelchairs or scooters, used by disabled people have a maximum speed of

⊙ 8 mph

⊙ 12 mph

⊙ 16 mph

⊙ 20 mph

⊙ **8 mph**

These are small battery powered vehicles, such as powered wheelchairs and mobility scooters, and can be used on the pavement and road. Due to their cheap cost a large number are now being used. They are generally used by the elderly, disabled or infirm. Take great care around these vehicles as they are extremely vulnerable because of their low speed, small size and low height.

7.21   *Mark **one** answer*

In front of you is a powered vehicle (powered wheelchair) driven by a disabled person. These vehicles have a maximum speed of

⊙ 8 mph

⊙ 18 mph

⊙ 28 mph

⊙ 38 mph

⊙ **8 mph**

These vehicles are battery powered and very vulnerable due to their slow speed, small size and low height. Take extra care and be patient if you are following one. Allow plenty of room when overtaking and do not go past unless you can do so safely.

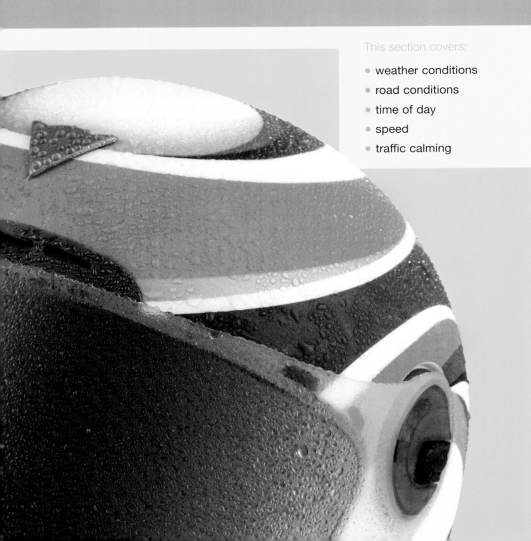

section eight
MOTORCYCLE HANDLING

This section covers:

- weather conditions
- road conditions
- time of day
- speed
- traffic calming

8.1
*Mark **one** answer*

When you are seated on a stationary motorcycle, your position should allow you to

 just touch the ground with your toes

place both feet on the ground

operate the centre stand

reach the switches by stretching

⊙ **place both feet on the ground**

When sitting astride a stationary motorcycle you should be able to place both feet on the ground for maximum control and stability.

8.2
*Mark **two** answers*

As a safety measure before starting your engine, you should

 push the motorcycle forward to check the rear wheel turns freely

engage first gear and apply the rear brake

engage first gear and apply the front brake

glance at the neutral light on your instrument panel

⊙ **push the motorcycle forward to check the rear wheel turns freely**

⊙ **glance at the neutral light on your instrument panel**

Before starting the engine you should ensure the motorcycle is in neutral. This can be done by

• moving the motorcycle to check that the rear wheel turns freely

• making sure the neutral warning light is lit when the ignition is turned on.

8.3
*Mark **two** answers*

You are approaching this junction. As the motorcyclist you should

prepare to slow down

sound your horn

keep near the left kerb

speed up to clear the junction

stop, as the car has right of way

⊙ **prepare to slow down**

⊙ **sound your horn**

Look out for road signs indicating side roads, even if you aren't turning off. A driver who is emerging might not be able to see you due to parked cars or heavy traffic. Always be prepared, and stop if necessary.

Remember, no one has priority at unmarked crossroads.

*Mark **one** answer*

What can you do to improve your safety on the road as a motorcyclist?

⊙ Anticipate the actions of others

⊙ Stay just above the speed limits

⊙ Keep positioned close to the kerbs

⊙ Remain well below speed limits

⊙ **Anticipate the actions of others**

Always ride defensively. This means looking and planning ahead as well as anticipating the actions of other road users.

8.5 *Mark **three** answers*

Which THREE of these can cause skidding?

⊙ Braking too gently

⊙ Leaning too far over when cornering

⊙ Staying upright when cornering

⊙ Braking too hard

⊙ Changing direction suddenly

⊙ **Leaning too far over when cornering**

⊙ **Braking too hard**

⊙ **Changing direction suddenly**

In order to keep control of your motorcycle and prevent skidding you must plan well ahead to prevent harsh, late braking. Try to avoid braking while changing direction, as this reduces the tyres' grip on the road.

Take the road and weather conditions into consideration and adjust your speed if necessary.

8.6 *Mark **two** answers*

It is very cold and the road looks wet. You cannot hear any road noise. You should

⊙ continue riding at the same speed

⊙ ride slower in as high a gear as possible

⊙ ride in as low a gear as possible

⊙ keep revving your engine

⊙ slow down as there may be black ice

⊙ **ride slower in as high a gear as possible**

⊙ **slow down as there may be black ice**

Rain freezing on roads is called black ice. It can be hard to see. Indications of black ice are when you can't hear tyre noise and the steering becomes very light.

You need to keep your speed down and avoid harsh steering, braking and acceleration. Riding in as high a gear as possible will help to reduce the risk of wheel-spin.

8.7   *Mark **one** answer*

When riding a motorcycle you should wear full protective clothing

- ⊙ at all times
- ⊙ only on faster, open roads
- ⊙ just on long journeys
- ⊙ only during bad weather

⊙ **at all times**

Protective clothing is designed to protect you from the cold and wet and also gives some protection from injury.

8.8   *Mark **two** answers*

You have to make a journey in fog. What are the TWO most important things you should do before you set out?

- ⊙ Fill up with fuel
- ⊙ Make sure that you have a warm drink with you
- ⊙ Check that your lights are working
- ⊙ Check the battery
- ⊙ Make sure that your visor is clean

⊙ **Check that your lights are working**

⊙ **Make sure that your visor is clean**

When you're riding a motorcycle, keep your visor as clean as possible to give you a clear view of the road. It's a good idea to carry a clean, damp cloth in a polythene bag for this purpose.

You need to ensure that your lights are clean and can be seen clearly by other road users. This is especially important when visibility is reduced, for example in fog or heavy rain.

8.9   *Mark **one** answer*

The best place to park your motorcycle is

- ⊙ on soft tarmac
- ⊙ on bumpy ground
- ⊙ on grass
- ⊙ on firm, level ground

⊙ **on firm, level ground**

Parking your motorcycle on soft ground might cause the stand to sink and the bike to fall over. The ground should also be level to ensure that the bike is stable.

Where off-road parking or motorcycle parking areas are available, use them.

*Mark **one** answer*

When riding in windy conditions, you should

- ⊙ stay close to large vehicles
- ⊙ keep your speed up
- ⊙ keep your speed down
- ⊙ stay close to the gutter

⊙ **keep your speed down**

Strong winds can blow motorcycles off course and even across the road. In windy conditions you need to

- slow down
- avoid riding on exposed roads
- watch for gaps in buildings and hedges where you may be affected by a sudden blast of wind.

*Mark **one** answer*

In normal riding your position on the road should be

- ⊙ about a foot from the kerb
- ⊙ about central in your lane
- ⊙ on the right of your lane
- ⊙ near the centre of the road

⊙ **about central in your lane**

If you're riding a motorcycle it's very important to ride where other road users can see you. In normal weather you should ride in the centre of your lane. This will

- help you to be seen in the mirror of the vehicle in front
- avoid uneven road surfaces in the gutter
- allow others to overtake on the right if they wish.

*Mark **one** answer*

Your motorcycle is parked on a two-way road. You should get on from the

- ⊙ right and apply the rear brake
- ⊙ left and leave the brakes alone
- ⊙ left and apply the front brake
- ⊙ right and leave the brakes alone

⊙ **left and apply the front brake**

When you get onto a motorcycle you should

- get on from the left side to avoid putting yourself in danger from passing traffic
- apply the front brake to prevent the motorcycle rolling either forwards or backwards.

8.13   *Mark **one** answer*

To gain basic skills in how to ride a
motorcycle you should

- ⊙ practise off-road with an approved
  training body
- ⊙ ride on the road on the first dry day
- ⊙ practise off-road in a public park or
  in a quiet cul-de-sac
- ⊙ ride on the road as soon as possible

⊙ **practise off-road with an**
approved training body

All new motorcyclists must complete a
course of basic training with an approved
training body before going on the road.
This training is given on a site which has
been authorised by the Driving Standards
Agency as being suitable for off-road
training.

8.14   *Mark **one** answer*

You should not ride with your clutch
lever pulled in for longer than necessary
because it

- ⊙ increases wear on the gearbox
- ⊙ increases petrol consumption
- ⊙ reduces your control of the motorcycle
- ⊙ reduces the grip of the tyres

⊙ **reduces your control of**
the motorcycle

Riding with the clutch lever pulled in is
known as coasting. It

- • gives you less steering control
- • reduces the traction on the road surface
- • causes the machine to pick up speed.

If you're travelling downhill your motorcycle
will gather speed quickly. If you are
coasting the engine won't be able to assist
the braking.

8.15   *Mark **one** answer*

You are approaching a road with a surface
of loose chippings. What should you do?

- ⊙ Ride normally
- ⊙ Speed up
- ⊙ Slow down
- ⊙ Stop suddenly

⊙ **Slow down**

The handling of your motorcycle will be
greatly affected by the road surface. Look
well ahead and be especially alert if the
road looks uneven or has loose chippings.

Slow down in good time as braking harshly
in these conditions will cause you to skid.
Avoid making sudden changes of direction
for the same reason.

8.16

8.16 *Mark **one** answer*

It rains after a long dry, hot spell. This may cause the road surface to

- ⊙ be unusually slippery
- ⊙ give better grip
- ⊙ become covered in grit
- ⊙ melt and break up

⊙ **be unusually slippery**

Oil and other substances build up on the road surface during long dry spells and when it rains this surface becomes very slippery.

8.17 *Mark **three** answers*

The main causes of a motorcycle skidding are

- ⊙ heavy and sharp braking
- ⊙ excessive acceleration
- ⊙ leaning too far when cornering
- ⊙ riding in wet weather
- ⊙ riding in the winter

⊙ **heavy and sharp braking**

⊙ **excessive acceleration**

⊙ **leaning too far when cornering**

Skids are a lot easier to get into than they are to get out of.

Riding at a speed that suits the conditions, looking ahead for hazards and braking in good time will all help you to avoid skidding or losing control of your vehicle.

8.18 *Mark **one** answer*

To stop your motorcycle quickly in an emergency you should apply

- ⊙ the rear brake only
- ⊙ the front brake only
- ⊙ the front brake just before the rear
- ⊙ the rear brake just before the front

⊙ **the front brake just before the rear**

You should plan ahead to avoid the need to stop suddenly. But if an emergency should arise you must be able to stop safely. Applying the correct amount of braking effort to each wheel will help you to stop safely and in control.

8.19 *Mark **one** answer*

Riding with the side stand down could cause an accident. This is most likely to happen when

- going uphill
- accelerating
- braking
- cornering

⊙ **cornering**

Cornering with the side stand down could lead to a serious accident. Most motorcycles have a device that stops the engine if you try to ride off with the side stand down, but don't rely on this.

8.20 *Mark **one** answer*

You leave the choke on for too long. This causes the engine to run too fast. When is this likely to make your motorcycle most difficult to control?

- Accelerating
- Going uphill
- Slowing down
- On motorways

⊙ **Slowing down**

Forgetting to switch the choke off will cause the engine to run too fast. This makes it difficult to control the motorcycle, especially when slowing down, for example when approaching junctions and bends.

You should NOT look down at the front wheel when riding because it can

- ⊙ make your steering lighter
- ⊙ improve your balance
- ⊙ use less fuel
- ⊙ upset your balance

⊙ **upset your balance**

When riding look ahead and around you, but don't look down at the front wheel as this can severely upset your balance.

You are entering a bend. Your side stand is not fully raised. This could

- ⊙ cause an accident
- ⊙ improve your balance
- ⊙ alter the motorcycle's centre of gravity
- ⊙ make the motorcycle more stable

⊙ **cause an accident**

If the stand isn't fully up it could dig into the road and cause an accident.

In normal riding conditions you should brake

- ⊙ by using the rear brake first and then the front
- ⊙ when the motorcycle is being turned or ridden through a bend
- ⊙ by pulling in the clutch before using the front brake
- ⊙ when the motorcycle is upright and moving in a straight line

⊙ **when the motorcycle is upright and moving in a straight line**

A motorcycle is most stable when it's upright and moving in a straight line. This is the best time to brake. Normally both brakes should be used, with the front brake being applied just before the rear.

8.24

*Mark **three** answers*

Which THREE of the following will affect your stopping distance?

- ☉ How fast you are going
- ☉ The tyres on your motorcycle
- ☉ The time of day
- ☉ The weather
- ☉ The street lighting

☉ **How fast you are going**

☉ **The tyres on your motorcycle**

☉ **The weather**

There are several factors that can affect the distance it takes to stop your motorcycle.

In wet weather you should double the separation distance from the vehicle in front. Your tyres will have less grip on the road and you therefore need to allow more time to stop. Always ride in accordance with the conditions.

8.25

*Mark **one** answer*

You are on a motorway at night. You MUST have your headlights switched on unless

- ☉ there are vehicles close in front of you
- ☉ you are travelling below 50 mph
- ☉ the motorway is lit
- ☉ your motorcycle is broken down on the hard shoulder

☉ **your motorcycle is broken down on the hard shoulder**

Always use your headlights at night on a motorway unless you have stopped on the hard shoulder. If you have to use the hard shoulder, switch off the headlights but leave the parking lights on so that other road users can see your motorcycle.

8.26

*Mark **one** answer*

You have to park on the road in fog. You should

- ☉ leave parking lights on
- ☉ leave no lights on
- ☉ leave dipped headlights on
- ☉ leave main beam headlights on

☉ **leave parking lights on**

If you have to park on the road in foggy conditions it's important that your motorcycle can be seen by other road users.

Try to find a place to park off the road. If this isn't possible leave your motorcycle facing in the same direction as the traffic. Make sure that your lights are clean and that you leave your parking lights on.

*Mark **one** answer*

You ride over broken glass and get a sudden puncture. What should you do?

- ⊙ Close the throttle and roll to a stop
- ⊙ Brake to a stop as quickly as possible
- ⊙ Release your grip on the handlebars
- ⊙ Steer from side to side to keep your balance

⊙ **Close the throttle and roll to a stop**

Your motorcycle will be very unstable if a tyre bursts. Try to keep a straight course and stop as gently as possible.

*Mark **one** answer*

You are riding in wet weather. You see diesel fuel on the road. What should you do?

- ⊙ Swerve to avoid the area
- ⊙ Accelerate through quickly
- ⊙ Brake sharply to a stop
- ⊙ Slow down in good time

⊙ **Slow down in good time**

Spilt diesel will show up in wet weather as a rainbow-coloured pattern on the road. You should try to avoid riding over this area if you can. Slow down in good time but don't swerve suddenly or change direction without taking proper observation.

*Mark **one** answer*

Spilt fuel on the road can be very dangerous for you as a motorcyclist. How can this hazard be seen?

- ⊙ By a rainbow pattern on the surface
- ⊙ By a series of skid marks
- ⊙ By a pitted road surface
- ⊙ By a highly polished surface

⊙ **By a rainbow pattern on the surface**

This rainbow-coloured pattern can be seen much more easily on a wet road. You should avoid riding over these areas if possible. If you have to go over them do so with extreme caution.

8.30
*Mark **one** answer*

You leave the choke on for too long. This could make the engine run faster than normal. This will make your motorcycle

- ⊙ handle much better
- ⊙ corner much safer
- ⊙ stop much more quickly
- ⊙ more difficult to control

⊙ **more difficult to control**

Leaving the choke on for longer than necessary will usually make the engine run too fast. This can lead to loss of control, which is especially dangerous when approaching junctions and bends in the road and whenever you need to slow down.

8.31
*Mark **four** answers*

Which FOUR types of road surface increase the risk of skidding for motorcyclists?

- ⊙ White lines
- ⊙ Dry tarmac
- ⊙ Tar banding
- ⊙ Yellow grid lines
- ⊙ Loose chippings

⊙ **White lines**

⊙ **Tar banding**

⊙ **Yellow grid lines**

⊙ **Loose chippings**

When riding a motorcycle make sure you look at the road surface ahead. If you see any slippery surfaces, you can then brake or change course in plenty of time.

Look out for

- potholes
- drain covers (especially in the wet)
- oily surfaces
- road markings
- tram tracks
- wet mud and leaves.

You are riding on a wet road. When braking you should

⊙ apply the rear brake well before the front

⊙ apply the front brake just before the rear

⊙ avoid using the front brake at all

⊙ avoid using the rear brake at all

⊙ **apply the front brake just before the rear**

On wet roads you will need to be especially careful: brake earlier and more smoothly.

Always try to brake when the motorcycle is upright. This is particularly important in wet conditions.

The road is wet. You are passing a line of queuing traffic and riding on the painted road markings. You should take extra care, particularly when

⊙ signalling

⊙ braking

⊙ carrying a passenger

⊙ checking your mirrors

⊙ **braking**

Take extra care when braking or cornering on wet roads and try to avoid slippery objects, such as drain covers and painted road markings.

You are going ahead and will have to cross tram lines. Why should you be especially careful?

⊙ Tram lines are always 'live'

⊙ Trams will be stopping here

⊙ Pedestrians will be crossing here

⊙ The steel rails can be slippery

⊙ **The steel rails can be slippery**

These rails can affect your steering and be a hazard when braking. The smooth surface of the rails makes them slippery and dangerous for motorcyclists, especially when wet.

8.35   *Mark **one** answer*

You have to brake sharply and your motorcycle starts to skid. You should

⊙ continue braking and select a low gear

⊙ apply the brakes harder for better grip

⊙ select neutral and use the front brake only

⊙ release the brakes and reapply

⊙ **release the brakes and reapply**

If you skid as a result of braking harshly you need to

• release the brakes to stop the skid

• reapply them progressively to stop.

8.36   *Mark **one** answer*

You see a rainbow-coloured pattern across the road. What will this warn you of?

⊙ A soft uneven road surface

⊙ A polished road surface

⊙ Fuel spilt on the road

⊙ Water on the road

⊙ **Fuel spilt on the road**

If fuel, especially diesel, is spilt on the road it will make the surface very slippery. In wet weather this can be seen as a rainbow-coloured pattern on the road.

8.37   *Mark **one** answer*

Traction Control Systems (TCS) are fitted to some motorcycles. What does this help to prevent?

⊙ Wheelspin when accelerating

⊙ Skidding when braking too hard

⊙ Uneven front tyre wear

⊙ Uneven rear tyre wear

⊙ **Wheelspin when accelerating**

Traction Control Systems (TCS) help to prevent the rear wheel from spinning, especially when accelerating on a slippery surface.

8.38 *Mark one answer*

Braking too hard has caused both wheels to skid. What should you do?

◉ Release both brakes together

◉ Release the front then the rear brake

◉ Release the front brake only

◉ Release the rear brake only

◉ **Release both brakes together**

Braking too hard will cause a skid. Release the brakes immediately to allow the wheels to turn, then reapply them as firmly as the road surface and conditions will allow.

8.39 *Mark one answer*

Your motorcycle does NOT have linked brakes. What should you do when braking to a normal stop?

◉ Only apply the front brake

◉ Rely just on the rear brake

◉ Apply both brakes smoothly

◉ Apply either of the brakes gently

◉ **Apply both brakes smoothly**

In normal riding you should always use both brakes.

Braking when the motorcycle is upright and travelling in a straight line helps you to keep control. If your motorcycle has linked brakes refer to the owner's manual.

8.40 *Mark three answers*

In which THREE of these situations may you overtake another vehicle on the left?

◉ When you are in a one-way street

◉ When approaching a motorway slip road where you will be turning off

◉ When the vehicle in front is signalling to turn right

◉ When a slower vehicle is travelling in the right-hand lane of a dual carriageway

◉ In slow-moving traffic queues when traffic in the right-hand lane is moving more slowly

◉ **When you are in a one-way street**

◉ **When the vehicle in front is signalling to turn right**

◉ **In slow-moving traffic queues when traffic in the right-hand lane is moving more slowly**

At certain times of the day traffic might be heavy. If traffic is moving slowly in queues and vehicles in the right-hand lane are moving more slowly, you may overtake on the left. Don't keep changing lanes to try and beat the queue.

8.41   *Mark **one** answer*

You are travelling in very heavy rain. Your overall stopping distance is likely to be

- ⊙ doubled
- ⊙ halved
- ⊙ up to ten times greater
- ⊙ no different

⊙ **doubled**

As well as visibility being reduced, the road will be extremely wet. This will reduce the grip the tyres have on the road and increase the distance it takes to stop. Double your separation distance.

8.42   *Mark **two** answers*

Which TWO of the following are correct? When overtaking at night you should

- ⊙ wait until a bend so that you can see the oncoming headlights
- ⊙ sound your horn twice before moving out
- ⊙ be careful because you can see less
- ⊙ beware of bends in the road ahead
- ⊙ put headlights on full beam

⊙ **be careful because you can see less**

⊙ **beware of bends in the road ahead**

Only overtake the vehicle in front if it's really necessary. At night the risks are increased due to the poor visibility. Don't overtake if there's a possibility of

- road junctions
- bends ahead
- the brow of a bridge or hill, except on a dual carriageway
- pedestrian crossings
- double white lines ahead
- vehicles changing direction
- any other potential hazard.

*Mark **one** answer*

When may you wait in a box junction?

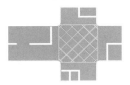

- ⊙ When you are stationary in a queue of traffic
- ⊙ When approaching a pelican crossing
- ⊙ When approaching a zebra crossing
- ⊙ When oncoming traffic prevents you turning right

⊙ **When oncoming traffic prevents you turning right**

The purpose of a box junction is to keep the junction clear by preventing vehicles from stopping in the path of crossing traffic.

You must not enter a box junction unless your exit is clear. But, you may enter the box and wait if you want to turn right and are only prevented from doing so by oncoming traffic.

*Mark **one** answer*

Which of these plates normally appear with this road sign?

⊙
Humps for
½ mile

⊙
Hump Bridge

⊙
Low Bridge

⊙
Soft Verge

⊙
Humps for
½ mile

Road humps are used to slow down the traffic. They are found in places where there are often pedestrians, such as

- in shopping areas
- near schools
- in residential areas.

Watch out for people close to the kerb or crossing the road.

8.45
*Mark **one** answer*

Traffic calming measures are used to

◉ stop road rage

◉ help overtaking

◉ slow traffic down

◉ help parking

◉ **slow traffic down**

Traffic calming measures are used to make the roads safer for vulnerable road users, such as cyclists, pedestrians and children. These can be designed as chicanes, road humps or other obstacles that encourage drivers and riders to slow down.

8.46
*Mark **one** answer*

You are on a motorway in fog. The left-hand edge of the motorway can be identified by reflective studs. What colour are they?

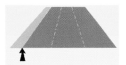

◉ Green

◉ Amber

◉ Red

◉ White

◉ **Red**

Be especially careful if you're on a motorway in fog. Reflective studs are used to help you in poor visibility. Different colours are used so that you'll know which lane you are in. These are

• red on the left-hand side of the road

• white between lanes

• amber on the right-hand edge of the carriageway

• green between the carriageway and slip roads.

8.47
*Mark **two** answers*

A rumble device is designed to

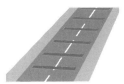

◉ give directions

◉ prevent cattle escaping

◉ alert you to low tyre pressure

◉ alert you to a hazard

◉ encourage you to reduce speed

◉ **alert you to a hazard**

◉ **encourage you to reduce speed**

A rumble device usually consists of raised markings or strips across the road. It gives an audible, visual and tactile warning of a hazard. These strips are found in places where traffic has constantly ignored warning or restriction signs. They are there for a good reason. Slow down and be ready to deal with a hazard.

8.48
*Mark **one** answer*

You are on a narrow road at night. A slower-moving vehicle ahead has been signalling right for some time. What should you do?

◉ Overtake on the left

◉ Flash your headlights before overtaking

◉ Signal right and sound your horn

◉ Wait for the signal to be cancelled before overtaking

◉ **Wait for the signal to be cancelled before overtaking**

If the vehicle in front has been indicating right for some time, but has made no attempt to turn, wait for the signal to be cancelled. The other driver may have misjudged the distance to the road junction or there might be a hidden hazard.

8.49
*Mark **one** answer*

You have to make a journey in foggy conditions. You should

◉ follow other vehicles' tail lights closely

◉ avoid using dipped headlights

◉ leave plenty of time for your journey

◉ keep two seconds behind other vehicles

◉ **leave plenty of time for your journey**

If you're planning to make a journey when it's foggy, listen to the weather reports on the radio or television. Don't travel if visibility is very poor or your trip isn't necessary.

If you do travel, leave plenty of time for your journey. If someone is expecting you at the other end, let them know that you'll be taking longer than normal to arrive.

8.50
*Mark **one** answer*

You are overtaking a car at night. You must be sure that

◉ you flash your headlights before overtaking

◉ you select a higher gear

◉ you have switched your lights to full beam before overtaking

◉ you do not dazzle other road users

◉ **you do not dazzle other road users**

To prevent your lights from dazzling the driver of the car in front, wait until you've overtaken before switching to full beam.

8.51   *Mark **one** answer*

You are on a road which has speed humps. A driver in front is travelling slower than you. You should

⊙ sound your horn

⊙ overtake as soon as you can

⊙ flash your headlights

⊙ slow down and stay behind

⊙ **slow down and stay behind**

Be patient and stay behind the car in front. Normally, you should not overtake other vehicles in traffic-calmed areas because if you overtake here your speed may exceed that which is safe along that road, defeating the purpose of the traffic calming measures.

8.52   *Mark **one** answer*

You are following other vehicles in fog with your lights on. How else can you reduce the chances of being involved in an accident?

⊙ Keep close to the vehicle in front

⊙ Use your main beam instead of dipped headlights

⊙ Keep together with the faster vehicles

⊙ Reduce your speed and increase the gap

⊙ **Reduce your speed and increase the gap**

When you're travelling in fog, always ensure that you have your dipped headlights and/or fog lights on so that you can be seen by other road users.

Keep at a sensible speed and don't follow the vehicle in front too closely. If the road is wet and slippery you'll need to allow twice the normal stopping distance.

8.53   *Mark **one** answer*

You see these markings on the road. Why are they there?

⊙ To show a safe distance between vehicles

⊙ To keep the area clear of traffic

⊙ To make you aware of your speed

⊙ To warn you to change direction

⊙ **To make you aware of your speed**

These lines may be painted on the road on the approach to a roundabout, village or a particular hazard. The lines are raised and painted yellow and their purpose is to make you aware of your speed. Reduce your speed in good time so that you avoid having to brake harshly over the last few metres before reaching the junction.

8.54 | Mark *three* answers

Areas reserved for trams may have

- metal studs around them
- white line markings
- zigzag markings
- a different coloured surface
- yellow hatch markings
- a different surface texture

- ⊙ **white line markings**

- ⊙ **a different coloured surface**

- ⊙ **a different surface texture**

Trams can run on roads used by other vehicles and pedestrians. The part of the road used by the trams is known as the reserved area and this should be kept clear. It has a coloured surface and is usually edged with white road markings. It might also have different surface texture.

8.55 | Mark *one* answer

You see a vehicle coming towards you on a single-track road. You should

- go back to the main road
- do an emergency stop
- stop at a passing place
- put on your hazard warning lights

- ⊙ **stop at a passing place**

You must take extra care when on single track roads. You may not be able to see around bends due to high hedges or fences. Proceed with caution and expect to meet oncoming vehicles around the next bend. If you do, pull into or opposite a passing place.

8.56 | Mark *one* answer

The road is wet. Why might a motorcyclist steer round drain covers on a bend?

- To avoid puncturing the tyres on the edge of the drain covers
- To prevent the motorcycle sliding on the metal drain covers
- To help judge the bend using the drain covers as marker points
- To avoid splashing pedestrians on the pavement

- ⊙ **To prevent the motorcycle sliding on the metal drain covers**

Other drivers or riders may have to change course due to the size or characteristics of their vehicle. Understanding this will help you to anticipate their actions. Motorcyclists and cyclists will be checking the road ahead for uneven or slippery surfaces, especially in wet weather. They may need to move across their lane to avoid surface hazards such as potholes and drain covers.

8.57   *Mark **one** answer*

After this hazard you should test your brakes. Why is this?

⊙ You will be on a slippery road

⊙ Your brakes will be soaking wet

⊙ You will be going down a long hill

⊙ You will have just crossed a long bridge

⊙ **Your brakes will be soaking wet**

A ford is a crossing over a stream that's shallow enough to go through. After you've gone through a ford or deep puddle the water will affect your brakes. To dry them out apply a light brake pressure while moving slowly. Don't travel at normal speeds until you are sure your brakes are working properly again.

8.58   *Mark **one** answer*

Why should you always reduce your speed when travelling in fog?

⊙ The brakes do not work as well

⊙ You will be dazzled by other headlights

⊙ The engine will take longer to warm up

⊙ It is more difficult to see events ahead

⊙ **It is more difficult to see events ahead**

You won't be able to see as far ahead in fog as you can on a clear day. You will need to reduce your speed so that, if a hazard looms out of the fog, you have the time and space to take avoiding action.

Travelling in fog is hazardous. If you can, try and delay your journey until it has cleared.

section nine
MOTORWAY RULES

This section covers:

- speed limits
- lane discipline
- stopping
- lighting
- parking

9.1   *Mark **one** answer*

On a motorway you may ONLY stop
on the hard shoulder

⊙ in an emergency

⊙ If you feel tired and need to rest

⊙ if you go past the exit that you wanted
to take

⊙ to pick up a hitchhiker

⊙ **in an emergency**

You MUST NOT stop on the hard shoulder
except in an emergency. Never use it to

• have a rest or a picnic

• pick up hitchhikers

• answer a mobile phone

• check a road map.

You must not ride back along the hard
shoulder if you accidentally go past the
exit you wanted.

9.2   *Mark **one** answer*

You are intending to leave the motorway at
the next exit. Before you reach the exit you
should normally position your motorcycle

⊙ in the middle lane

⊙ in the left-hand lane

⊙ on the hard shoulder

⊙ in any lane

⊙ **in the left-hand lane**

You'll see the first advance warning sign
for a junction one mile from the exit.
If you're travelling at 60 mph you'll only
have about 50 seconds before you reach
the countdown markers. Move in to the
left-hand lane in good time if you're not
there already. Don't cut across traffic at
the last moment.

9.3   *Mark **one** answer*

You are joining a motorway from a slip
road. You should

⊙ adjust your speed to the speed of the
traffic on the motorway

⊙ accelerate as quickly as you can and
ride straight out

⊙ ride onto the hard shoulder until a gap
appears

⊙ expect drivers on the motorway to
give way to you

⊙ **adjust your speed to the speed
of the traffic on the motorway**

Give way to the traffic already on the
motorway and join it where there's a
suitable gap in the traffic. Don't expect
traffic on the motorway to give way to
you, but try to avoid stopping at the end
of the slip road.

9.4 *Mark **one** answer*

A motorcycle is not allowed on a motorway if it has an engine size smaller than

- ☉ 50 cc
- ☉ 125 cc
- ☉ 150 cc
- ☉ 250 cc

☉ **50 cc**

Very small motorcycles are not allowed to use motorways due to their restricted speed, as this may cause a hazard to other vehicles.

9.5 *Mark **one** answer*

To ride on a motorway your motorcycle must be

- ☉ 50 cc or more
- ☉ 100 cc or more
- ☉ 125 cc or more
- ☉ 250 cc or more

☉ **50 cc or more**

Traffic on motorways travels at high speeds. Vehicles need to be capable of keeping up with the flow of traffic. For this reason low-powered vehicles are prohibited.

9.6 NI EXEMPT *Mark **one** answer*

You are travelling on a motorway. A red cross is shown above the hard shoulder. What does this mean?

- ☉ Use this lane as a rest area
- ☉ Use this as a normal running lane
- ☉ Do not use this lane to travel in
- ☉ National speed limit applies in this lane

☉ **Do not use this lane to travel in**

When a red cross is shown above the hard shoulder it should only be used for breakdowns or emergencies. Within Active Traffic Management (ATM) areas the hard shoulder may sometimes be used as a running lane. Speed limit signs directly above the hard shoulder will show that it's open.

9.7   *Mark **one** answer*

You are riding at 70 mph on a three-lane motorway. There is no traffic ahead. Which lane should you use?

⊙ Any lane

⊙ Middle lane

⊙ Right-hand lane

⊙ Left-hand lane

⊙ **Left-hand lane**

Use the left-hand lane if it's free, regardless of the speed you're travelling.

9.8   NI EXEMPT   *Mark **one** answer*

You are riding on a motorway. Unless signs show otherwise you must NOT exceed

⊙ 50 mph

⊙ 60 mph

⊙ 70 mph

⊙ 80 mph

⊙ **70 mph**

Ride in accordance with the conditions. Bad weather or heavy traffic may mean you have to lower your speed.

9.9   *Mark **one** answer*

Why is it particularly important to carry out a check of your motorcycle before making a long motorway journey?

⊙ You will have to do more harsh braking on motorways

⊙ Motorway service stations do not deal with breakdowns

⊙ The road surface will wear down the tyres faster

⊙ Continuous high speeds may increase the risk of your motorcycle breaking down

⊙ **Continuous high speeds may increase the risk of your motorcycle breaking down**

Before you start your journey, make sure that your motorcycle can cope with the demands of high-speed riding. Before setting off on a motorway journey, check the

• oil

• water

• tyres.

If you're travelling a long way it's a good idea to plan your rest stops in advance.

When joining a motorway you must always

⊙ use the hard shoulder

⊙ stop at the end of the acceleration lane

⊙ come to a stop before joining the motorway

⊙ give way to traffic already on the motorway

⊙ **give way to traffic already on the motorway**

You must give way to traffic already on the motorway. Don't try to force your way into the traffic stream.

You should join the motorway where there's a suitable gap in the left-hand lane. The traffic may be travelling at high speed so you should adjust your speed to fit in with the vehicles on the motorway.

What is the national speed limit for cars and motorcycles in the centre lane of a three-lane motorway?

⊙ 40 mph

⊙ 50 mph

⊙ 60 mph

⊙ 70 mph

⊙ **70 mph**

Unless otherwise indicated the speed limit for the motorway applies to all the lanes.

Be on the lookout for any indication of speed limit changes due to roadworks or traffic flow control.

What is the national speed limit on motorways for cars and motorcycles?

⊙ 30 mph

⊙ 50 mph

⊙ 60 mph

⊙ 70 mph

⊙ **70 mph**

Travelling at the national speed limit doesn't allow you to hog the right-hand lane. Always use the left-hand lane whenever possible. When leaving the motorway, always adjust your speed in good time to deal with

• bends or curves on the slip road

• traffic queuing at roundabouts.

9.13

*Mark **one** answer*

The left-hand lane on a three-lane motorway is for use by

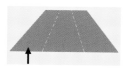

⊙ any vehicle

⊙ large vehicles only

⊙ emergency vehicles only

⊙ slow vehicles only

⊙ **any vehicle**

On a motorway all traffic should use the left-hand lane unless overtaking. Use the centre or right-hand lanes if you need to overtake.

Make sure that you move back to the left-hand lane when you've finished overtaking. Don't stay in the middle or right-hand lane if the left-hand lane is free.

9.14

*Mark **one** answer*

Which of these IS NOT allowed to travel in the right-hand lane of a three-lane motorway?

⊙ A small delivery van

⊙ A motorcycle

⊙ A vehicle towing a trailer

⊙ A motorcycle and side-car

⊙ **A vehicle towing a trailer**

A vehicle with a trailer is restricted to 60 mph. For this reason it isn't allowed in the right-hand lane as it might hold up the faster-moving traffic that wishes to overtake in that lane.

9.15

*Mark **two** answers*

You are travelling on a motorway. You decide you need a rest. You should

⊙ stop on the hard shoulder

⊙ go to a service area

⊙ park on the slip road

⊙ park on the central reservation

⊙ leave at the next exit

⊙ **go to a service area**

⊙ **leave at the next exit**

You must not stop on the motorway or hard shoulder except in an emergency, in a traffic queue or when signalled to do so by a police officer, Highways Agency Traffic Officer or traffic signals. You should plan your journey so that you have regular rest stops.

*Mark **one** answer*

You break down on a motorway. You need to call for help. Why may it be better to use an emergency roadside telephone rather than a mobile phone?

⊙ It connects you to a local garage

⊙ Using a mobile phone will distract other drivers

⊙ It allows easy location by the emergency services

⊙ Mobile phones do not work on motorways

⊙ **It allows easy location by the emergency services**

On a motorway it is best to use a roadside emergency telephone so that the emergency services are able to locate you easily. The nearest telephone is indicated by an arrow on the marker posts at the edge of the hard shoulder.

If you do use a mobile phone, the emergency services will want to know your exact location. Before you call, find out the number on the nearest marker post. This number will tell the emergency services your exact location.

*Mark **one** answer*

After a breakdown you need to rejoin the main carriageway of a motorway from the hard shoulder. You should

⊙ move out onto the carriageway then build up your speed

⊙ move out onto the carriageway using your hazard lights

⊙ gain speed on the hard shoulder before moving out onto the carriageway

⊙ wait on the hard shoulder until someone flashes their headlights at you

⊙ **gain speed on the hard shoulder before moving out onto the carriageway**

Wait for a safe gap in the traffic before you move out. Indicate your intention and use the hard shoulder to gain speed but don't force your way into the traffic.

*Mark **one** answer*

What colour are the reflective studs between a motorway and its slip road?

⊙ Amber

⊙ White

⊙ Green

⊙ Red

⊙ **Green**

The studs between the carriageway and the hard shoulder are normally red. These change to green where there is a slip road. They will help you identify slip roads when visibility is poor or when it is dark.

9.19

*Mark **one** answer*

A crawler lane on a motorway is found

- on a steep gradient
- before a service area
- before a junction
- along the hard shoulder

⊙ **on a steep gradient**

Slow-moving, large vehicles might slow down the progress of other traffic. On a steep gradient this extra lane is provided for these slow-moving vehicles to allow the faster-moving traffic to flow more easily.

9.20

*Mark **one** answer*

You have broken down on a motorway. To find the nearest emergency telephone you should always walk

- with the traffic flow
- facing oncoming traffic
- in the direction shown on the marker posts
- in the direction of the nearest exit

⊙ **in the direction shown on the marker posts**

Along the hard shoulder there are marker posts at 100-metre intervals. These will direct you to the nearest emergency telephone.

9.21

*Mark **one** answer*

How should you use the emergency telephone on a motorway?

- Stay close to the carriageway
- Face the oncoming traffic
- Keep your back to the traffic
- Stand on the hard shoulder

⊙ **Face the oncoming traffic**

Traffic is passing you at speed. If the draught from a large lorry catches you by surprise it could blow you off balance and even onto the carriageway. By facing the oncoming traffic you can see approaching lorries and so be prepared for their draught. You are also in a position to see other hazards approaching.

On a motorway the amber reflective studs can be found between

⊙ the hard shoulder and the carriageway

⊙ the acceleration lane and the carriageway

⊙ the central reservation and the carriageway

⊙ each pair of the lanes

⊙ **the central reservation and the carriageway**

On motorways reflective studs are fitted into the road to help you

• in the dark

• in conditions of poor visibility.

Amber-coloured studs are on the right-hand edge of the main carriageway, next to the central reservation.

What colour are the reflective studs between the lanes on a motorway?

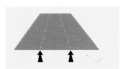

⊙ Green

⊙ Amber

⊙ White

⊙ Red

⊙ **White**

White studs are put between the lanes on motorways. The light from your headlights is reflected back and this is especially useful in bad weather, when visibility is restricted.

You are joining a motorway. Why is it important to make full use of the slip road?

⊙ Because there is space available to turn round if you need to

⊙ To allow you direct access to the overtaking lanes

⊙ To build up a speed similar to traffic on the motorway

⊙ Because you can continue on the hard shoulder

⊙ **To build up a speed similar to traffic on the motorway**

Try to join the motorway without affecting the progress of the traffic already travelling on it. Always give way to traffic already on the motorway. At busy times you may have to slow down to merge into slow-moving traffic.

9.25
*Mark **one** answer*

What do these motorway signs show?

- They are countdown markers to a bridge
- They are distance markers to the next telephone
- They are countdown markers to the next exit
- They warn of a police control ahead

⊙ **They are countdown markers to the next exit**

The exit from a motorway is indicated by countdown markers. These are positioned 90 metres (100 yards) apart, the first being 270 metres (300 yards) from the start of the slip road. Move into the left-hand lane well before you reach the start of the slip road.

9.26
*Mark **one** answer*

You are on a motorway. What colour are the reflective studs on the left of the carriageway?

- Green
- Red
- White
- Amber

⊙ **Red**

Red studs are placed between the edge of the carriageway and the hard shoulder. Where slip roads leave or join the motorway the studs are green.

9.27
*Mark **one** answer*

When may you stop on a motorway?

- If you have to read a map
- When you are tired and need a rest
- If your mobile phone rings
- In an emergency or breakdown

⊙ **In an emergency or breakdown**

You should not normally stop on a motorway but there may be occasions when you need to. If you are unfortunate enough to break down make every effort to pull up on the hard shoulder.

On a three-lane motorway which lane should you normally use?

⊙ Left

⊙ Right

⊙ Centre

⊙ Either the right or centre

⊙ **Left**

On a three-lane motorway you should travel in the left-hand lane unless you're overtaking. This applies regardless of the speed you're travelling at.

When going through a contraflow system on a motorway you should

⊙ ensure that you do not exceed 30 mph

⊙ keep a good distance from the vehicle ahead

⊙ switch lanes to keep the traffic flowing

⊙ stay close to the vehicle ahead to reduce queues

⊙ **keep a good distance from the vehicle ahead**

There's likely to be a speed restriction in force. Keep to this. Don't

• switch lanes

• get too close to traffic in front of you.

Be aware there will be no permanent barrier between you and the oncoming traffic.

You are approaching roadworks on a motorway. What should you do?

⊙ Speed up to clear the area quickly

⊙ Always use the hard shoulder

⊙ Obey all speed limits

⊙ Stay very close to the vehicle in front

⊙ **Obey all speed limits**

Accidents can often happen at roadworks. Be aware of the speed limits and reduce your speed in good time.

9.31
*Mark **one** answer*

You are on a three-lane motorway. There are red reflective studs on your left and white ones to your right. Where are you?

○ In the right-hand lane

○ In the middle lane

○ On the hard shoulder

○ In the left-hand lane

⊙ **In the left-hand lane**

The colours of the reflective studs on the motorway and their locations are

• red – between the hard shoulder and the carriageway

• white – lane markings

• amber – between the edge of the carriageway and the central reservation

• green – along slip road exits and entrances

• bright green/yellow – roadworks and contraflow systems.

9.32
*Mark **four** answers*

Which FOUR of these must NOT use motorways?

○ Learner car drivers

○ Motorcycles over 50cc

○ Double-deck buses

○ Farm tractors

○ Horse riders

○ Cyclists

⊙ **Learner car drivers**

⊙ **Farm tractors**

⊙ **Horse riders**

⊙ **Cyclists**

In addition, motorways MUST NOT be used by

• pedestrians

• motorcycles under 50 cc

• certain slow-moving vehicles, without permission

• invalid carriages weighing less than 254 kg (560 lbs).

Which FOUR of these must NOT use
motorways?

- ⊙ Learner car drivers
- ⊙ Motorcycles over 50cc
- ⊙ Double-deck buses
- ⊙ Farm tractors
- ⊙ Learner motorcyclists
- ⊙ Cyclists

- ⊙ **Learner car drivers**

- ⊙ **Farm tractors**

- ⊙ **Learner motorcyclists**

- ⊙ **Cyclists**

Learner car drivers and motorcyclists are
not allowed on the motorway until they
have passed their practical test.

Motorways have rules that you need to
know before you venture out for the first
time. When you've passed your practical
test it's a good idea to have some lessons
on motorways. Check with your instructor
about this.

Immediately after joining a motorway you
should normally

- ⊙ try to overtake
- ⊙ re-adjust your mirrors
- ⊙ position your vehicle in the centre lane
- ⊙ keep in the left-hand lane

- ⊙ **keep in the left-hand lane**

Stay in the left-hand lane long enough
to get used to the higher speeds of
motorway traffic.

What is the right-hand lane used for on
a three-lane motorway?

- ⊙ Emergency vehicles only
- ⊙ Overtaking
- ⊙ Vehicles towing trailers
- ⊙ Coaches only

- ⊙ **Overtaking**

You should keep to the left and only use
the right-hand lane if you're passing
slower-moving traffic.

9.36   *Mark **one** answer*

What should you use the hard shoulder
of a motorway for?

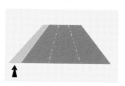

⊙ Stopping in an emergency

⊙ Leaving the motorway

⊙ Stopping when you are tired

⊙ Joining the motorway

⊙ **Stopping in an emergency**

Don't use the hard shoulder for stopping
unless it is an emergency. If you want to
stop for any other reason go to the next
exit or service station.

9.37   *Mark **one** answer*

You are in the right-hand lane on a
motorway. You see these overhead signs.
This means

⊙ move to the left and reduce your
  speed to 50 mph

⊙ there are roadworks 50 metres
  (55 yards) ahead

⊙ use the hard shoulder until you have
  passed the hazard

⊙ leave the motorway at the next exit

⊙ **move to the left and reduce
  your speed to 50 mph**

You must obey this sign. There might not
be any visible signs of a problem ahead.
However, there might be queuing traffic or
another hazard which you cannot yet see.

You are allowed to stop on a motorway
when you

- ⊙ need to walk and get fresh air
- ⊙ wish to pick up hitchhikers
- ⊙ are told to do so by flashing red lights
- ⊙ need to use a mobile telephone

⊙ **are told to do so by flashing
red lights**

You must stop if there are red lights
flashing above every lane on the motorway.
However, if any of the other lanes show a
green arrow you may move into that lane
and continue if it is safe to do so.

You are travelling along the left-hand lane
of a three-lane motorway. Traffic is joining
from a slip road. You should

- ⊙ race the other vehicles
- ⊙ move to another lane
- ⊙ maintain a steady speed
- ⊙ switch on your hazard flashers

⊙ **move to another lane**

You should move to another lane if it is
safe to do so. This can greatly assist the
flow of traffic joining the motorway,
especially at peak times.

On motorways you should never overtake
on the left unless

- ⊙ you can see well ahead that the hard
  shoulder is clear
- ⊙ the traffic in the right-hand lane is
  signalling right
- ⊙ you warn drivers behind by signalling
  left
- ⊙ there is a queue of slow-moving traffic
  to your right that is moving more slowly
  than you are

⊙ **there is a queue of slow-moving
traffic to your right that is moving
more slowly than you are**

Only overtake on the left if traffic is moving
slowly in queues and the traffic on your
right is moving more slowly than the traffic
in your lane.

9.41

A basic rule when on motorways is

- use the lane that has least traffic
- keep to the left-hand lane unless overtaking
- overtake on the side that is clearest
- try to keep above 50 mph to prevent congestion

⊙ **keep to the left-hand lane unless overtaking**

You should normally travel in the left-hand lane unless you are overtaking a slower-moving vehicle. When you are past that vehicle move back into the left-hand lane as soon as it's safe to do so. Don't cut across in front of the vehicle that you're overtaking.

9.42 NI EXEMPT

Motorway emergency telephones are usually linked to the police. In some areas they are now linked to

- the Highways Agency Control Centre
- the Driver Vehicle Licensing Agency
- the Driving Standards Agency
- the local Vehicle Registration Office

⊙ **the Highways Agency Control Centre**

In some areas motorway telephones are now linked to a Highways Agency Control Centre, instead of the police. Highways Agency Traffic Officers work in partnership with the police and assist at motorway emergencies and accidents. They are recognised by a high-visibility orange and yellow jacket and high-visibility vehicle with yellow and black chequered markings.

9.43

An Emergency Refuge Area is an area

- on a motorway for use in cases of emergency or breakdown
- for use if you think you will be involved in a road rage incident
- on a motorway for a police patrol to park and watch traffic
- for construction and road workers to store emergency equipment

⊙ **on a motorway for use in cases of emergency or breakdown**

Emergency Refuge Areas may be found at the side of the hard shoulder about 500 metres apart. If you break down you should use them rather than the hard shoulder if you are able to. When re-joining the motorway you must remember to take extra care especially when the hard shoulder is being used as a running lane within an Active Traffic Management area. Try to match your speed to that of traffic in the lane you are joining.

9.44

*Mark **one** answer*

What is an Emergency Refuge Area on a motorway for?

- ⊙ An area to park in when you want to use a mobile phone

- ⊙ To use in cases of emergency or breakdown
- ⊙ For an emergency recovery vehicle to park in a contra-flow system
- ⊙ To drive in when there is queuing traffic ahead

⊙ **To use in cases of emergency or breakdown**

In cases of breakdown or emergency try to get your vehicle into an Emergency Refuge Area. This is safer than just stopping on the hard shoulder as it gives you greater distance from the main carriageway. If you are able to re-join the motorway you must take extra care, especially when the hard shoulder is being used as a running lane.

9.45   NI EXEMPT   *Mark **one** answer*

Highways Agency Traffic Officers

- ⊙ will not be able to assist at a breakdown or emergency
- ⊙ are not able to stop and direct anyone on a motorway
- ⊙ will tow a broken down vehicle and it's passengers home
- ⊙ are able to stop and direct anyone on a motorway

⊙ **are able to stop and direct anyone on a motorway**

Highways Agency Traffic Officers (HATOs) do not have enforcement powers but are able to stop and direct anyone on the motorway. They work in partnership with the police at motorway incidents and provide a highly-trained and visible service. Their role is to help keep traffic moving and make your journey as safe and reliable as possible. They are recognised by an orange and yellow jacket and their vehicle has yellow and black markings.

9.46   NI EXEMPT   *Mark **one** answer*

You are travelling on a motorway. Unless signs show a lower speed limit you must NOT exceed

- ⊙ 50 mph
- ⊙ 60 mph
- ⊙ 70 mph
- ⊙ 80 mph

⊙ **70 mph**

The national speed limit for a car or motorcycle on the motorway is 70 mph. Lower speed limits may be in force, for example at roadworks, so look out for the signs. Variable speed limits operate in some areas to control very busy stretches of motorway. The speed limit may change depending on the volume of traffic.

9.47   NI EXEMPT   *Mark one answer*

You are on a motorway. A red cross is displayed above the hard shoulder. What does this mean?

⊙ Pull up in this lane to answer your mobile phone

⊙ Use this lane as a running lane

⊙ This lane can be used if you need a rest

⊙ You should not travel in this lane

⊙ **You should not travel in this lane**

Active Traffic Management schemes are being introduced on motorways. Within these areas at certain times the hard shoulder will be used as a running lane. A red cross above the hard shoulder shows that this lane should NOT be used, except for emergencies and breakdowns.

9.48   *Mark one answer*

Motorway emergency telephones are usually linked to the police. In some areas they are now linked to

⊙ the local ambulance service

⊙ an Highways Agency control centre

⊙ the local fire brigade

⊙ a breakdown service control centre

⊙ **an Highways Agency control centre**

The controller will ask you

• the make and colour of your vehicle

• whether you are a member of an emergency breakdown service

• the number shown on the emergency telephone casing

• whether you are travelling alone.

9.49   NI EXEMPT   *Mark one answer*

You are in an Active Traffic Management area on a motorway. When the Actively Managed mode is operating

⊙ speed limits are only advisory

⊙ the national speed limit will apply

⊙ the speed limit is always 30 mph

⊙ all speed limit signals are set

⊙ **all speed limit signals are set**

When an Active Traffic Management (ATM) scheme is operating on a motorway you must follow the mandatory instructions shown on the gantries above each lane. This includes the hard shoulder.

The aim of an Active Traffic Management scheme on a motorway is to

⊙ prevent overtaking

⊙ reduce rest stops

⊙ prevent tailgating

⊙ reduce congestion

⊙ **reduce congestion**

Active Traffic Management schemes are intended to reduce congestion and make journey times more reliable. In these areas the hard shoulder may be used as a running lane to ease congestion at peak times or in the event of an incident. It may appear that you could travel faster for a short distance, but keeping traffic flow at a constant speed may improve your journey time.

On a three-lane motorway why should you normally ride in the left-hand lane?

⊙ The left-hand lane is only for lorries and motorcycles

⊙ The left-hand lane should only be used by smaller vehicles

⊙ The lanes on the right are for overtaking

⊙ Motorcycles are not allowed in the far right-hand lane

⊙ **The lanes on the right are for overtaking**

Change lanes only if necessary. When you do change lanes make sure you observe, signal and manoeuvre in good time. Always remember your 'lifesaver' check. This is a final, quick rearward glance before you pull out.

When should you stop on a motorway?

⊙ If you have to read a map

⊙ When you are tired and need a rest

⊙ If red lights show above every lane

⊙ When told to by the police

⊙ If your mobile phone rings

⊙ When signalled by a Highways Agency Traffic Officer

⊙ **If red lights show above every lane**

⊙ **When told to by the police**

⊙ **When signalled by a Highways Agency Traffic Officer**

There are some occasions when you may have to stop on the carriageway of a motorway. These include, when signalled by the police or a Highways Agency Traffic Officer, when flashing red lights show above every lane and in traffic jams.

9.53   NI EXEMPT   *Mark one answer*

You are travelling on a motorway. A red cross is shown above the hard shoulder and mandatory speed limits above all other lanes. This means

- ◉ the hard shoulder can be used as a rest area if you feel tired
- ◉ the hard shoulder is for emergency or breakdown use only
- ◉ the hard shoulder can be used as a normal running lane
- ◉ the hard shoulder has a speed limit of 50 mph

- ◉ **the hard shoulder is for emergency or breakdown use only**

A red cross above the hard shoulder shows it is closed as a running lane and should only be used for emergencies or breakdowns. At busy times within an Active Traffic Management area the hard shoulder may be used as a running lane. This will be shown by a mandatory speed limit on the gantry above.

9.54   NI EXEMPT   *Mark one answer*

You are on a motorway in an Active Traffic Management (ATM) area. A mandatory speed limit is displayed above the hard shoulder. What does this mean?

- ◉ You should not travel in this lane
- ◉ The hard shoulder can be used as a running lane
- ◉ You can park on the hard shoulder if you feel tired
- ◉ You can pull up in this lane to answer a mobile phone

- ◉ **The hard shoulder can be used as a running lane**

A mandatory speed limit sign above the hard shoulder shows that it can be used as a running lane between junctions. You must stay within the speed limit. Look out for vehicles that may have broken down and be blocking the hard shoulder.

You see this sign on a motorway. It means you can use

⊙ any lane except the hard shoulder

⊙ the hard shoulder only

⊙ the three right hand lanes only

⊙ all the lanes including the hard shoulder

⊙ **all the lanes including the hard shoulder**

Mandatory speed limit signs above all lanes including the hard shoulder, show that you are in an Active Traffic Management (ATM) area. In this case you can use the hard shoulder as a running lane. You must stay within the speed limit shown. Look out for any vehicles that may have broken down and be blocking the hard shoulder.

Why can it be an advantage for traffic speed to stay constant over a longer distance?

⊙ You will do more stop-start driving

⊙ You will use far more fuel

⊙ You will be able to use more direct routes

⊙ Your overall journey time will normally improve

⊙ **Your overall journey time will normally improve**

When traffic travels at a constant speed over a longer distance, journey times normally improve. You may feel that you could travel faster for short periods but this won't generally make your overall time better. Signs will show the maximum speed at which you should travel.

You are on a motorway. There are red flashing lights above every lane. You must

⊙ pull onto the hard shoulder

⊙ slow down and watch for further signals

⊙ leave at the next exit

⊙ stop and wait

⊙ **stop and wait**

Red flashing lights above every lane mean you must not go on any further. You'll also see a red cross illuminated. Stop and wait. Don't

• change lanes

• continue

• pull onto the hard shoulder (unless in an emergency).

9.58   NI EXEMPT   *Mark **one** answer*

You should not normally travel on the hard shoulder of a motorway. When can you use it?

- ⊙ When taking the next exit
- ⊙ When traffic is stopped
- ⊙ When signs direct you to
- ⊙ When traffic is slow moving

⊙ **When signs direct you to**

Normally you should only use the hard shoulder for emergencies and breakdowns, and at roadworks when signs direct you to. Active Traffic Management (ATM) areas are being introduced to ease traffic congestion. In these areas the hard shoulder may be used as a running lane when speed limit signs are shown directly above.

9.59   *Mark **one** answer*

For what reason may you use the right-hand lane of a motorway?

- ⊙ For keeping out of the way of lorries
- ⊙ For travelling at more than 70 mph
- ⊙ For turning right
- ⊙ For overtaking other vehicles

⊙ **For overtaking other vehicles**

The right-hand lane of the motorway is for overtaking.

Sometimes you may be directed into a right-hand lane as a result of roadworks or an accident. This will be indicated by signs or police directing the traffic.

9.60   *Mark **one** answer*

On a motorway what is used to reduce traffic bunching?

- ⊙ Variable speed limits
- ⊙ Contraflow systems
- ⊙ National speed limits
- ⊙ Lane closures

⊙ **Variable speed limits**

Congestion can be reduced by keeping traffic at a constant speed. At busy times maximum speed limits are displayed on overhead gantries. These can be varied quickly depending on the amount of traffic. By keeping to a constant speed on busy sections of motorway overall journey times are normally improved.

section ten
RULES OF THE ROAD

This section covers:

- speed limits
- lane discipline
- lighting
- parking

10.1
*Mark **one** answer*

You are riding slowly in a town centre. Before turning left you should glance over your left shoulder to

- ⊙ check for cyclists
- ⊙ help keep your balance
- ⊙ look for traffic signs
- ⊙ check for potholes

⊙ **check for cyclists**

When riding slowly you must remember cyclists. They can travel quickly and fit through surprisingly narrow spaces. Before you turn left in slow-moving traffic it's important to check that a cyclist isn't trying to overtake on your left.

10.2
*Mark **two** answers*

As a motorcycle rider which TWO lanes must you NOT use?

- ⊙ Crawler lane
- ⊙ Overtaking lane
- ⊙ Acceleration lane
- ⊙ Cycle lane
- ⊙ Tram lane

⊙ **Cycle lane**

⊙ **Tram lane**

In some towns motorcycles are permitted to use bus lanes. Check the signs carefully.

10.3
*Mark **one** answer*

You are turning right at a large roundabout. Just before you leave the roundabout you should

- ⊙ take a 'lifesaver' glance over your left shoulder
- ⊙ take a 'lifesaver' glance over your right shoulder
- ⊙ put on your right indicator
- ⊙ cancel the left indicator

⊙ **take a 'lifesaver' glance over your left shoulder**

You need to be aware of what's happening behind and alongside you. Take a final quick rearward glance: this will give you the chance to react if it isn't safe to make the manoeuvre.

*Mark **one** answer*

What does this sign mean?

- ⊙ No parking for solo motorcycles
- ⊙ Parking for solo motorcycles
- ⊙ Passing place for motorcycles
- ⊙ Police motorcycles only

⊙ **Parking for solo motorcycles**

In some towns and cities there are special areas reserved for parking motorcycles. Look out for these signs.

---

*Mark **one** answer*

You are riding on a busy dual carriageway. When changing lanes you should

- ⊙ rely totally on mirrors
- ⊙ always increase your speed
- ⊙ signal so others will give way
- ⊙ use mirrors and shoulder checks

⊙ **use mirrors and shoulder checks**

Before you change lanes, you need to see if it is safe to move across. There are areas behind and to the side of you which are not covered by the mirrors. As well as using your mirrors, you need to check over your shoulder to see if a vehicle is in one of your blind spots before changing direction.

---

*Mark **one** answer*

You are looking for somewhere to park your motorcycle. The area is full EXCEPT for spaces marked 'disabled use'. You can

- ⊙ use these spaces when elsewhere is full
- ⊙ park if you stay with your motorcycle
- ⊙ use these spaces, disabled or not
- ⊙ not park there unless permitted

⊙ **not park there unless permitted**

Don't be selfish. These spaces are intended for people with limited mobility. Find somewhere else to park, even if it means that you have to walk further.

10.7
*Mark **three** answers*

On which THREE occasions MUST you stop your motorcycle?

- ⊙ When involved in an accident
- ⊙ At a red traffic light
- ⊙ When signalled to do so by a police officer
- ⊙ At a junction with double broken white lines
- ⊙ At a pelican crossing when the amber light is flashing and no pedestrians are crossing

⊙ **When involved in an accident**

⊙ **At a red traffic light**

⊙ **When signalled to do so by a police officer**

Don't stop or hold up traffic unnecessarily. However, you MUST stop when signalled to do so by

- a police officer
- a school crossing patrol
- a red traffic light.

If you are in an accident in which injury or damage is caused, you must stop by law.

10.8
*Mark **one** answer*

You are on a road with passing places. It is only wide enough for one vehicle. There is a car coming towards you. What should you do?

- ⊙ Pull into a passing place on your right
- ⊙ Force the other driver to reverse
- ⊙ Turn round and ride back to the main road
- ⊙ Pull into a passing place on your left

⊙ **Pull into a passing place on your left**

If you meet another vehicle in a narrow road and the passing place is on your left, pull into it. If the passing place is on the right, wait opposite it.

10.9
*Mark **one** answer*

You are both turning right at this crossroads. It is safer to keep the car to your right so you can

- ⊙ see approaching traffic
- ⊙ keep close to the kerb
- ⊙ keep clear of following traffic
- ⊙ make oncoming vehicles stop

⊙ **see approaching traffic**

When turning right at this crossroads you should keep the oncoming car on your right. This will give you a clear view of the road ahead and any oncoming traffic.

10.10
*Mark **three** answers*

When filtering through slow-moving or stationary traffic you should

- ⊙ watch for hidden vehicles emerging from side roads
- ⊙ continually use your horn as a warning
- ⊙ look for vehicles changing course suddenly
- ⊙ always ride with your hazard lights on
- ⊙ stand up on the footrests for a good view ahead
- ⊙ look for pedestrians walking between vehicles

⊙ **watch for hidden vehicles emerging from side roads**

⊙ **look for vehicles changing course suddenly**

⊙ **look for pedestrians walking between vehicles**

Other road users may not expect or look for motorcycles filtering through slow-moving or stationary traffic.

Your view will be reduced by the vehicles around you: you will need to watch out for

- pedestrians walking between the vehicles
- vehicles suddenly changing direction
- vehicles pulling out of side roads.

10.11

*Mark **one** answer*

You are riding towards roadworks. The temporary traffic lights are at red. The road ahead is clear. What should you do?

⊙ Ride on with extreme caution

⊙ Ride on at normal speed

⊙ Carry on if approaching cars have stopped

⊙ Wait for the green light

⊙ **Wait for the green light**

You must obey all traffic signs and signals. Just because the lights are temporary it does not mean that you can disregard them.

10.12

*Mark **one** answer*

You intend to go abroad and will be riding on the right-hand side of the road. What should you fit to your motorcycle?

⊙ Twin headlights

⊙ Headlight deflectors

⊙ Tinted yellow brake lights

⊙ Tinted red indicator lenses

⊙ **Headlight deflectors**

When abroad and riding on the right, deflectors are usually required to prevent your headlight dazzling approaching drivers.

10.13

*Mark **one** answer*

You want to tow a trailer with your motorcycle. Your engine must be more than

⊙ 50 cc

⊙ 125 cc

⊙ 525 cc

⊙ 1000 cc

⊙ **125 cc**

You must remember that towing a trailer requires special care. You must obey the restrictions which apply to all vehicles towing trailers.

Do not forget it is there, especially when negotiating bends and junctions.

What is the national speed limit on a single carriageway?

⊙ 40 mph
⊙ 50 mph
⊙ 60 mph
⊙ 70 mph

⊙ **60 mph**

You don't have to ride at the speed limit. Use your own judgement and ride at a speed that suits the prevailing road, weather and traffic conditions.

What is the meaning of this sign?

⊙ Local speed limit applies
⊙ No waiting on the carriageway
⊙ National speed limit applies
⊙ No entry to vehicular traffic

⊙ **National speed limit applies**

This sign doesn't tell you the speed limit in figures. You should know the speed limit for the type of road that you're on. Study your copy of *The Highway Code*.

What is the national speed limit for cars and motorcycles on a dual carriageway?

⊙ 30 mph
⊙ 50 mph
⊙ 60 mph
⊙ 70 mph

⊙ **70 mph**

Ensure that you know the speed limit for the road that you're on. The speed limit on a dual carriageway or motorway is 70 mph for cars and motorcycles, unless there are signs to indicate otherwise. The speed limits for different types of vehicles are listed in *The Highway Code*.

10.17
*Mark **one** answer*

There are no speed limit signs on the road. How is a 30 mph limit indicated?

- By hazard warning lines
- By street lighting
- By pedestrian islands
- By double or single yellow lines

⊙ **By street lighting**

There is usually a 30 mph speed limit where there are street lights unless there are signs showing another limit.

10.18
*Mark **one** answer*

Where you see street lights but no speed limit signs the limit is usually

- 30 mph
- 40 mph
- 50 mph
- 60 mph

⊙ **30 mph**

A 30 mph limit usually applies where there are street lights but no speed limit signs.

10.19
*Mark **one** answer*

What does this sign mean?

- Minimum speed 30 mph
- End of maximum speed
- End of minimum speed
- Maximum speed 30 mph

⊙ **End of minimum speed**

A red slash through this sign indicates that the restriction has ended. In this case the restriction was a minimum speed limit of 30 mph.

There is a tractor ahead of you. You wish to overtake but you are NOT sure if it is safe to do so. You should

- ⊙ follow another overtaking vehicle through
- ⊙ sound your horn to the slow vehicle to pull over
- ⊙ speed through but flash your lights to oncoming traffic
- ⊙ not overtake if you are in doubt

⊙ **not overtake if you are in doubt**

Never overtake if you're not sure if it's safe to do so. Can you see far enough down the road to ensure that you can complete the manoeuvre safely? If the answer is no, don't go.

Which three of the following are most likely to take an unusual course at roundabouts?

- ⊙ Horse riders
- ⊙ Milk floats
- ⊙ Delivery vans
- ⊙ Long vehicles
- ⊙ Estate cars
- ⊙ Cyclists

⊙ **Horse riders**

⊙ **Long vehicles**

⊙ **Cyclists**

Long vehicles might have to take a slightly different position when approaching the roundabout or going around it. This is to stop the rear of the vehicle cutting in and mounting the kerb.

Horse riders and cyclists might stay in the left-hand lane although they are turning right. Be aware of this and allow them room.

On a clearway you must not stop

- ⊙ at any time
- ⊙ when it is busy
- ⊙ in the rush hour
- ⊙ during daylight hours

⊙ **at any time**

Clearways are in place so that traffic can flow without the obstruction of parked vehicles. Just one parked vehicle will cause an obstruction for all other traffic. Do not stop where a clearway is in force, not even to pick up or set down passengers.

10.23

*Mark **one** answer*

What is the meaning of this sign?

- ⊙ No entry
- ⊙ Waiting restrictions
- ⊙ National speed limit
- ⊙ School crossing patrol

⊙ **Waiting restrictions**

This sign indicates that there are waiting restrictions. It is normally accompanied by details of when restrictions are in force.

Details of most signs which are in common use are shown in The Highway Code and a more comprehensive selection is available in Know Your Traffic Signs.

10.24

*Mark **one** answer*

You can park on the right-hand side of a road at night

- ⊙ in a one-way street
- ⊙ with your sidelights on
- ⊙ more than 10 metres (32 feet) from a junction
- ⊙ under a lamp-post

⊙ **in a one-way street**

Red rear reflectors show up when headlights shine on them. These are useful when you are parked at night but will only reflect if you park in the same direction as the traffic flow. Normally you should park on the left, but if you're in a one-way street you may also park on the right-hand side.

10.25

*Mark **one** answer*

What is the national speed limit on a single carriageway road for cars and motorcycles?

- ⊙ 30 mph
- ⊙ 50 mph
- ⊙ 60 mph
- ⊙ 70 mph

⊙ **60 mph**

Exceeding the speed limit is dangerous and can result in you receiving penalty points on your licence. It isn't worth it. You should know the speed limit for the road that you're on by observing the road signs. Different speed limits apply if you are towing a trailer.

209

On a three-lane dual carriageway the right-hand lane can be used for

- ⊙ overtaking only, never turning right
- ⊙ overtaking or turning right
- ⊙ fast-moving traffic only
- ⊙ turning right only, never overtaking

⊙ **overtaking or turning right**

You should normally use the left-hand lane on any dual carriageway unless you are overtaking or turning right.

When overtaking on a dual carriageway, look for vehicles ahead that are turning right. They're likely to be slowing or stopped. You need to see them in good time so that you can take appropriate action.

You are approaching a busy junction. There are several lanes with road markings. At the last moment you realise that you are in the wrong lane. You should

- ⊙ continue in that lane
- ⊙ force your way across
- ⊙ stop until the area has cleared
- ⊙ use clear arm signals to cut across

⊙ **continue in that lane**

There are times where road markings can be obscured by queuing traffic, or you might be unsure which lane you need to be in.

If you realise that you're in the wrong lane, don't cut across lanes or bully other drivers to let you in. Follow the lane you're in and find somewhere safe to turn around if you need to.

Where may you overtake on a one-way street?

- ⊙ Only on the left-hand side
- ⊙ Overtaking is not allowed
- ⊙ Only on the right-hand side
- ⊙ Either on the right or the left

⊙ **Either on the right or the left**

You can overtake other traffic on either side when travelling in a one-way street. Make full use of your mirrors and ensure that it's clear all around before you attempt to overtake. Look for signs and road markings and use the most suitable lane for your destination.

10.29
*Mark **one** answer*

When going straight ahead at a roundabout you should

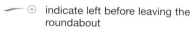

- ⊙ indicate left before leaving the roundabout
- ⊙ not indicate at any time
- ⊙ indicate right when approaching the roundabout
- ⊙ indicate left when approaching the roundabout

⊙ **indicate left before leaving the roundabout**

When you want to go straight on at a roundabout, don't signal as you approach it, but indicate left just after you pass the exit before the one you wish to take.

10.30
*Mark **one** answer*

Which vehicle might have to use a different course to normal at roundabouts?

- ⊙ Sports car
- ⊙ Van
- ⊙ Estate car
- ⊙ Long vehicle

⊙ **Long vehicle**

A long vehicle may have to straddle lanes either on or approaching a roundabout so that the rear wheels don't cut in over the kerb.

If you're following a long vehicle, stay well back and give it plenty of room.

10.31

*Mark **one** answer*

You are going straight ahead at a roundabout. How should you signal?

- ⊙ Signal right on the approach and then left to leave the roundabout
- ⊙ Signal left as you leave the roundabout
- ⊙ Signal left on the approach to the roundabout and keep the signal on until you leave
- ⊙ Signal left just after you pass the exit before the one you will take

⊙ **Signal left just after you pass the exit before the one you will take**

To go straight ahead at a roundabout you should normally approach in the left-hand lane without signalling. Where there are road markings, use the lane indicated.

Ensure that you signal correctly when you are travelling around the roundabout. Other road users need to know your intentions.

10.32

You may only enter a box junction when

- ⊙ there are less than two vehicles in front of you
- ⊙ the traffic lights show green
- ⊙ your exit road is clear
- ⊙ you need to turn left

⊙ **your exit road is clear**

Box junctions are marked on the road to prevent the road becoming blocked. Don't enter the box unless your exit road is clear. You may only wait in the box if your exit road is clear but oncoming traffic is preventing you from completing the turn.

10.33

You may wait in a yellow box junction when

- ⊙ oncoming traffic is preventing you from turning right
- ⊙ you are in a queue of traffic turning left
- ⊙ you are in a queue of traffic to go ahead
- ⊙ you are on a roundabout

⊙ **oncoming traffic is preventing you from turning right**

The purpose of this road marking is to keep the junction clear of queuing traffic. You may only wait in the marked area when you're turning right and your exit lane is clear but you can't complete the turn because of oncoming traffic.

10.34

Who can use a toucan crossing?

- ⊙ Trains
- ⊙ Cyclists
- ⊙ Buses
- ⊙ Pedestrians
- ⊙ Trams

⊙ **Cyclists**

⊙ **Pedestrians**

Toucan crossings are similar to pelican crossings but there is no flashing amber phase. Cyclists share the crossing with pedestrians and are allowed to cycle across when the green cycle symbol is shown.

10.35 *Mark **three** answers*

You MUST stop when signalled to do so by which THREE of these?

- A police officer
- A pedestrian
- A school crossing patrol
- A bus driver
- A red traffic light

- ⊙ **A police officer**
- ⊙ **A school crossing patrol**
- ⊙ **A red traffic light**

Looking well ahead and 'reading' the road will help you to anticipate hazards. This will enable you to stop safely at traffic lights or if ordered to do so by an authorised person.

10.36 *Mark **one** answer*

Someone is waiting to cross at a zebra crossing. They are standing on the pavement. You should normally

- ⊙ go on quickly before they step onto the crossing
- ⊙ stop before you reach the zigzag lines and let them cross
- ⊙ stop, let them cross, wait patiently
- ⊙ ignore them as they are still on the pavement

- ⊙ **stop, let them cross, wait patiently**

By standing on the pavement, the pedestrian is showing an intention to cross. If you are looking well down the road you will give yourself enough time to slow down and stop safely. Don't forget to check your mirrors before slowing down.

10.37 *Mark **one** answer*

At toucan crossings, apart from pedestrians you should be aware of

- ⊙ emergency vehicles emerging
- ⊙ buses pulling out
- ⊙ trams crossing in front
- ⊙ cyclists riding across

- ⊙ **cyclists riding across**

The use of cycles is being encouraged and more toucan crossings are being installed. These crossings enable pedestrians and cyclists to cross the path of other traffic. Watch out as cyclists will approach the crossing faster than pedestrians.

At a pelican crossing, what does a flashing amber light mean?

⊙ You must not move off until the lights stop flashing

⊙ You must give way to pedestrians still on the crossing

⊙ You can move off, even if pedestrians are still on the crossing

⊙ You must stop because the lights are about to change to red

⊙ **You must give way to pedestrians still on the crossing**

If there is no-one on the crossing when the amber light is flashing, you may proceed over the crossing. You don't need to wait for the green light to show.

You are waiting at a pelican crossing. The red light changes to flashing amber. This means you must

⊙ wait for pedestrians on the crossing to clear

⊙ move off immediately without any hesitation

⊙ wait for the green light before moving off

⊙ get ready and go when the continuous amber light shows

⊙ **wait for pedestrians on the crossing to clear**

This light allows time for the pedestrians already on the crossing to get to the other side in their own time, without being rushed. Don't rev your engine or start to move off while they are still crossing.

You park at night on a road with a 40 mph speed limit. You should park

⊙ facing the traffic

⊙ with parking lights on

⊙ with dipped headlights on

⊙ near a street light

⊙ **with parking lights on**

You must use parking lights when parking at night on a road or lay-by with a speed limit greater than 30 mph. You must also park in the direction of the traffic flow.

10.41

*Mark **one** answer*

When can you park on the left opposite these road markings?

⊙ If the line nearest to you is broken

⊙ When there are no yellow lines

⊙ To pick up or set down passengers

⊙ During daylight hours only

⊙ **To pick up or set down passengers**

You must not park or stop on a road marked with double white lines (even where one of the lines is broken) except to pick up or set down passengers.

10.42

*Mark **one** answer*

You are intending to turn right at a crossroads. An oncoming driver is also turning right. It will normally be safer to

⊙ keep the other vehicle to your RIGHT and turn behind it (offside to offside)

⊙ keep the other vehicle to your LEFT and turn in front of it (nearside to nearside)

⊙ carry on and turn at the next junction instead

⊙ hold back and wait for the other driver to turn first

⊙ **keep the other vehicle to your RIGHT and turn behind it (offside to offside)**

At some junctions the layout may make it difficult to turn offside to offside. If this is the case, be prepared to pass nearside to nearside, but take extra care as your view ahead will be obscured by the vehicle turning in front of you.

10.43

*Mark **one** answer*

You are on a road that has no traffic signs. There are street lights. What is the speed limit?

⊙ 20 mph

⊙ 30 mph

⊙ 40 mph

⊙ 60 mph

⊙ **30 mph**

If you aren't sure of the speed limit a good indication is the presence of street lights. If there is street lighting the speed limit will be 30 mph unless otherwise indicated.

10.44   *Mark **three** answers*

You are going along a street with parked vehicles on the left-hand side. For which THREE reasons should you keep your speed down?

- So that oncoming traffic can see you more clearly
- You may set off car alarms
- Vehicles may be pulling out
- Drivers' doors may open
- Children may run out from between the vehicles

⊙ **Vehicles may be pulling out**

⊙ **Drivers' doors may open**

⊙ **Children may run out from between the vehicles**

Travel slowly and carefully where there are parked vehicles in a built-up area.

Beware of

- vehicles pulling out, especially bicycles and other motorcycles
- pedestrians, especially children, who may run out from between cars
- drivers opening their doors.

10.45   *Mark **one** answer*

You meet an obstruction on your side of the road. You should

- carry on, you have priority
- give way to oncoming traffic
- wave oncoming vehicles through
- accelerate to get past first

⊙ **give way to oncoming traffic**

Take care if you have to pass a parked vehicle on your side of the road. Give way to oncoming traffic if there isn't enough room for you both to continue safely.

10.46   *Mark **two** answers*

You are on a two-lane dual carriageway. For which TWO of the following would you use the right-hand lane?

- Turning right
- Normal progress
- Staying at the minimum allowed speed
- Constant high speed
- Overtaking slower traffic
- Mending punctures

⊙ **Turning right**

⊙ **Overtaking slower traffic**

Normally you should travel in the left-hand lane and only use the right-hand lane for overtaking or turning right. Move back into the left lane as soon as it's safe but don't cut in across the path of the vehicle you've just passed.

10.47 *Mark one answer*

Who has priority at an unmarked crossroads?

⊙ The larger vehicle

⊙ No one has priority

⊙ The faster vehicle

⊙ The smaller vehicle

⊙ **No one has priority**

Practise good observation in all directions before you emerge or make a turn. Proceed only when you're sure it's safe to do so.

10.48 NI EXEMPT *Mark one answer*

What is the nearest you may park to a junction?

⊙ 10 metres (32 feet)

⊙ 12 metres (39 feet)

⊙ 15 metres (49 feet)

⊙ 20 metres (66 feet)

⊙ **10 metres (32 feet)**

Don't park within 10 metres (32 feet) of a junction (unless in an authorised parking place). This is to allow drivers emerging from, or turning into, the junction a clear view of the road they are joining. It also allows them to see hazards such as pedestrians or cyclists at the junction.

10.49 NI EXEMPT *Mark three answers*

In which THREE places must you NOT park?

⊙ Near the brow of a hill

⊙ At or near a bus stop

⊙ Where there is no pavement

⊙ Within 10 metres (32 feet) of a junction

⊙ On a 40 mph road

⊙ **Near the brow of a hill**

⊙ **At or near a bus stop**

⊙ **Within 10 metres (32 feet) of a junction**

Other traffic will have to pull out to pass you. They may have to use the other side of the road and if you park near the brow of a hill they may not be able to see oncoming traffic.

It's important not to park at or near a bus stop as this could inconvenience passengers and may put them at risk as they get on or off the bus.

Parking near a junction could restrict the view for emerging vehicles.

10.50 *Mark **one** answer*

You are waiting at a level crossing. A train has passed but the lights keep flashing. You must

⊙ carry on waiting

⊙ phone the signal operator

⊙ edge over the stop line and look for trains

⊙ park and investigate

⊙ **carry on waiting**

If the lights at a level crossing continue to flash after a train has passed, wait as there might be another train coming. Time seems to pass slowly when you're held up in a queue. Be patient and wait until the lights stop flashing.

10.51 *Mark **one** answer*

At a crossroads there are no signs or road markings. Two vehicles approach. Which has priority?

⊙ Neither of the vehicles

⊙ The vehicle travelling the fastest

⊙ Oncoming vehicles turning right

⊙ Vehicles approaching from the right

⊙ **Neither of the vehicles**

At a crossroads where there are no 'give way' signs or road markings be very careful. No vehicle has priority, even if the sizes of the roads are different.

10.52 *Mark **one** answer*

What does this sign tell you?

⊙ That it is a no-through road

⊙ End of traffic calming zone

⊙ Free parking zone ends

⊙ No waiting zone ends

⊙ **No waiting zone ends**

The blue and red circular sign on its own means that waiting restrictions are in force. This sign shows that you are leaving the controlled zone and waiting restrictions no longer apply.

10.53

*Mark **one** answer*

You are entering an area of roadworks. There is a temporary speed limit displayed. You should

- not exceed the speed limit
- obey the limit only during rush hour
- ignore the displayed limit
- obey the limit except at night

⊙ **not exceed the speed limit**

Where there are extra hazards such as roadworks, it's often necessary to slow traffic down by imposing a temporary speed limit. These speed limits aren't advisory – they must be adhered to.

10.54

*Mark **two** answers*

In which TWO places should you NOT park?

- Near a school entrance
- Near a police station
- In a side road
- At a bus stop
- In a one-way street

⊙ **Near a school entrance**

⊙ **At a bus stop**

It may be tempting to park where you shouldn't while you run a quick errand. Careless parking is a selfish act and could endanger other road users.

10.55

*Mark **one** answer*

You are travelling on a well-lit road at night in a built-up area. By using dipped headlights you will be able to

- see further along the road
- go at a much faster speed
- switch to main beam quickly
- be easily seen by others

⊙ **be easily seen by others**

You may be difficult to see when you're travelling at night, even on a well lit road. If you use dipped headlights rather than sidelights other road users will see you more easily.

*Mark **one** answer*

The dual carriageway you are turning right onto has a very narrow central reservation. What should you do?

- ⊙ Proceed to the central reservation and wait
- ⊙ Wait until the road is clear in both directions
- ⊙ Stop in the first lane so that other vehicles give way
- ⊙ Emerge slightly to show your intentions

⊙ **Wait until the road is clear in both directions**

When the central reservation is narrow you should treat a dual carriageway as one road. Wait until the road is clear in both directions before emerging to turn right. If you try to treat it as two separate roads and wait in the middle, you are likely to cause an obstruction and possibly an accident.

---

*Mark **one** answer*

You are travelling on a motorway. You MUST stop when signalled to do so by which of these?

- ⊙ Flashing amber lights above your lane
- ⊙ A Highways Agency Traffic Officer
- ⊙ Pedestrians on the hard shoulder
- ⊙ A driver who has broken down

⊙ **A Highways Agency Traffic Officer**

You will find Highways Agency Traffic Officers on many of Britain's motorways. They work in partnership with the police, helping to keep traffic moving and to make your journey as safe as possible. It is an offence not to comply with the directions given by a Traffic Officer.

---

*Mark **one** answer*

At a busy unmarked crossroads, which of the following has priority?

- ⊙ Vehicles going straight ahead
- ⊙ Vehicles turning right
- ⊙ None of the vehicles
- ⊙ The vehicles that arrived first

⊙ **None of the vehicles**

If there are no road signs or markings do not assume that you have priority. Remember that other drivers may assume they have the right to go. No type of vehicle has priority but it's courteous to give way to large vehicles. Also look out in particular for cyclists and motorcyclists.

10.59   *Mark **one** answer*

You will see these red and white markers when approaching

- the end of a motorway
- a concealed level crossing
- a concealed speed limit sign
- the end of a dual carriageway

⊙ **a concealed level crossing**

If there is a bend just before the level crossing you may not be able to see the level crossing barriers or waiting traffic. These signs give you an early warning that you may find these hazards just around the bend.

section eleven
ROAD AND TRAFFIC SIGNS

This section covers:

- road signs
- speed limits
- road markings
- regulations

11.1
*Mark **one** answer*

What shape is a STOP sign at a junction?

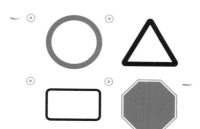

To make it easy to recognise, the 'stop' sign is the only sign of this shape. You must stop and make effective observation before proceeding.

11.2
*Mark **one** answer*

What does this sign mean?

⊙ Ring road
⊙ Mini-roundabout
⊙ No vehicles
⊙ Roundabout

⊙ **Roundabout**

As you approach a roundabout look well ahead and check all signs. Decide which exit you wish to take and move into the correct position as you approach the roundabout, signalling as required.

11.3
*Mark **one** answer*

What does this sign mean?

⊙ Turn left ahead
⊙ T-junction
⊙ No through road
⊙ Give way

⊙ **T-junction**

This type of sign will warn you of hazards ahead.

Make sure you look at each sign that you pass on the road, so that you do not miss any vital instructions or information.

*Mark **one** answer*

What does this sign mean?

⊙ Crossroads
⊙ Level crossing with gate
⊙ Level crossing without gate
⊙ Ahead only

⊙ **Crossroads**

The priority through the junction is shown by the broader line. You need to be aware of the hazard posed by traffic crossing or pulling out onto a major road.

*Mark **one** answer*

At a junction you see this sign partly covered by snow. What does it mean?

⊙ Cross roads
⊙ Give way
⊙ Stop
⊙ Turn right

⊙ **Stop**

The STOP sign is the only road sign that is octagonal. This is so that it can be recognised and obeyed even if it is obscured, for example by snow.

*Mark **one** answer*

Which of these signs means there is a double bend ahead?

Triangular signs give you a warning of hazards ahead. They are there to give you time to prepare for the hazard, for example by adjusting your speed.

11.7   *Mark **one** answer*

What does this sign mean?

- Low bridge ahead
- Tunnel ahead
- Ancient monument ahead
- Accident black spot ahead

⊙ **Tunnel ahead**

When approaching a tunnel switch on your dipped headlights and reduce your speed. Be aware that your eyes might need to adjust to the sudden darkness.

11.8   *Mark **one** answer*

Which sign means 'two-way traffic crosses a one-way road'?

⊙

Traffic could be joining the road you're in from either direction. Unless you need to turn, don't change lanes as you approach the junction.

11.9   *Mark **one** answer*

Which of these signs means the end of a dual carriageway?

⊙

If you're travelling in the right-hand lane, prepare and move over into the left-hand lane as soon as it's safe to do so.

What does this sign mean?

⊙ End of dual carriageway
⊙ Tall bridge
⊙ Road narrows
⊙ End of narrow bridge

⊙ **End of dual carriageway**

Don't leave moving into the left-hand lane until the last moment. Plan ahead and don't rely on other traffic letting you in.

What does this sign mean?

⊙ Adverse camber
⊙ Steep hill downwards
⊙ Uneven road
⊙ Steep hill upwards

⊙ **Steep hill downwards**

This sign will give you an early warning that the road ahead will slope downhill. Prepare to alter your speed and gear. Looking at the sign from left to right will show you whether the road slopes uphill or downhill.

Which sign means 'no through road'?

⊙

This sign is found at the entrance to a road that can only be used for access.

226

11.13

Mark **one** answer

What does this sign mean?

- ⊙ Turn left for parking area
- ⊙ No through road on the left
- ⊙ No entry for traffic turning left
- ⊙ Turn left for ferry terminal

⊙ **No through road on the left**

If you intend to take a left turn, this sign shows you that you can't get through to another route using the left-turn junction ahead.

11.14

Mark **one** answer

What does this sign mean?

- ⊙ T-junction
- ⊙ No through road
- ⊙ Telephone box ahead
- ⊙ Toilet ahead

⊙ **No through road**

You will not be able to find a through route to another road. Use this road only for access.

11.15

Mark **one** answer

What does this sign mean?

- ⊙ Bus station on the right
- ⊙ Contraflow bus lane
- ⊙ With-flow bus lane
- ⊙ Give way to buses

⊙ **Contraflow bus lane**

There will also be markings on the road surface to indicate the bus lane. You must not use this lane for parking or overtaking.

What does this sign mean?

- ⊙ Uneven road surface
- ⊙ Bridge over the road
- ⊙ Road ahead ends
- ⊙ Water across the road

⊙ **Water across the road**

This sign is found where a shallow stream crosses the road. Heavy rainfall could increase the flow of water. If the water looks too deep or the stream has spread over a large distance, stop and find another route.

What does this sign mean?

- ⊙ Buses turning
- ⊙ Ring road
- ⊙ Mini-roundabout
- ⊙ Keep right

⊙ **Mini-roundabout**

When you see this sign, look out for any direction signs and judge whether you need to signal your intentions. Do this in good time so that other road users approaching the roundabout know what you're planning to do.

What does this sign mean?

- ⊙ Two-way traffic straight ahead
- ⊙ Two-way traffic crosses a one-way road
- ⊙ Two-way traffic over a bridge
- ⊙ Two-way traffic crosses a two-way road

⊙ **Two-way traffic crosses a one-way road**

Be prepared for traffic approaching from junctions on either side of you. Try to avoid unnecessary changing of lanes just before the junction.

11.19   *Mark **one** answer*

What does this sign mean?

- ⊙ Two-way traffic ahead across a one-way road
- ⊙ Traffic approaching you has priority
- ⊙ Two-way traffic straight ahead
- ⊙ Motorway contraflow system ahead

⊙ **Two-way traffic straight ahead**

This sign may be at the end of a dual carriageway or a one-way street. It is there to warn you of oncoming traffic.

11.20   *Mark **one** answer*

What does this sign mean?

- ⊙ Hump-back bridge
- ⊙ Traffic calming hump
- ⊙ Low bridge
- ⊙ Uneven road

⊙ **Hump-back bridge**

You will need to slow down. At humpback bridges your view ahead will be restricted and the road will often be narrow on the bridge. If the bridge is very steep be prepared to sound your horn to warn others of your approach. Going fast over the bridge is highly dangerous to other road users and could even cause your wheels to leave the road, with a resulting loss of control.

11.21   *Mark **one** answer*

Which of the following signs informs you that you are coming to a 'no through road'?

⊙
⊙

⊙
⊙

⊙

This sign is found at the entrance to a road that can only be used for access.

What does this sign mean?

- ⊙ Level crossing with gate or barrier
- ⊙ Gated road ahead
- ⊙ Level crossing without gate or barrier
- ⊙ Cattle grid ahead

⊙ **Level crossing with gate or barrier**

Some crossings have gates but no attendant or signals. You should

- stop
- look both ways
- listen and make sure that there is no train approaching.

If there is a telephone, contact the signal operator to make sure that it's safe to cross.

At a railway level crossing the red light signal continues to flash after a train has gone by. What should you do?

- ⊙ Phone the signal operator
- ⊙ Alert drivers behind you
- ⊙ Wait
- ⊙ Proceed with caution

⊙ **Wait**

You must always obey red flashing stop lights. If a train passes but the lights continue to flash, another train will be passing soon. Cross only when the lights go off and the barriers open.

You are in a tunnel and you see this sign. What does it mean?

- ⊙ Direction to emergency pedestrian exit
- ⊙ Beware of pedestrians, no footpath ahead
- ⊙ No access for pedestrians
- ⊙ Beware of pedestrians crossing ahead

⊙ **Direction to emergency pedestrian exit**

If you find yourself having to evacuate a tunnel, do so as quickly as you can. Follow the signs directing you to the nearest exit point. If there are several people using the exit, don't panic but try to leave in a calm and orderly manner.

11.25
*Mark **one** answer*

What does this traffic sign mean?

- ⊙ No overtaking allowed
- ⊙ Give priority to oncoming traffic
- ⊙ Two way traffic
- ⊙ One-way traffic only

⊙ **Give priority to oncoming traffic**

Priority signs are normally shown where the road is narrow and there isn't enough room for two vehicles to pass, such as at

- • a narrow bridge
- • roadworks
- • a width restriction.

Make sure that you know who has priority. Comply with the sign and don't force your way through. Show courtesy and consideration to other road users.

11.26
*Mark **one** answer*

What does this sign mean?

- ⊙ Leave motorway at next exit
- ⊙ Lane for heavy and slow vehicles
- ⊙ All lorries use the hard shoulder
- ⊙ Rest area for lorries

⊙ **Lane for heavy and slow vehicles**

Where there's a long, steep, uphill gradient on a motorway, a crawler lane may be provided. This helps the traffic to flow by diverting the slower heavy vehicles into a dedicated lane on the left.

11.27
*Mark **one** answer*

What does this sign mean?

- ⊙ No overtaking
- ⊙ You are entering a one-way street
- ⊙ Two-way traffic ahead
- ⊙ You have priority over vehicles from the opposite direction

⊙ **You have priority over vehicles from the opposite direction**

Don't force your way through if oncoming vehicles fail to give way. If necessary, slow down and give way to avoid confrontation or an accident.

What are triangular signs for?

- ◉ To give warnings
- ◉ To give information
- ◉ To give orders
- ◉ To give directions

◉ **To give warnings**

This type of sign will warn you of hazards ahead.

Make sure you look at each sign that you pass on the road, so that you do not miss any vital instructions or information.

Which FOUR of these would be indicated by a triangular road sign?

- ◉ Road narrows
- ◉ Ahead only
- ◉ Low bridge
- ◉ Minimum speed
- ◉ Children crossing
- ◉ T-junction

◉ **Road narrows**

◉ **Low bridge**

◉ **Children crossing**

◉ **T-junction**

Warning signs are there to make you aware of potential hazards on the road ahead. Act on the signs so you are prepared and can take whatever action is necessary.

What does this traffic sign mean?

- ◉ Slippery road ahead
- ◉ Tyres liable to punctures ahead
- ◉ Danger ahead
- ◉ Service area ahead

◉ **Danger ahead**

This sign is there to alert you to the likelihood of danger ahead. It may be accompanied by a plate indicating the type of hazard. Be ready to reduce your speed and take avoiding action.

11.31
*Mark **one** answer*

You are about to overtake when you see this sign. You should

Hidden dip

- ⊙ overtake the other driver as quickly as possible
- ⊙ move to the right to get a better view
- ⊙ switch your headlights on before overtaking
- ⊙ hold back until you can see clearly ahead

⊙ **hold back until you can see clearly ahead**

You won't be able to see any hazards that might be hidden in the dip. As well as oncoming traffic the dip may conceal

- cyclists
- horse riders
- parked vehicles
- pedestrians in the road.

11.32
*Mark **one** answer*

What does this sign mean?

- ⊙ Quayside or river bank
- ⊙ Steep hill downwards
- ⊙ Uneven road surface
- ⊙ Road liable to flooding

⊙ **Quayside or river bank**

You should be careful in these locations as the road surface is likely to be wet and slippery. There may be a steep drop to the water and there may not be a barrier along the edge of the road.

11.33
*Mark **one** answer*

Where can you find reflective amber studs on a motorway?

- ⊙ Separating the slip road from the motorway
- ⊙ On the left-hand edge of the road
- ⊙ On the right-hand edge of the road
- ⊙ Separating the lanes

⊙ **On the right-hand edge of the road**

At night or in poor visibility reflective studs on the road help you to judge your position on the carriageway.

*Mark **one** answer*

Which shape is used for a 'give way' sign?

Other warning signs are the same shape and colour, but the 'give way' sign is the only triangular one that points downwards. When you see this sign you must give way to traffic on the road which you are about to enter.

*Mark **one** answer*

Which of these signs means that you are entering a one-way street?

If the road has two lanes you can use either lane and overtake on either side. Use the lane that's more convenient for your destination unless road markings indicate otherwise.

*Mark **one** answer*

Where would you see a contraflow bus and cycle lane?

⊙ On a dual carriageway

⊙ On a roundabout

⊙ On an urban motorway

⊙ On a one-way street

⊙ **On a one-way street**

In a contraflow lane the traffic permitted to use it travels in the opposite direction to traffic in the other lanes on the road.

234

11.37
*Mark **one** answer*

Which sign means you have priority over oncoming vehicles?

Even though you have priority, be prepared to give way if complying with the sign is likely to cause an accident, congestion or confrontation.

11.38
*Mark **one** answer*

What does this sign mean?

⊙ **With-flow bus and cycle lane**

Buses, taxis and cycles are permitted to travel in this lane in the same direction as other traffic. They will be on your left. There may be times shown on the sign to indicate when the lane is in operation.

- ⊙ With-flow bus and cycle lane
- ⊙ Contraflow bus and cycle lane
- ⊙ No buses and cycles allowed
- ⊙ No waiting for buses and cycles

11.39
*Mark **one** answer*

Which is the sign for a ring road?

Ring roads are designed to relieve congestion in towns and city centres.

11.40

*Mark **one** answer*

What does this sign mean?

⊙ The right-hand lane ahead is narrow
⊙ Right-hand lane for buses only
⊙ Right-hand lane for turning right
⊙ The right-hand lane is closed

⊙ **The right-hand lane is closed**

Yellow and black temporary signs may be used to inform you of roadworks or lane restrictions. Look well ahead. If you have to change lanes, do so in good time.

11.41

*Mark **one** answer*

What does this sign mean?

⊙ Change to the left lane
⊙ Leave at the next exit
⊙ Contraflow system
⊙ One-way street

⊙ **Contraflow system**

If you use the right-hand lane in a contraflow system, you'll be travelling with no permanent barrier between you and the oncoming traffic. Observe speed limits and keep a good distance from the vehicle ahead.

11.42

*Mark **one** answer*

What is the meaning of this traffic sign?

⊙ End of two-way road
⊙ Give priority to vehicles coming towards you
⊙ You have priority over vehicles coming towards you
⊙ Bus lane ahead

⊙ **You have priority over vehicles coming towards you**

Don't force your way through. Show courtesy and consideration to other road users. Although you have priority, make sure oncoming traffic is going to give way before you continue.

11.43
*Mark **one** answer*

What does this sign mean?

- ⊙ Direction to park-and-ride car park
- ⊙ No parking for buses or coaches
- ⊙ Directions to bus and coach park
- ⊙ Parking area for cars and coaches

⊙ **Direction to park-and-ride car park**

To ease the congestion in town centres, some cities and towns provide park-and-ride schemes. These allow you to park in a designated area and ride by bus into the centre.

Park-and-ride schemes are usually cheaper and easier than car parking in the town centre.

11.44
*Mark **one** answer*

What does this motorway sign mean?

- ⊙ Change to the lane on your left
- ⊙ Leave the motorway at the next exit
- ⊙ Change to the opposite carriageway
- ⊙ Pull up on the hard shoulder

⊙ **Change to the lane on your left**

On the motorway, signs sometimes show temporary warnings due to traffic or weather conditions. They may be used to indicate

- lane closures
- temporary speed limits
- weather warnings.

11.45
*Mark **one** answer*

What does this motorway sign mean?

- ⊙ Temporary minimum speed 50 mph
- ⊙ No services for 50 miles
- ⊙ Obstruction 50 metres (164 feet) ahead
- ⊙ Temporary maximum speed 50 mph

⊙ **Temporary maximum speed 50 mph**

Look out for signs above your lane or on the central reservation. These will give you important information or warnings about the road ahead. Due to the high speeds of motorway traffic these signs may light up some distance from any hazard. Don't ignore the signs just because the road looks clear to you.

*Mark **one** answer*

What does this sign mean?

- ⊙ Through traffic to use left lane
- ⊙ Right-hand lane T-junction only
- ⊙ Right-hand lane closed ahead
- ⊙ 11 tonne weight limit

⊙ **Right-hand lane closed ahead**

Move over as soon as you see the sign and it's safe to do so. Don't stay in a lane that is closed ahead until the last moment to beat a queue of traffic.

*Mark **one** answer*

On a motorway this sign means

- ⊙ move over onto the hard shoulder
- ⊙ overtaking on the left only
- ⊙ leave the motorway at the next exit
- ⊙ move to the lane on your left

⊙ **move to the lane on your left**

It is important to know and obey temporary signs on the motorway: they are there for a reason. You may not be able to see the hazard straight away, as the signs give warnings well in advance due to the speed of traffic on the motorway.

*Mark **one** answer*

What does '25' mean on this motorway sign?

- ⊙ The distance to the nearest town
- ⊙ The route number of the road
- ⊙ The number of the next junction
- ⊙ The speed limit on the slip road

⊙ **The number of the next junction**

Before you set out on your journey use a road map to plan your route. When you see advance warning of your junction, make sure you get into the correct lane in plenty of time. Last-minute harsh braking and cutting across lanes at speed is extremely hazardous.

11.49
*Mark **one** answer*

At this junction there is a stop sign with a solid white line on the road surface. Why is there a stop sign here?

- ⊙ Speed on the major road is de-restricted
- ⊙ It is a busy junction
- ⊙ Visibility along the major road is restricted
- ⊙ There are hazard warning lines in the centre of the road

⊙ **Visibility along the major road is restricted**

If your view is restricted at a road junction you must stop. There may also be a 'stop' sign. Don't emerge until you're sure there's no traffic approaching.

IF YOU DON'T KNOW, DON'T GO.

11.50
*Mark **one** answer*

The right-hand lane of a three-lane motorway is

- ⊙ for lorries only
- ⊙ an overtaking lane
- ⊙ the right-turn lane
- ⊙ an acceleration lane

⊙ **an overtaking lane**

You should stay in the left-hand lane of a motorway unless overtaking. The right-hand lane of a motorway is an overtaking lane and not a 'fast lane'.

After overtaking, move back to the left when it is safe to do so.

11.51
*Mark **one** answer*

Where on a motorway would you find green reflective studs?

- ⊙ Separating driving lanes
- ⊙ Between the hard shoulder and the carriageway
- ⊙ At slip road entrances and exits
- ⊙ Between the carriageway and the central reservation

⊙ **At slip road entrances and exits**

Knowing the colours of the reflective studs on the road will help you judge your position in foggy conditions or when visibility is poor.

*Mark **one** answer*

You are travelling along a motorway. You see this sign. You should

- ⊙ leave the motorway at the next exit
- ⊙ turn left immediately
- ⊙ change lane
- ⊙ move onto the hard shoulder

⊙ **leave the motorway at the next exit**

You'll see this sign if the motorway is closed ahead. Pull into the nearside lane as soon as it is safe to do so. Don't leave it to the last moment.

*Mark **one** answer*

What does this sign mean?

- ⊙ No motor vehicles
- ⊙ End of motorway
- ⊙ No through road
- ⊙ End of bus lane

⊙ **End of motorway**

When you leave the motorway make sure that you check your speedometer. You may be going faster than you realise. Slow down and look out for speed limit signs.

*Mark **one** answer*

What does this sign mean?

- ⊙ End of motorway
- ⊙ End of restriction
- ⊙ Lane ends ahead
- ⊙ Free recovery ends

⊙ **End of restriction**

Temporary restrictions on motorways are shown on signs which have flashing amber lights. At the end of the restriction you will see this sign without any flashing lights.

11.55
*Mark **one** answer*

You are on a motorway. You see this sign on a lorry that has stopped in the right-hand lane. You should

⊙ move into the right-hand lane
⊙ stop behind the flashing lights
⊙ pass the lorry on the left
⊙ leave the motorway at the next exit

⊙ **pass the lorry on the left**

Sometimes work is carried out on the motorway without closing the lanes. When this happens, signs are mounted on the back of lorries to warn other road users of roadworks ahead.

11.56
*Mark **one** answer*

You are on a motorway. Red flashing lights appear above your lane only. What should you do?

⊙ Continue in that lane and look for further information
⊙ Move into another lane in good time
⊙ Pull onto the hard shoulder
⊙ Stop and wait for an instruction to proceed

⊙ **Move into another lane in good time**

Flashing red lights above your lane show that your lane is closed. You should move into another lane as soon as you can do so safely.

11.57
*Mark **one** answer*

You are riding on a motorway. There is a slow-moving vehicle ahead. On the back you see this sign. What should you do?

⊙ Pass on the right
⊙ Pass on the left
⊙ Leave at the next exit
⊙ Drive no further

⊙ **Pass on the left**

If this vehicle is in your lane you will have to move to the left. Use your mirrors and signal if necessary. When it's safe move into the lane on your left. You should always look well ahead so that you can spot such hazards early, giving yourself time to react safely.

241

You see this signal overhead on the motorway. What does it mean?

- ⊙ Leave the motorway at the next exit
- ⊙ All vehicles use the hard shoulder
- ⊙ Sharp bend to the left ahead
- ⊙ Stop, all lanes ahead closed

⊙ **Leave the motorway at the next exit**

You will see this sign if there has been an incident ahead and the motorway is closed. You must obey the sign. Make sure that you prepare to leave as soon as you see the warning sign.

Don't pull over at the last moment or cut across other traffic.

Which type of vehicle does this sign apply to?

- ⊙ Wide vehicles
- ⊙ Long vehicles
- ⊙ High vehicles
- ⊙ Heavy vehicles

⊙ **High vehicles**

The triangular shapes above and below the dimensions indicate a height restriction that applies to the road ahead.

Which of these signs warn you of a pedestrian crossing?

⊙

Look well ahead and check the pavements and surrounding areas for pedestrians. Look for anyone walking towards the crossing. Check your mirrors for traffic behind, in case you have to slow down or stop.

11.61
*Mark **one** answer*

When may you NOT overtake on the left?

- On a free-flowing motorway or dual carriageway
- When the traffic is moving slowly in queues
- On a one-way street
- When the car in front is signalling to turn right

⊙ **On a free-flowing motorway or dual carriageway**

You should normally overtake on the right but there are some occasions when you may overtake on the left. These include when traffic is moving slowly in queues, or when a vehicle ahead is positioned to turn right and there's room to pass on the left.

On motorways and dual carriageways, do not overtake on the left if traffic is flowing freely.

11.62
*Mark **one** answer*

Which sign means that pedestrians may be walking along the road?

⊙

When you pass pedestrians in the road, leave plenty of room. You might have to use the right-hand side of the road, so look well ahead, as well as in your mirrors, before pulling out. Take great care if there is a bend in the road obscuring your view ahead.

11.63
*Mark **one** answer*

What does this sign mean?

- Cyclists must dismount
- Cycles are not allowed
- Cycle route ahead
- Cycle in single file

⊙ **Cycle route ahead**

Where there's a cycle route ahead, a sign will show a bicycle in a red warning triangle. Watch out for children on bicycles and cyclists rejoining the main road.

11.64 *Mark one answer*

What does this sign mean?

- ⊙ No footpath ahead
- ⊙ Pedestrians only ahead
- ⊙ Pedestrian crossing ahead
- ⊙ School crossing ahead

⊙ **Pedestrian crossing ahead**

There are many signs relating to pedestrians that you need to be aware of. You will find these in *The Highway Code* and *Know Your Traffic Signs*. Some of the signs look similar but give different warnings. Make sure you know what they all mean so that you're prepared for any potential hazard.

11.65 *Mark one answer*

What does this sign mean?

- ⊙ School crossing patrol
- ⊙ No pedestrians allowed
- ⊙ Pedestrian zone – no vehicles
- ⊙ Pedestrian crossing ahead

⊙ **Pedestrian crossing ahead**

Look well ahead and be ready to stop for any pedestrians crossing the road. Also check the pavements for anyone who looks like they might step into the road.

11.66 *Mark one answer*

What do these zigzag lines at pedestrian crossings mean?

- ⊙ No parking at any time
- ⊙ Parking allowed only for a short time
- ⊙ Slow down to 20 mph
- ⊙ Sounding horns is not allowed

⊙ **No parking at any time**

The approach to and exit from a pedestrian crossing is marked with zigzag lines. You must not

- park on them or
- overtake the leading vehicle when approaching the crossing.

Parking here would block the view for pedestrians and the approaching traffic.

11.67

A white line like this along the centre of the road is a

- ⊙ bus lane marking
- ⊙ hazard warning
- ⊙ give way marking
- ⊙ lane marking

⊙ **hazard warning**

The centre of the road is usually marked by a broken white line, with lines that are shorter than the gaps. When the lines become longer than the gaps this is a hazard warning line. Look well ahead for these, especially when you are planning to overtake or turn off.

11.68

What does this road marking mean?

- ⊙ Do not cross the line
- ⊙ No stopping allowed
- ⊙ You are approaching a hazard
- ⊙ No overtaking allowed

⊙ **You are approaching a hazard**

Road markings will warn you of a hazard ahead. A single, broken line along the centre of the road, with long markings and short gaps, is a hazard warning line. Don't cross it unless you can see that the road is clear well ahead.

11.69

Where would you see this road marking?

- ⊙ At traffic lights
- ⊙ On road humps
- ⊙ Near a level crossing
- ⊙ At a box junction

⊙ **On road humps**

Due to the dark colour of the road, changes in level aren't easily seen. White triangles painted on the road surface give you an indication of where there are road humps.

Which is a hazard warning line?

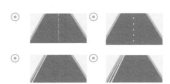

You need to know the difference between the normal centre line and a hazard warning line. If there is a hazard ahead, the markings are longer and the gaps shorter. This gives you advanced warning of an unspecified hazard ahead.

You see this line across the road at the entrance to a roundabout. What does it mean?

⊙ Give way to traffic from the right
⊙ Traffic from the left has right of way
⊙ You have right of way
⊙ Stop at the line

⊙ **Give way to traffic from the right**

Slow down as you approach the roundabout checking for traffic coming from the right. If you need to stop and give way, stay behind the broken line until it is safe to emerge onto the roundabout.

Where would you see these road markings?

⊙ At a level crossing
⊙ On a motorway slip road
⊙ At a pedestrian crossing
⊙ On a single-track road

⊙ **On a motorway slip road**

When driving on a motorway or slip road, you must not enter into an area marked with chevrons and bordered by a solid white line for any reason, except in an emergency.

11.73

*Mark **one** answer*

When may you cross a double solid white line in the middle of the road?

⊙ To pass traffic that is queuing back at a junction

⊙ To pass a car signalling to turn left ahead

⊙ To pass a road maintenance vehicle travelling at 10 mph or less

⊙ To pass a vehicle that is towing a trailer

⊙ **To pass a road maintenance vehicle travelling at 10 mph or less**

You may cross the solid white line to pass a stationary vehicle, pedal cycle, horse or road maintenance vehicle if they are travelling at 10 mph or less. You may also cross the solid line to enter into a side road or access a property.

11.74

*Mark **one** answer*

What is the reason for the yellow criss-cross lines painted on the road here?

⊙ To mark out an area for trams only

⊙ To prevent queuing traffic from blocking the junction on the left

⊙ To mark the entrance lane to a car park

⊙ To warn you of the tram lines crossing the road

⊙ **To prevent queuing traffic from blocking the junction on the left**

Yellow 'box junctions' like this are often used where it's busy. Their purpose is to keep the junction clear for crossing traffic. Don't enter the painted area unless your exit is clear. The exception to this is when you are turning right and are only prevented from doing so by oncoming traffic or by other vehicles waiting to turn right.

11.75
*Mark **one** answer*

What is the reason for the area marked in red and white along the centre of this road?

- ⊙ It is to separate traffic flowing in opposite directions
- ⊙ It marks an area to be used by overtaking motorcyclists
- ⊙ It is a temporary marking to warn of the roadworks
- ⊙ It is separating the two sides of the dual carriageway

⊙ **It is to separate traffic flowing in opposite directions**

Areas of 'hatched markings' such as these are to separate traffic streams which could be a danger to each other. They are often seen on bends or where the road becomes narrow. If the area is bordered by a solid white line, you must not enter it except in an emergency.

11.76
*Mark **one** answer*

Where would you find these road markings?

- ⊙ At a railway crossing
- ⊙ At a junction
- ⊙ On a motorway
- ⊙ On a pedestrian crossing

⊙ **At a junction**

These markings show the direction in which the traffic should go at a mini-roundabout.

11.77

*Mark **one** answer*

This broken white line painted in the centre of the road means

⊙ oncoming vehicles have priority over you

⊙ you should give priority to oncoming vehicles

⊙ there is a hazard ahead of you

⊙ the area is a national speed limit zone

⊙ **there is a hazard ahead of you**

A long white line with short gaps means that you are approaching a hazard. If you do need to cross it, make sure that the road is clear well ahead.

11.78

*Mark **one** answer*

What is the purpose of these yellow criss-cross lines on the road?

⊙ To make you more aware of the traffic lights

⊙ To guide you into position as you turn

⊙ To prevent the junction becoming blocked

⊙ To show you where to stop when the lights change

⊙ **To prevent the junction becoming blocked**

You must not enter a box junction until your exit road or lane is clear. The exception to this is if you want to turn right and are only prevented from doing so by oncoming traffic or by other vehicles waiting to turn right.

This marking appears on the road just before a

⊙ 'no entry' sign
⊙ 'give way' sign
⊙ 'stop' sign
⊙ 'no through road' sign

⊙ **'give way' sign**

Where you see this road marking you must give way to traffic on the main road. It might not be used at junctions where there is relatively little traffic. However, if there is a double broken line across the junction the 'give way' rules still apply.

What does a sign with a brown background show?

⊙ Tourist directions
⊙ Primary roads
⊙ Motorway routes
⊙ Minor routes

⊙ **Tourist directions**

Signs with a brown background give directions to places of interest. They will often be seen on the motorway directing you along the easiest route to the attraction.

This sign means

⊙ tourist attraction
⊙ beware of trains
⊙ level crossing
⊙ beware of trams

⊙ **tourist attraction**

These signs indicate places of interest and are designed to guide you by the easiest route. They are particularly useful if you are unfamiliar with the area.

11.82 — *Mark **one** answer*

Which of these signs means that the national speed limit applies?

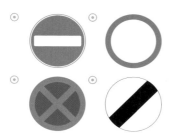

⊙ You should know the speed limit for the road that you're travelling on and the vehicle that you're driving. The different speed limits are shown in *The Highway Code*.

11.83 — *Mark **one** answer*

What is the maximum speed on a single carriageway road?

⊙ 50 mph
⊙ 60 mph
⊙ 40 mph
⊙ 70 mph

⊙ **60 mph**

If you're travelling on a dual carriageway that becomes a single carriageway road, reduce your speed gradually so that you aren't exceeding the limit as you enter. There might not be a sign to remind you of the limit, so make sure you know what the speed limits are for different types of roads and vehicles.

11.84 — *Mark **one** answer*

This sign is advising you to

⊙ follow the route diversion
⊙ follow the signs to the picnic area
⊙ give way to pedestrians
⊙ give way to cyclists

⊙ **follow the route diversion**

When a diversion route has been put in place, drivers are advised to follow a symbol which may be a triangle, square, circle or diamond shape on a yellow background.

*Mark **one** answer*

Why would this temporary speed limit sign be shown?

- ⊙ To warn of the end of the motorway
- ⊙ To warn you of a low bridge
- ⊙ To warn you of a junction ahead
- ⊙ To warn of road works ahead

⊙ **To warn of road works ahead**

In the interests of road safety, temporary speed limits are imposed at all major road works. Signs like this, giving advanced warning of the speed limit, are normally placed about three quarters of a mile ahead of where the speed limit comes into force.

*Mark **one** answer*

This traffic sign means there is

- ⊙ a compulsory maximum speed limit
- ⊙ an advisory maximum speed limit
- ⊙ a compulsory minimum speed limit
- ⊙ an advised separation distance

⊙ **a compulsory maximum speed limit**

The sign gives you an early warning of a speed restriction. If you are travelling at a higher speed, slow down in good time. You could come across queuing traffic due to roadworks or a temporary obstruction.

*Mark **one** answer*

How should you give an arm signal to turn left?

⊙   ⊙

⊙ ⊙

⊙

Arm signals can be effective during daylight, especially when you're wearing bright clothing. Practise giving arm signals when you're learning. You need to be able to keep full control of your motorcycle with one hand off the handlebars.

11.88 *Mark **one** answer*

You are giving an arm signal ready to turn left. Why should you NOT continue with the arm signal while you turn?

⊙ Because you might hit a pedestrian on the corner

⊙ Because you will have less steering control

⊙ Because you will need to keep the clutch applied

⊙ Because other motorists will think that you are stopping on the corner

⊙ **Because you will have less steering control**

Consider giving an arm signal if it will help other road users to understand your intentions, for example

• approaching a pedestrian crossing

• in bright sunshine when your direction indicators may be difficult to see

• if your direction indicators may be obscured, for example in a traffic queue

• where your direction indicators could cause confusion, such as when pulling up close to a side road.

Don't maintain an arm signal when turning. To keep full control of your motorcycle make sure you have both hands on the handlebars when you make the turn.

11.89 *Mark **one** answer*

Which of these signals should you give when slowing or stopping your motorcycle?

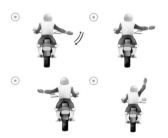

Arm signals can be given to reinforce your flashing indicators, especially if the indicator signal could cause confusion, for example if you intend to pull up close to a side road.

You approach a junction. The traffic lights are not working. A police officer gives this signal. You should

⊙ turn left only

⊙ turn right only

⊙ stop level with the officer's arm

⊙ stop at the stop line

⊙ **stop at the stop line**

If a police officer or traffic warden is directing traffic you must obey them. They will use the arm signals shown in *The Highway Code*. Learn what these mean and act accordingly.

The driver of the car in front is giving this arm signal. What does it mean?

⊙ The driver is slowing down

⊙ The driver intends to turn right

⊙ The driver wishes to overtake

⊙ The driver intends to turn left

⊙ **The driver intends to turn left**

There might be an occasion where another driver uses an arm signal. This may be because the vehicle's indicators are obscured by other traffic. In order for such signals to be effective, all drivers should know the meaning of them.

Be aware that the 'left turn' signal might look similar to the 'slowing down' signal.

You are signalling to turn right in busy traffic. How would you confirm your intention safely?

⊙ Sound the horn

⊙ Give an arm signal

⊙ Flash your headlights

⊙ Position over the centre line

⊙ **Give an arm signal**

In some situations you may feel your indicators cannot be seen by other road users. If you think you need to make your intention more clearly seen, give the arm signal shown in *The Highway Code*.

11.93
*Mark **one** answer*

The driver of this car is giving an arm signal. What are they about to do?

⊙ Turn to the right

⊙ Turn to the left

⊙ Go straight ahead

⊙ Let pedestrians cross

⊙ **Turn to the left**

In some situations drivers may need to give arm signals, in addition to indicators, to make their intentions clear. For arm signals to be effective, all road users should know their meaning.

11.94
*Mark **one** answer*

Which arm signal tells you that the car you are following is going to turn left?

There may be occasions when drivers need to give an arm signal in addition to an indicator. For example

• in bright sunshine

• at a complex road layout

• when stopping at a pedestrian crossing

• to confirm an indicator

• when turning right just after passing a parked vehicle.

You should understand what each arm signal means. If you give arm signals, make them clear, correct and decisive.

Why should you make sure that you cancel your indicators after turning?

⊙ To avoid flattening the battery

⊙ To avoid misleading other road users

⊙ To avoid dazzling other road users

⊙ To avoid damage to the indicator relay

⊙ **To avoid misleading other road users**

Always check that you have cancelled your indicators after turning. Failing to cancel your indicators could lead to a serious or even fatal accident. Other road users may pull out in front of you if they think you are going to turn off before you reach them.

Your indicators are difficult to see due to bright sunshine. When using them you should

⊙ also give an arm signal

⊙ sound your horn

⊙ flash your headlight

⊙ keep both hands on the handlebars

⊙ **also give an arm signal**

Arm signals should be used to confirm your intentions when you aren't sure that your indicators can be seen by other road users. Use the signals shown in *The Highway Code* and return your hand to the handlebars before you turn.

You are approaching a red traffic light. The signal will change from red to

⊙ red and amber, then green

⊙ green, then amber

⊙ amber, then green

⊙ green and amber, then green

⊙ **red and amber, then green**

If you know which light is going to show next you can plan your approach accordingly. This can help prevent excessive braking or hesitation at the junction.

11.98 *Mark **one** answer*

A red traffic light means

- ⊙ you should stop unless turning left
- ⊙ stop, if you are able to brake safely
- ⊙ you must stop and wait behind the stop line
- ⊙ proceed with caution

⊙ **you must stop and wait behind the stop line**

Learn the sequence of traffic lights.

- RED means stop and wait behind the stop line.
- RED-AND-AMBER also means stop. Don't go until the green light shows.
- GREEN means you may go if your way is clear. Don't proceed if your exit road is blocked and don't block the junction. Look out for pedestrians.
- AMBER means stop at the stop line. You may go if the amber light appears after you've crossed the stop line or you're so close to it that to pull up might cause an accident.

11.99 *Mark **one** answer*

At traffic lights, amber on its own means

- ⊙ prepare to go
- ⊙ go if the way is clear
- ⊙ go if no pedestrians are crossing
- ⊙ stop at the stop line

⊙ **stop at the stop line**

If the lights have been on green for a while they're likely to change to red as you approach. Be ready for this so that you're able to stop in time.

You are at a junction controlled by traffic lights. When should you NOT proceed at green?

- ⊙ When pedestrians are waiting to cross
- ⊙ When your exit from the junction is blocked
- ⊙ When you think the lights may be about to change
- ⊙ When you intend to turn right

⊙ **When your exit from the junction is blocked**

As you approach the lights look into the road you wish to take. Only proceed if your exit road is clear. If the road is blocked hold back, even if you have to wait for the next green signal.

You are in the left-hand lane at traffic lights. You are waiting to turn left. At which of these traffic lights must you NOT move on?

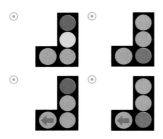

At some junctions there may be a separate signal for different lanes. These are called 'filter' lights. They're designed to help traffic flow at major junctions. Make sure that you're in the correct lane and proceed if the way is clear and the green light shows for your lane.

11.102
*Mark **one** answer*

What does this sign mean?

⊙ Traffic lights out of order
⊙ Amber signal out of order
⊙ Temporary traffic lights ahead
⊙ New traffic lights ahead

⊙ **Traffic lights out of order**

Where traffic lights are out of order you might see this sign. Proceed with caution as nobody has priority at the junction.

11.103
*Mark **one** answer*

When traffic lights are out of order, who has priority?

⊙ Traffic going straight on
⊙ Traffic turning right
⊙ Nobody
⊙ Traffic turning left

⊙ **Nobody**

When traffic lights are out of order you should treat the junction as an unmarked crossroads. Be cautious as you may need to give way or stop. Keep a look out for traffic attempting to cross the junction at speed.

11.104
*Mark **three** answers*

These flashing red lights mean STOP. In which THREE of the following places could you find them?

⊙ Pelican crossings
⊙ Lifting bridges
⊙ Zebra crossings
⊙ Level crossings
⊙ Motorway exits
⊙ Fire stations

⊙ **Lifting bridges**

⊙ **Level crossings**

⊙ **Fire stations**

You must always stop when the red lights are flashing, whether or not the way seems to be clear.

*Mark **one** answer*

You see this sign at a crossroads.
You should

◉ maintain the same speed

◉ carry on with great care

◉ find another route

◉ telephone the police

◉ **carry on with great care**

When traffic lights are out of order treat the junction as an unmarked crossroad.
Be very careful as no one has priority and be prepared to stop.

---

*Mark **one** answer*

You see this amber traffic light ahead.
Which light or lights, will come on next?

◉ Red alone

◉ Red and amber together

◉ Green and amber together

◉ Green alone

◉ **Red alone**

At junctions controlled by traffic lights you must stop behind the white line until the lights change to green. Red and amber lights showing together also mean stop.

You may proceed when the light is green unless your exit road is blocked or pedestrians are crossing in front of you.

If you're approaching traffic lights that are visible from a distance and the light has been green for some time, they are likely to change. Be ready to slow down and stop.

---

*Mark **one** answer*

At a junction you see this signal. It means

◉ cars must stop

◉ trams must stop

◉ both trams and cars must stop

◉ both trams and cars can continue

◉ **trams must stop**

The white light shows that trams must stop, but the green light shows that other vehicles may go if the way is clear.

You may not live in an area where there are trams but you should still learn the signs. You never know when you may go to a town with trams.

11.108

*Mark **one** answer*

A red traffic light means

⊙ you must stop behind the white stop line

⊙ you may go straight on if there is no other traffic

⊙ you may turn left if it is safe to do so

⊙ you must slow down and prepare to stop if traffic has started to cross

⊙ **you must stop behind the white stop line**

The white line is generally positioned so that pedestrians have room to cross in front of waiting traffic. Don't move off while pedestrians are crossing even if the lights change to green.

11.109

*Mark **one** answer*

You are approaching traffic lights. Red and amber are showing. This means

⊙ pass the lights if the road is clear

⊙ there is a fault with the lights – take care

⊙ wait for the green light before you cross the stop line

⊙ the lights are about to change to red

⊙ **wait for the green light before you cross the stop line**

Be aware that other traffic might still be clearing the junction. Make sure the way is clear before continuing.

What does this sign mean?

- ☉ Maximum speed limit with traffic calming
- ☉ Minimum speed limit with traffic calming
- ☉ '20 cars only' parking zone
- ☉ Only 20 cars allowed at any one time

☉ **Maximum speed limit with traffic calming**

If you're in places where there are likely to be pedestrians such as outside schools, near parks, residential areas and shopping areas, you should be extra-cautious and keep your speed down.

Many local authorities have taken measures to slow traffic down by creating traffic calming measures such as speed humps. They are there for a reason; slow down.

What does this sign mean?

- ☉ New speed limit 20 mph
- ☉ No vehicles over 30 tonnes
- ☉ Minimum speed limit 30 mph
- ☉ End of 20 mph zone

☉ **End of 20 mph zone**

Where you see this sign the 20 mph restriction ends. Check all around for possible hazards and only increase your speed if it's safe to do so.

11.112 — Mark **one** answer

What does this sign mean?

⊙ End of restricted speed area
⊙ End of restricted parking area
⊙ End of clearway
⊙ End of cycle route

⊙ **End of restricted parking area**

Even though you have left the restricted area, make sure that you park where you won't endanger other road users or cause an obstruction.

11.113 — Mark **one** answer

What does this sign mean?

⊙ Humpback bridge
⊙ Humps in the road
⊙ Entrance to tunnel
⊙ Soft verges

⊙ **Humps in the road**

These have been put in place to slow the traffic down. They're usually found in residential areas. Slow down to an appropriate speed.

11.114 — Mark **one** answer

In some narrow residential streets you may find a speed limit of

⊙ 20 mph
⊙ 25 mph
⊙ 35 mph
⊙ 40 mph

⊙ **20 mph**

In some built-up areas, you may find the speed limit reduced to 20 mph. Driving at a slower speed will help give you the time and space to see and deal safely with hazards such as pedestrians and parked cars.

What does this sign mean?

⊙ Route for trams only

⊙ Route for buses only

⊙ Parking for buses only

⊙ Parking for trams only

⊙ **Route for trams only**

Avoid blocking tram routes. Trams are fixed on their route and can't manoeuvre around other vehicles and pedestrians. Modern trams travel quickly and are quiet so you might not hear them approaching.

What does this sign mean?

⊙ Route for trams

⊙ Give way to trams

⊙ Route for buses

⊙ Give way to buses

⊙ **Route for trams**

Take extra care when you encounter trams. Look out for road markings and signs that alert you to them. Modern trams are very quiet and you may not hear them approaching.

What does this sign mean?

⊙ No trams ahead

⊙ Oncoming trams

⊙ Trams crossing ahead

⊙ Trams only

⊙ **Trams crossing ahead**

This sign warns you to beware of trams. If you don't usually drive in a town where there are trams, remember to look out for them at junctions and look for tram rails, signs and signals.

11.118
*Mark **one** answer*

What does this sign mean?

⊙ Wait at the barriers
⊙ Wait at the crossroads
⊙ Give way to trams
⊙ Give way to farm vehicles

⊙ **Give way to trams**

Obey the 'give way' signs. Trams are unable to steer around you if you misjudge when it is safe to enter the junction.

11.119
*Mark **one** answer*

What does this sign mean?

⊙ Waiting restrictions apply
⊙ Waiting permitted
⊙ National speed limit applies
⊙ Clearway (no stopping)

⊙ **Waiting restrictions apply**

There will be a plate or additional sign to tell you when the restrictions apply.

11.120
*Mark **one** answer*

Which sign means 'no stopping'?

⊙

Stopping where this clearway restriction applies is likely to cause congestion. Allow the traffic to flow by obeying the signs.

*Mark **one** answer*

What does this sign mean?

⊙ Roundabout
⊙ Crossroads
⊙ No stopping
⊙ No entry

⊙ **No stopping**

This sign is in place to ensure a clear route for traffic. Don't stop except in an emergency.

*Mark **one** answer*

You see this sign ahead. It means

⊙ national speed limit applies
⊙ waiting restrictions apply
⊙ no stopping
⊙ no entry

⊙ **no stopping**

Clearways are stretches of road where you aren't allowed to stop unless in an emergency. You'll see this sign. Stopping where these restrictions apply may be dangerous and likely to cause an obstruction. Restrictions might apply for several miles and this may be indicated on the sign.

*Mark **one** answer*

What does this sign mean?

⊙ Distance to parking place ahead
⊙ Distance to public telephone ahead
⊙ Distance to public house ahead
⊙ Distance to passing place ahead

⊙ **Distance to parking place ahead**

If you intend to stop and rest, this sign allows you time to reduce speed and pull over safely.

11.124 — Mark *one* answer

What does this sign mean?

⊙ Vehicles may not park on the verge or footway

⊙ Vehicles may park on the left-hand side of the road only

⊙ Vehicles may park fully on the verge or footway

⊙ Vehicles may park on the right-hand side of the road only

⊙ **Vehicles may park fully on the verge or footway**

In order to keep roads free from parked cars, there are some areas where you're allowed to park on the verge. Only do this where you see the sign. Parking on verges or footways anywhere else could lead to a fine.

11.125 — Mark *one* answer

What does this sign mean?

⊙ You can park on the days and times shown

⊙ No parking on the days and times shown

⊙ No parking at all from Monday to Friday

⊙ End of the urban clearway restrictions

⊙ **No parking on the days and times shown**

Urban clearways are provided to keep traffic flowing at busy times. You may stop only briefly to set down or pick up passengers. Times of operation will vary from place to place so always check the signs.

*Mark **one** answer*

This sign is of particular importance to motorcyclists. It means

- ⊙ side winds
- ⊙ airport
- ⊙ slippery road
- ⊙ service area

⊙ **side winds**

Strong crosswinds can suddenly blow you off course. Keep your speed down when it's very windy, especially on exposed roads.

*Mark **one** answer*

What does this sign mean?

- ⊙ Multi-exit roundabout
- ⊙ Risk of ice
- ⊙ Six roads converge
- ⊙ Place of historical interest

⊙ **Risk of ice**

It will take up to ten times longer to stop when it's icy. Where there is a risk of icy conditions you need to be aware of this and take extra care.

If you think the road may be icy don't brake or steer harshly as your tyres could lose their grip on the road.

*Mark **one** answer*

What does this sign mean?

- ⊙ Crosswinds
- ⊙ Road noise
- ⊙ Airport
- ⊙ Adverse camber

⊙ **Crosswinds**

A warning sign with a picture of a windsock will indicate there may be strong crosswinds. This sign is often found on exposed roads.

11.129 *Mark one answer*

When drivers flash their headlights at
you it means

- ⊙ that there is a radar speed trap ahead
- ⊙ that they are giving way to you
- ⊙ that they are warning you of their
  presence
- ⊙ that there is something wrong
  with your motorcycle

⊙ **that they are warning
you of their presence**

A driver flashing their headlights has
the same meaning as sounding the horn –
it's a warning of their presence.

11.130 *Mark one answer*

When may you sound the horn?

- ⊙ To give you right of way
- ⊙ To attract a friend's attention
- ⊙ To warn others of your presence
- ⊙ To make slower drivers move over

⊙ **To warn others of
your presence**

Don't use the horn aggressively.
You MUST NOT sound it

- between 11.30 pm and 7 am
- when you are stationary, unless a
  moving vehicle poses a danger.

11.131 *Mark one answer*

You must not use your horn when you
are stationary

- ⊙ unless a moving vehicle may cause
  you danger
- ⊙ at any time whatsoever
- ⊙ unless it is used only briefly
- ⊙ except for signalling that you have
  just arrived

⊙ **unless a moving vehicle may
cause you danger**

Only sound you horn when stationary if
you think there is a risk of an accident.

Don't use it to attract someone's attention,
as this causes unnecessary noise and
could be misleading to other road users.

11.132

*Mark **one** answer*

Other drivers may sometimes flash their headlights at you. In which situation are they allowed to do this?

- ⊙ To warn of a radar speed trap ahead
- ⊙ To show that they are giving way to you
- ⊙ To warn you of their presence
- ⊙ To let you know there is a fault with your vehicle

⊙ **To warn you of their presence**

If other drivers flash their headlights this isn't a signal to show priority. The flashing of headlights has the same meaning as sounding the horn – it's a warning of their presence.

11.133

*Mark **one** answer*

Which one of these signs are you allowed to ride past on a solo motorcycle?

Most regulatory signs are circular; a red circle tells you what you MUST NOT do.

11.134

*Mark **one** answer*

What does this sign mean?

- ⊙ You have priority
- ⊙ No motor vehicles
- ⊙ Two-way traffic
- ⊙ No overtaking

⊙ **No overtaking**

Road signs that prohibit overtaking are placed in locations where passing the vehicle in front is dangerous. If you see this sign don't attempt to overtake. The sign is there for a reason and you must obey it.

11.135
*Mark **one** answer*

Traffic signs giving orders are generally which shape?

Road signs in the shape of a circle give orders. Those with a red circle are mostly prohibitive. The 'stop' sign is octagonal to give it greater prominence. Signs giving orders must always be obeyed.

11.136
*Mark **one** answer*

Which type of sign tells you NOT to do something?

Signs in the shape of a circle give orders. A sign with a red circle means that you aren't allowed to do something. Study *Know Your Traffic Signs* to ensure that you understand what the different traffic signs mean.

11.137
*Mark **one** answer*

Which sign means no motor vehicles are allowed?

You would generally see this sign at the approach to a pedestrian-only zone.

*Mark **one** answer*

Which of these signs means no motor vehicles?

If you are driving a motor vehicle or riding a motorcycle you must not travel past this sign. This area has been designated for use by pedestrians.

*Mark **one** answer*

What does this sign mean?

⊙ No overtaking
⊙ No motor vehicles
⊙ Clearway (no stopping)
⊙ Cars and motorcycles only

⊙ **No motor vehicles**

A sign will indicate which types of vehicles are prohibited from certain roads. Make sure that you know which signs apply to the vehicle you're using.

*Mark **one** answer*

What does this sign mean?

⊙ No parking
⊙ No road markings
⊙ No through road
⊙ No entry

⊙ **No entry**

'No entry' signs are used in places such as one-way streets to prevent vehicles driving against the traffic. To ignore one would be dangerous, both for yourself and other road users, as well as being against the law.

11.141

*Mark **one** answer*

What does this sign mean?

- ⊙ Bend to the right
- ⊙ Road on the right closed
- ⊙ No traffic from the right
- ⊙ No right turn

⊙ **No right turn**

The 'no right turn' sign may be used to warn road users that there is a 'no entry' prohibition on a road to the right ahead.

11.142

*Mark **one** answer*

Which sign means 'no entry'?

⊙   ⊙

⊙   ⊙

⊙

Look out for traffic signs. Disobeying or not seeing a sign could be dangerous. It may also be an offence for which you could be prosecuted.

11.143

*Mark **one** answer*

Which sign means NO motor vehicles allowed?

⊙   ⊙

⊙   ⊙

⊙

This sign is used to enable pedestrians to walk free from traffic. It's often found in shopping areas.

Mark one answer

You MUST obey signs giving orders. These signs are mostly in

- green rectangles
- red triangles
- blue rectangles
- red circles

⊙ **red circles**

Traffic signs can be divided into three classes – those giving orders, those warning and those informing.

Warning signs are usually triangular and direction signs are generally rectangular. One noteable exception to these classes is the eight-sided 'stop' sign.

Mark one answer

What does this sign mean?

- Keep in one lane
- Give way to oncoming traffic
- Do not overtake
- Form two lanes

⊙ **Do not overtake**

If you're behind a slow-moving vehicle be patient. Wait until the restriction no longer applies and you can overtake safely.

Mark one answer

How will a police officer in a patrol vehicle normally get you to stop?

- Flash the headlights, indicate left and point to the left
- Wait until you stop, then approach you
- Use the siren, overtake, cut in front and stop
- Pull alongside you, use the siren and wave you to stop

⊙ **Flash the headlights, indicate left and point to the left**

You must obey signals given by the police. If a police officer in a patrol vehicle wants you to pull over they will indicate this without causing danger to you or other traffic.

11.147

*Mark **one** answer*

What does this sign mean?

- Service area 30 miles ahead
- Maximum speed 30 mph
- Minimum speed 30 mph
- Lay-by 30 miles ahead

⊙ **Minimum speed 30 mph**

This sign is shown where slow-moving vehicles would impede the flow of traffic. However, if you need to slow down to avoid a potential accident, do so.

11.148

*Mark **one** answer*

Which of these signs means turn left ahead?

⊙

Blue circles tell you what you must do and this sign gives a clear instruction. Turn left ahead.

You should be looking out for signs at all times and know what they mean.

11.149

*Mark **one** answer*

What does this sign mean?

- Give way to oncoming vehicles
- Approaching traffic passes you on both sides
- Turn off at the next available junction
- Pass either side to get to the same destination

⊙ **Pass either side to get to the same destination**

These signs are often seen in one-way streets that have more than one lane. When you see this sign, use the route that's the most convenient and doesn't require a late change of direction.

What does a circular traffic sign with a blue background do?

⊙ Give warning of a motorway ahead

⊙ Give directions to a car park

⊙ Give motorway information

⊙ Give an instruction

⊙ **Give an instruction**

Signs with blue circles give a positive instruction. These are often found in urban areas and include signs for mini-roundabouts and directional arrows.

Which sign means no overtaking?

⊙   ⊙

⊙   ⊙

⊙

This sign indicates that overtaking here is not allowed and you could face prosecution if you ignore this prohibition.

What does this sign mean?

⊙ Motorcycles only

⊙ No cars

⊙ Cars only

⊙ No motorcycles

⊙ **No motorcycles**

You must comply with all traffic signs and be especially aware of those signs which apply specifically to the type of vehicle you are using.

11.153
*Mark **three** answers*

At roadworks which of the following can control traffic flow?

- ⊙ A STOP–GO board
- ⊙ Flashing amber lights
- ⊙ A police officer
- ⊙ Flashing red lights
- ⊙ Temporary traffic lights

⊙ **A STOP–GO board**

⊙ **A police officer**

⊙ **Temporary traffic lights**

As you approach the warning signs you should be considering what actions you need to take. You might have to slow right down or stop. Obey any instructions you are given and don't try to beat any lights by speeding up.

11.154
*Mark **one** answer*

There is a police car following you. The police officer flashes the headlights and points to the left. What should you do?

- ⊙ Turn left at the next junction
- ⊙ Pull up on the left
- ⊙ Stop immediately
- ⊙ Move over to the left

⊙ **Pull up on the left**

You must pull up on the left as soon as it's safe to do so and switch off your engine.

11.155
*Mark **one** answer*

What MUST you do when you see this sign?

- ⊙ Stop, only if traffic is approaching
- ⊙ Stop, even if the road is clear
- ⊙ Stop, only if children are waiting to cross
- ⊙ Stop, only if a red light is showing

⊙ **Stop, even if the road is clear**

'Stop' signs are situated at junctions where visibility is restricted or there is heavy traffic. They must be obeyed: you must stop.

Take good all-round observation before moving off.

section twelve
DOCUMENTS

This section covers:

- licences
- insurance
- MOT certificate

12.1
*Mark **one** answer*

After passing your motorcycle test you must exchange the pass certificate for a full motorcycle licence within

- six months
- one year
- two years
- five years

⊙ **two years**

When you pass your practical motorcycle test you'll be issued with a pass certificate. You must exchange the certificate for a full licence within two years of passing your test. If you don't

- the certificate will lapse
- you'll have to retake your test if you wish to resume full motorcycle licence entitlement.

12.2
*Mark **two** answers*

For which TWO of these must you show your motorcycle insurance certificate?

- When you are taking your motorcycle test
- When buying or selling a machine
- When a police officer asks you for it
- When you are taxing your machine
- When having an MOT inspection

⊙ **When a police officer asks you for it**

⊙ **When you are taxing your machine**

You don't have to carry your vehicle insurance certificate with you at all times. However, it must be valid and available to present at a police station if requested.

12.3
*Mark **three** answers*

Which of the following information is found on your motorcycle registration document?

- Make and model
- Service history record
- Ignition key security number
- Engine size and number
- Purchase price
- Year of first registration

⊙ **Make and model**

⊙ **Engine size and number**

⊙ **Year of first registration**

Each motorcycle has a registration document which describes the vehicle's make, model and other details; it also gives details of the registered keeper.

If you buy a new motorcycle the dealer will register your motorcycle with the licensing authority, who will send the registration document to you.

12.4

A theory test pass certificate is valid for

⊙ two years

⊙ three years

⊙ four years

⊙ five years

⊙ **two years**

Your theory test pass certificate is valid for two years. If you don't pass your practical test for the same category of vehicle within two years, you will have to retake your theory test.

12.5
NI EXEMPT   *Mark **one** answer*

Compulsory Basic Training (CBT) can only be carried out by

⊙ any ADI (Approved Driving Instructor)

⊙ any road safety officer

⊙ any DSA (Driving Standards Agency) approved training body

⊙ any motorcycle main dealer

⊙ **any DSA (Driving Standards Agency) approved training body**

DSA approves bodies to provide basic motorcycle training in a safe environment. Frequent checks are made to ensure a high standard of instruction. Taking a CBT course will provide you with the right start to your motorcycling life.

12.6
*Mark **one** answer*

Before riding anyone else's motorcycle you should make sure that

⊙ the owner has third party insurance cover

⊙ your own motorcycle has insurance cover

⊙ the motorcycle is insured for your use

⊙ the owner has the insurance documents with them

⊙ **the motorcycle is insured for your use**

If you borrow a motorcycle you must make sure that you are insured. Find out yourself. Don't take anyone else's word for it.

12.7

*Mark **one** answer*

Vehicle excise duty is often called 'Road Tax' or 'The Tax Disc'. You must

- keep it with your registration document
- display it clearly on your motorcycle
- keep it concealed safely in your motorcycle
- carry it on you at all times

⊙ **display it clearly on your motorcycle**

You must display a current, valid tax disc on your vehicle. It can't be transferred from one vehicle to another.

A vehicle that is exempt from duty must display a valid nil licence instead.

12.8   NI EXEMPT   *Mark **one** answer*

Motorcycles must FIRST have an MOT test certificate when they are

- one year old
- three years old
- five years old
- seven years old

⊙ **three years old**

Any motorcycle you ride must be in good condition and roadworthy. If it's over three years old it must have a valid MOT test certificate.

12.9

*Mark **one** answer*

Your motorcycle needs a current MOT certificate. You do not have one. Until you do have one you will not be able to renew your

- driving licence
- motorcycle insurance
- road tax disc
- motorcycle registration document

⊙ **road tax disc**

If your motorcycle needs an MOT certificate you will need to produce it when renewing your tax disc (also known as vehicle excise duty).

281

Which THREE of the following do you need
before you can ride legally?

⊙ A valid driving licence with signature

⊙ A valid tax disc displayed on your
motorcycle

⊙ Proof of your identity

⊙ Proper insurance cover

⊙ Breakdown cover

⊙ A vehicle handbook

⊙ **A valid driving licence
with signature**

⊙ **A valid tax disc displayed
on your motorcycle**

⊙ **Proper insurance cover**

Riding a motorcycle without

• a valid driving licence

• displaying a current, valid tax disc

• insurance

could carry a heavy fine and lead to penalty
points on your licence.

Which THREE pieces of information are
found on a registration document?

⊙ Registered keeper

⊙ Make of the motorcycle

⊙ Service history details

⊙ Date of the MOT

⊙ Type of insurance cover

⊙ Engine size

⊙ **Registered keeper**

⊙ **Make of the motorcycle**

⊙ **Engine size**

Every motorcycle used on the road has a
registration document issued by the Driver
and Vehicle Licensing Agency (DVLA) or
Driver and Vehicle Licensing Northern
Ireland (DVLNI). It is used to record any
change of ownership and gives the

• date of first registration

• registration number

• previous keeper

• registered keeper

• make of motorcycle

• engine size and frame number

• year of manufacture

• colour.

12.12

*Mark **three** answers*

You have a duty to contact the licensing authority when

- ⊙ you go abroad on holiday
- ⊙ you change your motorcycle
- ⊙ you change your name
- ⊙ your job status is changed
- ⊙ your permanent address changes
- ⊙ your job involves travelling abroad

⊙ **you change your motorcycle**

⊙ **you change your name**

⊙ **your permanent address changes**

The licensing authority will need to keep their records up to date. They send out a reminder when your road tax is due and need your current address for this purpose. Every motorcycle in the country is registered, so it is possible to trace its history.

12.13

*Mark **two** answers*

Your motorcycle is insured third party only. This covers

- ⊙ damage to your motorcycle
- ⊙ damage to other vehicles
- ⊙ injury to yourself
- ⊙ injury to others
- ⊙ all damage and injury

⊙ **damage to other vehicles**

⊙ **injury to others**

Third party insurance cover is usually cheaper than fully comprehensive. However, it does not cover any damage to your own motorcycle or property and it does not provide cover if your motorcycle is stolen.

12.14

*Mark **one** answer*

Your motorcycle insurance policy has an excess of £100. What does this mean?

- ⊙ The insurance company will pay the first £100 of any claim
- ⊙ You will be paid £100 if you do not have an accident
- ⊙ Your motorcycle is insured for a value of £100 if it is stolen
- ⊙ You will have to pay the first £100 of any claim

⊙ **You will have to pay the first £100 of any claim**

This is a method used by insurance companies to keep annual premiums down. Generally, the higher the excess you choose to pay, the lower the annual premium you will be charged.

When you apply to renew your motorcycle excise licence (tax disc) you must produce

⊙ a valid insurance certificate
⊙ the old tax disc
⊙ the motorcycle handbook
⊙ a valid driving licence

⊙ **a valid insurance certificate**

Tax discs can be renewed at most post offices, your nearest vehicle registration office or by post to the licensing authority. Make sure you take all the relevant documents with your application.

What is the legal minimum insurance cover you must have to ride on public roads?

⊙ Third party, fire and theft
⊙ Fully comprehensive
⊙ Third party only
⊙ Personal injury cover

⊙ **Third party only**

The minimum insurance cover required by law is third party only. This covers other people and vehicles involved in an accident, but not you or your motorcycle. Basic third party insurance won't cover you for theft or fire damage.

Check with your insurance company for advice on the best cover for you. Make sure that you read the policy carefully.

Your motorcycle road tax is due to expire. As well as the renewal form and fee you will also need to produce an MOT (if required). What else will you need?

⊙ Proof of purchase receipt
⊙ Compulsory Basic Training certificate
⊙ A valid certificate of insurance
⊙ The Vehicle Registration Document

⊙ **A valid certificate of insurance**

You will normally be sent a reminder automatically by the DVLA (DVLNI in Northern Ireland) close to the time of renewal. Make sure that all your documentation is correct, up to date and valid.

12.18
Mark one answer

A Vehicle Registration Document will show

⊙ the service history

⊙ the year of first registration

⊙ the purchase price

⊙ the tyre sizes

⊙ **the year of first registration**

A Vehicle Registration Document contains a number of details that are unique to a particular vehicle. You must notify DVLA (or DVLNI in Northern Ireland) of any changes to, for example, the registered keeper, registration number or any modifications to the vehicle.

12.19
Mark one answer

What is the purpose of having a vehicle test certificate (MOT)?

⊙ To make sure your motorcycle is roadworthy

⊙ To certify how many miles per gallon it does

⊙ To prove you own the motorcycle

⊙ To allow you to park in restricted areas

⊙ **To make sure your motorcycle is roadworthy**

It is your responsibility to make sure that any motorcycle you ride is in a roadworthy condition. Any faults that develop should be promptly corrected.

If your motorcycle fails an MOT test, it should not be used on the road unless you're taking it to have the faults repaired or for a previously arranged retest.

12.20   NI EXEMPT   *Mark one answer*

Before taking a practical motorcycle test you need

⊙ a full moped licence

⊙ a full car licence

⊙ a CBT (Compulsory Basic Training) certificate

⊙ 12 months riding experience

⊙ **a CBT (Compulsory Basic Training) certificate**

You can find out about a CBT course by asking your motorcycle dealer or by telephoning 0115 901 2595.

You must notify the licensing authority when

- ⊙ your health affects your riding
- ⊙ your eyesight does not meet a set standard
- ⊙ you intend lending your motorcycle
- ⊙ your motorcycle requires an MOT certificate
- ⊙ you change your motorcycle

- ⊙ **your health affects your riding**
- ⊙ **your eyesight does not meet a set standard**
- ⊙ **you change your motorcycle**

The Driver and Vehicle Licensing Agency (DVLA) hold the records of all vehicles, drivers and riders in Great Britain (DVLNI in Northern Ireland). They need to know of any change in circumstances so they can keep their records up to date.

Your health might affect your ability to ride safely. Don't put yourself or other road users at risk.

You have just passed your practical motorcycle test. This is your first full licence. Within two years you get six penalty points. You will have to

- ⊙ retake only your theory test
- ⊙ retake your theory and practical tests
- ⊙ retake only your practical test
- ⊙ reapply for your full licence immediately
- ⊙ reapply for your provisional licence

- ⊙ **retake your theory and practical tests**
- ⊙ **reapply for your provisional licence**

If, during your first two years of holding a full licence, the number of points on your licence reaches six or more, your licence will be revoked. This includes offences you committed before you passed your test.

You may ride only as a learner until you pass both the theory and practical tests again.

12.23
*Mark **one** answer*

You are a learner motorcyclist. The law states that you can carry a passenger when

⊙ your motorcycle is no larger than 125 cc

⊙ your pillion passenger is a full licence-holder

⊙ you have passed your test for a full licence

⊙ you have had three years' experience of riding

⊙ **you have passed your test for a full licence**

When you're a learner motorcyclist you must comply with certain legal restrictions. The law states that you must

• display L-plates (or D-plates in Wales) to the front and rear on your motorcycle

• not carry pillion passengers

• not use the motorway.

12.24
*Mark **three** answers*

You hold a provisional motorcycle licence. This means you must NOT

⊙ exceed 30 mph

⊙ ride on a motorway

⊙ ride after dark

⊙ carry a pillion passenger

⊙ ride without 'L' plates displayed

⊙ **ride on a motorway**

⊙ **carry a pillion passenger**

⊙ **ride without 'L' plates displayed**

Provisional entitlement means that restrictions apply to your use of motorcycles.

The requirements are there to protect you and other road users. Make sure you are aware of all the restrictions that apply before you ride your motorcycle on the road.

12.25
*Mark **one** answer*

A full category A1 licence will allow you to ride a motorcycle up to

⊙ 125 cc

⊙ 250 cc

⊙ 350 cc

⊙ 425 cc

⊙ **125 cc**

When you pass your test on a motorcycle between 75 cc and 125 cc you will be issued with a full light motorcycle licence of category A1. You will then be allowed to ride any motorcycle up to 125 cc and with a power output of 11 Kw (14.6 bhp).

12.26
*Mark **one** answer*

Which one of these details would you expect to see on an MOT?

- Your name, address and telephone number
- The vehicle registration and chassis number
- The previous owners' details
- The next due date for servicing

⊙ **The vehicle registration and chassis number**

The MOT test applies to all scooters, mopeds and motorcycles over three years old. Once your vehicle is three years old or older, you must take it to an appointed vehicle testing station to have this test carried out annually. You will need to produce this document when you renew your road tax.

12.27 NI EXEMPT
*Mark **one** answer*

You want a licence to ride a large motorcycle via Direct Access. You will

- not require L-plates if you have passed a car test
- require L-plates only when learning on your own machine
- require L-plates while learning with a qualified instructor
- not require L-plates if you have passed a moped test

⊙ **require L-plates while learning with a qualified instructor**

While training through the Direct Access scheme you must be accompanied by an instructor on another motorcycle and be in radio contact. You must display L-plates on your motorcycle and follow all normal learner restrictions.

12.28
*Mark **one** answer*

A theory test pass certificate will not be valid after

- six months
- one year
- eighteen months
- two years

⊙ **two years**

A theory test pass certificate is valid for two years. If after two years you have not passed your practical test you will have to take your theory test again.

12.29   NI EXEMPT   *Mark **three** answers*

A motorcyclist may only carry a pillion passenger when

- the rider has successfully completed CBT (Compulsory Basic Training)
- the rider holds a full licence for the category of motorcycle
- the motorcycle is fitted with rear footrests
- the rider has a full car licence and is over 21
- there is a proper passenger seat fitted
- there is no sidecar fitted to the machine

- **the rider holds a full licence for the category of motorcycle**
- **the motorcycle is fitted with rear footrests**
- **there is a proper passenger seat fitted**

Before carrying a passenger on a motorcycle the rider must hold a full licence for the category being ridden and make sure that

- passenger footrests are fitted
- a proper passenger seat is fitted.

12.30   NI EXEMPT   *Mark **one** answer*

You have a CBT (Compulsory Basic Training) certificate. How long is it valid?

- one year
- two years
- three years
- four years

- **two years**

All new learner motorcycle and moped riders must complete a Compulsory Basic Training (CBT) course before riding on the road. This can only be given by an Approved Training Body (ATB). If you don't pass your practical test within two years you will need to retake and pass CBT to continue riding.

12.31   *Mark **one** answer*

An MOT certificate is normally valid for

- three years after the date it was issued
- 10,000 miles
- one year after the date it was issued
- 30,000 miles

- **one year after the date it was issued**

Make a note of the date that your MOT certificate expires. Some garages remind you that your vehicle is due an MOT but not all do.

12.32

*Mark **one** answer*

A cover note is a document issued before you receive your

- ⊙ driving licence
- ⊙ insurance certificate
- ⊙ registration document
- ⊙ MOT certificate

⊙ **insurance certificate**

Sometimes an insurance company will issue a temporary insurance certificate called a cover note. It gives you the same insurance cover as your certificate, but lasts for a limited period, usually one month.

12.33

*Mark **two** answers*

You have just passed your practical test. You do not hold a full licence in another category. Within two years you get six penalty points on your licence. What will you have to do?

- ⊙ Retake only your theory test
- ⊙ Retake your theory and practical tests
- ⊙ Retake only your practical test
- ⊙ Reapply for your full licence immediately
- ⊙ Reapply for your provisional licence

⊙ **Retake your theory and practical tests**

⊙ **Reapply for your provisional licence**

If you accumulate six or more penalty points within two years of gaining your first full licence it will be revoked. The six or more points include any gained due to offences you committed before passing your test.

If this happens you may only drive as a learner until you pass both the theory and practical tests again.

12.34

*Mark **one** answer*

A police officer asks to see your documents. You do not have them with you. You may produce them at a police station within

- ⊙ 5 days
- ⊙ 7 days
- ⊙ 14 days
- ⊙ 21 days

⊙ **7 days**

You don't have to carry the documents for your vehicle around with you. If a police officer asks to see them and you don't have them with you, you may produce them at a police station within seven days.

12.35   Mark *one* answer

How long will a Statutory Off Road Notification (SORN) last for?

- ⊙ 12 months
- ⊙ 24 months
- ⊙ 3 years
- ⊙ 10 years

⊙ **12 months**

A SORN declaration allows you to keep a vehicle off road and untaxed for 12 months. If you want to keep your vehicle off road beyond that you must send a further SORN form to DVLA or DVLNI.

12.36   NI EXEMPT   Mark *one* answer

What is a Statutory Off Road Notification (SORN) declaration?

- ⊙ A notification to tell VOSA that a vehicle does not have a current MOT
- ⊙ Information kept by the police about the owner of the vehicle
- ⊙ A notification to tell DVLA that a vehicle is not being used on the road
- ⊙ Information held by insurance companies to check the vehicle is insured

⊙ **A notification to tell DVLA that a vehicle is not being used on the road**

If you want to keep a vehicle off the public road you must declare SORN. It is an offence not to do so. You then won't have to pay road tax. If you don't renew the SORN declaration or re-license the vehicle, you will incur a penalty.

12.37   NI EXEMPT   Mark *one* answer

A Statutory Off Road Notification (SORN) declaration is

- ⊙ to tell DVLA that your vehicle is being used on the road but the MOT has expired
- ⊙ to tell DVLA that you no longer own the vehicle
- ⊙ to tell DVLA that your vehicle is not being used on the road
- ⊙ to tell DVLA that you are buying a personal number plate

⊙ **to tell DVLA that your vehicle is not being used on the road**

This will enable you to keep a vehicle off the public road for 12 months without having to pay road tax. You must send a further SORN declaration after 12 months.

12.38

A Statutory Off Road Notification (SORN) is valid

- ⊙ for as long as the vehicle has an MOT
- ⊙ for 12 months only
- ⊙ only if the vehicle is more than 3 years old
- ⊙ provided the vehicle is insured

⊙ **for 12 months only**

If you want to keep a vehicle off the public road you must declare SORN. It is an offence not to do so. You then won't have to pay road tax for that vehicle. You will incur a penalty after 12 months if you don't renew the SORN declaration, or re-license the vehicle. If you sell the vehicle the SORN declaration ends and the new owner should declare SORN or re-license the vehicle.

12.39

A Statutory Off Road Notification (SORN) will last

- ⊙ for the life of the vehicle
- ⊙ for as long as you own the vehicle
- ⊙ for 12 months only
- ⊙ until the vehicle warranty expires

⊙ **for 12 months only**

If you are keeping a vehicle, or vehicles, off road and don't want to pay road tax you must declare SORN. You must still do this even if the vehicle is incapable of being used, for example it may be under restoration or being stored. After 12 months you must send another SORN declaration or re-license your vehicle. You will be fined if you don't do this. The SORN will end if you sell the vehicle and the new owner will be responsible immediately.

12.40   NI EXEMPT

What is the maximum specified fine for driving without insurance?

- ⊙ £50
- ⊙ £500
- ⊙ £1000
- ⊙ £5000

⊙ **£5000**

It is a serious offence to drive without insurance. As well as a heavy fine you may be disqualified or incur penalty points.

12.41
*Mark **one** answer*

When should you update your Vehicle Registration Certificate (V5C)?

⊙ When you pass your driving test
⊙ When you move house
⊙ When your vehicle needs an MOT
⊙ When you have an accident

⊙ **When you move house**

As the registered keeper of a vehicle it is up to you to inform DVLA of any changes in your vehicle or personal details, for example, change of name or address. You do this by completing the relevant section of your Registration Certificate and sending it to DVLA.

12.42
*Mark **one** answer*

Who is legally responsible for ensuring that a Vehicle Registration Certificate (V5C) is updated?

⊙ The registered vehicle keeper
⊙ The vehicle manufacturer
⊙ Your insurance company
⊙ The licensing authority

⊙ **The registered vehicle keeper**

It is your legal responsibility to keep the details of your Vehicle Registration Certificate (V5C) up to date. You should tell the licensing authority of any changes. These include your name, address, or vehicle details. If you don't do this you may have problems when you sell your vehicle.

section thirteen
ACCIDENTS

This section covers:

- first aid
- warning devices
- reporting procedures
- safety regulations

13.1
*Mark **one** answer*

Your motorcycle has broken down on a motorway. How will you know the direction of the nearest emergency telephone?

⊙ By walking with the flow of traffic

⊙ By following an arrow on a marker post

⊙ By walking against the flow of traffic

⊙ By remembering where the last phone was

⊙ **By following an arrow on a marker post**

If you break down on a motorway you should

• pull onto the hard shoulder and stop as far over to the left as you can

• switch on hazard lights (if they are fitted)

• make your way to the nearest emergency telephone.

Marker posts spaced every 100 metres will direct you to the nearest telephone.

13.2
*Mark **one** answer*

You are travelling on a motorway. A bag falls from your motorcycle. There are valuables in the bag. What should you do?

⊙ Go back carefully and collect the bag as quickly as possible

⊙ Stop wherever you are and pick up the bag, but only when there is a safe gap

⊙ Stop on the hard shoulder and use the emergency telephone to inform the police

⊙ Stop on the hard shoulder and then retrieve the bag yourself

⊙ **Stop on the hard shoulder and use the emergency telephone to inform the police**

You must never walk on a motorway, however important you think retrieving your property may be. Your bag might be creating a hazard but not as great a hazard as you would be.

13.3
*Mark **one** answer*

You should use the engine cut-out switch to

⊙ stop the engine in an emergency

⊙ stop the engine on short journeys

⊙ save wear on the ignition switch

⊙ start the engine if you lose the key

⊙ **stop the engine in an emergency**

Most motorcycles are fitted with an engine cut-out switch. This is designed to stop the engine in an emergency and so reduce the risk of fire.

*Mark **one** answer*

You are riding on a motorway. The car in front switches on its hazard warning lights whilst moving. This means

⊙ they are going to take the next exit

⊙ there is a danger ahead

⊙ there is a police car in the left lane

⊙ they are trying to change lanes

⊙ **there is a danger ahead**

When riding on a motorway, or a dual carriageway subject to a national speed limit, vehicles may switch on their hazard warning lights to warn following traffic of an obstruction ahead.

*Mark **one** answer*

You are on the motorway. Luggage falls from your motorcycle. What should you do?

⊙ Stop at the next emergency telephone and contact the police

⊙ Stop on the motorway and put on hazard lights whilst you pick it up

⊙ Walk back up the motorway to pick it up

⊙ Pull up on the hard shoulder and wave traffic down

⊙ **Stop at the next emergency telephone and contact the police**

If any of your luggage falls onto the motorway carriageway, pull over onto the hard shoulder near an emergency telephone and phone for assistance. Don't

• stop on the carriageway

• attempt to retrieve anything.

*Mark **three** answers*

You have broken down on a motorway. When you use the emergency telephone you will be asked

⊙ for the number on the telephone that you are using

⊙ for your driving licence details

⊙ for the name of your vehicle insurance company

⊙ for details of yourself and your motorcycle

⊙ whether you belong to a motoring organisation

⊙ **for the number on the telephone that you are using**

⊙ **for details of yourself and your motorcycle**

⊙ **whether you belong to a motoring organisation**

Have these details ready before you phone and be sure to give the correct information. Face the traffic when you speak on the telephone.

13.7   *Mark **four** answers*

You are involved in an accident with another vehicle. Someone is injured. Your motorcycle is damaged. Which FOUR of the following should you find out?

⊙ Whether the driver owns the other vehicle involved

⊙ The other driver's name, address and telephone number

⊙ The make and registration number of the other vehicle

⊙ The occupation of the other driver

⊙ The details of the other driver's vehicle insurance

⊙ Whether the other driver is licensed to drive

⊙ **Whether the driver owns the other vehicle involved**

⊙ **The other driver's name, address and telephone number**

⊙ **The make and registration number of the other vehicle**

⊙ **The details of the other driver's vehicle insurance**

If you are involved in an accident where someone is injured, your first priority is to warn other traffic and call the emergency services.

When exchanging details, make sure you have all the information you need before you leave the scene. Don't ride your motorcycle if it is unroadworthy.

13.8   *Mark **one** answer*

You are on a motorway. When can you use hazard warning lights?

⊙ When a vehicle is following too closely

⊙ When you slow down quickly because of danger ahead

⊙ When you are being towed by another vehicle

⊙ When riding on the hard shoulder

⊙ **When you slow down quickly because of danger ahead**

Hazard lights will warn the traffic behind you that there is a potential hazard ahead. Don't forget to turn them off again when your signal has been seen.

Your motorcycle breaks down in a tunnel. What should you do?

⊙ Stay with your motorcycle and wait for the Police

⊙ Stand in the lane behind your motorcycle to warn others

⊙ Stand in front of your motorcycle to warn oncoming drivers

⊙ Switch on hazard lights then go and call for help immediately

⊙ **Switch on hazard lights then go and call for help immediately**

Any broken down vehicle in a tunnel can cause serious congestion and danger to other traffic and drivers. If you break down you should get help without delay. Switch on your hazard warning lights and then go to an emergency telephone point to call for help.

You are riding through a tunnel. Your motorcycle breaks down. What should you do?

⊙ Switch on hazard warning lights

⊙ Remain on your motorcycle

⊙ Wait for the police to find you

⊙ Rely on CCTV cameras seeing you

⊙ **Switch on hazard warning lights**

If your motorcycle breaks down in a tunnel it could present a danger to other traffic. First switch on your hazard warning lights and then call for help from an emergency telephone point.

Don't rely on being found by the police or being seen by a CCTV camera.

You are involved in an accident. How can you reduce the risk of fire to your motorcycle?

⊙ Keep the engine running

⊙ Open the choke

⊙ Turn the fuel tap to reserve

⊙ Use the engine cut-out switch

⊙ **Use the engine cut-out switch**

The engine cut-out switch is used to stop the engine in an emergency. In the event of an accident this will help to reduce any fire hazard.

13.12
*Mark **one** answer*

At the scene of an accident you should

- not put yourself at risk
- go to those casualties who are screaming
- pull everybody out of their vehicles
- leave vehicle engines switched on

⊙ **not put yourself at risk**

It's important that people at the scene of an accident do not create a further risk to themselves or other road users. If the accident has occurred on a motorway or major road, traffic will be approaching at speed. Do not put yourself at risk when trying to help casualties or warning other road users.

13.13
*Mark **four** answers*

You are the first to arrive at the scene of an accident. Which FOUR of these should you do?

- Leave as soon as another motorist arrives
- Switch off the vehicle engine(s)
- Move uninjured people away from the vehicle(s)
- Call the emergency services
- Warn other traffic

⊙ **Switch off the vehicle engine(s)**

⊙ **Move uninjured people away from the vehicle(s)**

⊙ **Call the emergency services**

⊙ **Warn other traffic**

At an accident scene you can help in practical ways, even if you don't know how to do first aid. Make sure you do not put yourself or anyone else in danger.

The safest way to warn other traffic is by switching on your hazard warning lights.

13.14
*Mark **one** answer*

You arrive at the scene of a motorcycle accident. The rider is injured. When should the helmet be removed?

- Only when it is essential
- Always straight away
- Only when the motorcyclist asks
- Always, unless they are in shock

⊙ **Only when it is essential**

If a motorcyclist has been injured in an accident, it's important not to remove their helmet unless it is necessary to do so to keep them alive.

You are the first person to arrive at an accident where people are badly injured. Which THREE should you do?

- Switch on your own hazard warning lights
- Make sure that someone telephones for an ambulance
- Try and get people who are injured to drink something
- Move the people who are injured clear of their vehicles
- Get people who are not injured clear of the scene

⊙ **Switch on your own hazard warning lights**

⊙ **Make sure that someone telephones for an ambulance**

⊙ **Get people who are not injured clear of the scene**

If you're the first person to arrive at the scene of an accident, the risk of further collision and fire are the first concerns.

Switching off vehicle engines will reduce the risk of fire. Your hazard warning lights will let approaching traffic know that there's a need for caution.

Make sure that the emergency services are contacted, as you can't assume this has already been done.

You arrive at a serious motorcycle accident. The motorcyclist is unconscious and bleeding. Your main priorities should be to

- try to stop the bleeding
- make a list of witnesses
- check the casualty's breathing
- take the numbers of the vehicles involved
- sweep up any loose debris
- check the casualty's airways

⊙ **try to stop the bleeding**

⊙ **check the casualty's breathing**

⊙ **check the casualty's airways**

At a road accident, first deal with the danger of further collisions and fire.

Injuries should be dealt with in the following order

- Airway
- Breathing
- Circulation and bleeding.

13.17 — *Mark **one** answer*

You arrive at an accident. A motorcyclist is unconscious. Your FIRST priority is the casualty's

- breathing
- bleeding
- broken bones
- bruising

⊙ **breathing**

At the scene of an accident you must make sure there is no danger from further collisions or fire before attempting to give first aid to any casualties.

The first priority when dealing with an unconscious person is to make sure they can breathe. This may involve clearing their airway if they're having difficulty or you can see that there is some obstruction.

13.18 — *Mark **three** answers*

At an accident a casualty is unconscious. Which THREE of the following should you check urgently?

- Circulation
- Airway
- Shock
- Breathing
- Broken bones

⊙ **Circulation**

⊙ **Airway**

⊙ **Breathing**

An unconscious casualty may have difficulty breathing. Check that their airway is clear by tilting the head back gently and unblock it if necessary. Then make sure they are breathing.

If there is bleeding, stem the flow by placing clean material over any wounds but without pressing on any objects in the wound.

13.19 — *Mark **three** answers*

At an accident someone is unconscious. Your main priorities should be to

- sweep up the broken glass
- take the names of witnesses
- count the number of vehicles involved
- check the airway is clear
- make sure they are breathing
- stop any heavy bleeding

⊙ **check the airway is clear**

⊙ **make sure they are breathing**

⊙ **stop any heavy bleeding**

Remember this procedure by saying ABC which stands for Airway, Breathing, Circulation.

13.20
*Mark **three** answers*

You arrive at the scene of an accident. It has just happened and someone is unconscious. Which of the following should be given urgent priority to help them?

- ⊙ Clear the airway and keep it open
- ⊙ Try to get them to drink water
- ⊙ Check that they are breathing
- ⊙ Look for any witnesses
- ⊙ Stop any heavy bleeding
- ⊙ Take the numbers of vehicles involved

- ⊙ **Clear the airway and keep it open**
- ⊙ **Check that they are breathing**
- ⊙ **Stop any heavy bleeding**

Once emergency first aid has been administered, stay with the casualty; make sure someone rings for an ambulance.

13.21
*Mark **three** answers*

You have stopped at the scene of an accident to give help. Which THREE things should you do?

- ⊙ Keep injured people warm and comfortable
- ⊙ Keep injured people calm by talking to them reassuringly
- ⊙ Keep injured people on the move by walking them around
- ⊙ Give injured people a warm drink
- ⊙ Make sure that injured people are not left alone

- ⊙ **Keep injured people warm and comfortable**
- ⊙ **Keep injured people calm by talking to them reassuringly**
- ⊙ **Make sure that injured people are not left alone**

If you stop at the scene of an accident to give help and there are casualties, don't move injured people unless there is a risk of further danger. Make sure no one gives casualties anything to eat or drink.

13.22 — Mark **three** answers

You arrive at the scene of an accident. It has just happened and someone is injured. Which THREE of the following should be given urgent priority?

- ⊙ Stop any severe bleeding
- ⊙ Get them a warm drink
- ⊙ Check that their breathing is OK
- ⊙ Take numbers of vehicles involved
- ⊙ Look for witnesses
- ⊙ Clear their airway and keep it open

⊙ **Stop any severe bleeding**

⊙ **Check that their breathing is OK**

⊙ **Clear their airway and keep it open**

Your first priority is to make sure the casualty's airway is clear and they are breathing. Then stem any bleeding using clean material.

Make sure someone calls the emergency services: they are the experts.

If you feel you are not capable of carrying out first aid, you could consider getting some training. It might save a life.

13.23 — Mark **one** answer

Which of the following should you NOT do at the scene of an accident?

- ⊙ Warn other traffic by switching on your hazard warning lights
- ⊙ Call the emergency services immediately
- ⊙ Offer someone a cigarette to calm them down
- ⊙ Ask drivers to switch off their engines

⊙ **Offer someone a cigarette to calm them down**

Keeping casualties or witnesses calm is important, but never offer a cigarette because of the risk of fire.

Don't offer an injured person anything to eat or drink. They may have internal injuries or need surgery.

13.24 — Mark **two** answers

There has been an accident. The driver is suffering from shock. You should

- ⊙ give them a drink
- ⊙ reassure them
- ⊙ not leave them alone
- ⊙ offer them a cigarette
- ⊙ ask who caused the accident

⊙ **reassure them**

⊙ **not leave them alone**

Be aware that they could have an injury that is not immediately obvious. Stay with casualties and talk to them to reassure them.

13.25 *Mark one answer*

You have to treat someone for shock at the scene of an accident. You should

⊙ reassure them constantly

⊙ walk them around to calm them down

⊙ give them something cold to drink

⊙ cool them down as soon as possible

⊙ **reassure them constantly**

Stay with the casualty and talk to them quietly and firmly to calm and reassure them.

Avoid moving them unnecessarily in case they are injured. Keep them warm, but don't give them anything to eat or drink.

13.26 *Mark one answer*

You arrive at the scene of a motorcycle accident. No other vehicle is involved. The rider is unconscious, lying in the middle of the road. The first thing you should do is

⊙ move the rider out of the road

⊙ warn other traffic

⊙ clear the road of debris

⊙ give the rider reassurance

⊙ **warn other traffic**

The motorcyclist is in an extremely vulnerable position, exposed to further danger from traffic. Approaching vehicles need advance warning in order to slow right down and safely take avoiding action.

Don't put yourself or anyone else at risk. Use the hazard warning lights on your vehicle to alert other road users to the danger.

13.27 *Mark one answer*

At an accident a small child is not breathing. When giving mouth to mouth you should breathe

⊙ sharply

⊙ gently

⊙ heavily

⊙ rapidly

⊙ **gently**

If a young child has stopped breathing, first check that the airway is clear, then begin mouth to mouth resuscitation. Breathe very gently and continue the resuscitation procedure until they can breathe without help.

13.28
*Mark **one** answer*

When you are giving mouth to mouth you should only stop when

- ⊙ you think the casualty is dead
- ⊙ the casualty can breathe without help
- ⊙ the casualty has turned blue
- ⊙ you think the ambulance is coming

⊙ **the casualty can breathe without help**

Don't give up. Look for signs of recovery and check the casualty's pulse. Continue resuscitation until the casualty is breathing unaided. Avoid moving them unless it's necessary for their safety.

13.29
*Mark **one** answer*

You arrive at the scene of an accident. There has been an engine fire and someone's hands and arms have been burnt. You should NOT

- ⊙ douse the burn thoroughly with cool liquid
- ⊙ lay the casualty down
- ⊙ remove anything sticking to the burn
- ⊙ reassure them constantly

⊙ **remove anything sticking to the burn**

This could cause further damage and infection to the wound. Your first priorities are to cool the burn and check the patient for shock.

13.30
*Mark **one** answer*

You arrive at an accident where someone is suffering from severe burns. You should

- ⊙ apply lotions to the injury
- ⊙ burst any blisters
- ⊙ remove anything stuck to the burns
- ⊙ douse the burns with cool liquid

⊙ **douse the burns with cool liquid**

Try to find fluid that is clean, cold and non-toxic. Its coolness will help take the heat out of the burn and relieve the pain. Keep the wound doused for at least ten minutes. If blisters appear don't attempt to burst them as this could lead to infection.

13.31

You arrive at the scene of an accident. A pedestrian has a severe bleeding wound on their leg, although it is not broken. What should you do?

- Dab the wound to stop bleeding
- Keep both legs flat on the ground
- Apply firm pressure to the wound
- Raise the leg to lessen bleeding
- Fetch them a warm drink

⊙ **Apply firm pressure to the wound**

⊙ **Raise the leg to lessen bleeding**

As soon as you can, apply a pad of clean material to the wound with a bandage or a clean length of cloth. Raising the leg will lessen the flow of blood.

Avoid tying anything tightly round the leg, as any restriction to blood circulation for more than a short period of time can result in long-term injury.

13.32

You arrive at the scene of an accident. A passenger is bleeding badly from an arm wound. What should you do?

- Apply pressure over the wound and keep the arm down
- Dab the wound
- Get them a drink
- Apply pressure over the wound and raise the arm

⊙ **Apply pressure over the wound and raise the arm**

If possible, lay the casualty down. Apply firm pressure to the wound using clean material, without pressing on anything which might be caught in it. Raising the arm above the level of the heart will also help to stem the flow of blood.

13.33

You arrive at the scene of an accident. A pedestrian is bleeding heavily from a leg wound but the leg is not broken. What should you do?

- Dab the wound to stop the bleeding
- Keep both legs flat on the ground
- Apply firm pressure to the wound
- Fetch them a warm drink

⊙ **Apply firm pressure to the wound**

Use clean material to apply pressure to the wound ensuring there is nothing caught in it. Lifting and supporting the casualty's leg, so that the wound is higher than their heart, should also help reduce the flow of blood.

13.34
*Mark **one** answer*

At an accident a casualty is unconscious but still breathing. You should only move them if

- ⊙ an ambulance is on its way
- ⊙ bystanders advise you to
- ⊙ there is further danger
- ⊙ bystanders will help you to

⊙ **there is further danger**

At an accident only move a casualty if they are in danger where they are. Moving a casualty unnecessarily could cause further injury.

13.35
*Mark **one** answer*

At an accident you suspect a casualty has back injuries. The area is safe. You should

- ⊙ offer them a drink
- ⊙ not move them
- ⊙ raise their legs
- ⊙ offer them a cigarette

⊙ **not move them**

Talk to the casualty and keep them calm. Do not attempt to move them as this could cause further injury. Call an ambulance at the first opportunity.

13.36
*Mark **one** answer*

At an accident it is important to look after the casualty. When the area is safe, you should

- ⊙ get them out of the vehicle
- ⊙ give them a drink
- ⊙ give them something to eat
- ⊙ keep them in the vehicle

⊙ **keep them in the vehicle**

Don't move casualties who are trapped in vehicles unless they are in danger.

A tanker is involved in an accident. Which sign would show that the tanker is carrying dangerous goods?

There will be an orange label on the side and rear of the lorry. Look at this carefully and report what it says when you phone the emergency services. Full details of hazard warning plates are given in *The Highway Code*.

The police may ask you to produce which three of these documents following an accident?

- Vehicle registration document
- Driving licence
- Theory test certificate
- Insurance certificate
- MOT test certificate
- Road tax disc

- **Driving licence**
- **Insurance certificate**
- **MOT test certificate**

You must stop if you have been involved in a collision which results in any injury or damage.

You see a car on the hard shoulder of a motorway with a HELP pennant displayed. This means the driver is most likely to be

- a disabled person
- first aid trained
- a foreign visitor
- a rescue patrol person

- **a disabled person**

If a disabled driver's vehicle breaks down and they are unable to walk to an emergency phone, they are advised to stay in their car and switch on the hazard warning lights. They may also display a 'Help' pennant in their vehicle.

13.40
*Mark **two** answers*

For which TWO should you use hazard warning lights?

- When you slow down quickly on a motorway because of a hazard ahead
- When you have broken down
- When you wish to stop on double yellow lines
- When you need to park on the pavement

- ⊙ **When you slow down quickly on a motorway because of a hazard ahead**
- ⊙ **When you have broken down**

Hazard warning lights are fitted to all modern cars and some motorcycles. They should only be used to warn other road users of a hazard ahead.

13.41
*Mark **one** answer*

When are you allowed to use hazard warning lights?

- When stopped and temporarily obstructing traffic
- When travelling during darkness without headlights
- When parked for shopping on double yellow lines
- When travelling slowly because you are lost

- ⊙ **When stopped and temporarily obstructing traffic**

You must not use hazard warning lights when moving, except when slowing suddenly on a motorway or unrestricted dual carriageway to warn the traffic behind.

Never use hazard warning lights to excuse dangerous or illegal parking.

13.42
*Mark **one** answer*

You are on a motorway. A large box falls onto the road from a lorry. The lorry does not stop. You should

- go to the next emergency telephone and inform the police
- catch up with the lorry and try to get the driver's attention
- stop close to the box until the police arrive
- pull over to the hard shoulder, then remove the box

- ⊙ **go to the next emergency telephone and inform the police**

Lorry drivers are sometimes unaware of objects falling from their vehicles. If you see something fall off a lorry onto the motorway, watch to see if the driver pulls over. If they don't stop, do not attempt to retrieve it yourself. You should

- pull over onto the hard shoulder near an emergency telephone
- report the hazard to the police.

13.43

Mark **one** answer

After an accident, someone is unconscious in their vehicle. When should you call the emergency services?

- ⊙ Only as a last resort
- ⊙ As soon as possible
- ⊙ After you have woken them up
- ⊙ After checking for broken bones

⊙ **As soon as possible**

It is important to make sure that emergency services arrive on the scene as soon as possible. When a person is unconscious, they could have serious injuries that are not immediately obvious.

13.44

Mark **one** answer

An accident casualty has an injured arm. They can move it freely, but it is bleeding. Why should you get them to keep it in a raised position?

- ⊙ Because it will ease the pain
- ⊙ It will help them to be seen more easily
- ⊙ To stop them touching other people
- ⊙ It will help to reduce the bleeding

⊙ **It will help to reduce the bleeding**

If a casualty is bleeding heavily, raise the limb to a higher position. This will help to reduce the blood flow. Before raising the limb you should make sure that it is not broken.

13.45

Mark **one** answer

You are going through a congested tunnel and have to stop. What should you do?

- ⊙ Pull up very close to the vehicle in front to save space
- ⊙ Ignore any message signs as they are never up to date
- ⊙ Keep a safe distance from the vehicle in front
- ⊙ Make a U-turn and find another route

⊙ **Keep a safe distance from the vehicle in front**

It's important to keep a safe distance from the vehicle in front at all times. This still applies in congested tunnels even if you are moving very slowly or have stopped. If the vehicle in front breaks down you may need room to manoeuvre past it.

13.46
*Mark **one** answer*

You are going through a tunnel. What should you look out for that warns of accidents or congestion?

- ⊙ Hazard warning lines
- ⊙ Other drivers flashing their lights
- ⊙ Variable message signs
- ⊙ Areas marked with hatch markings

⊙ **Variable message signs**

Follow the instructions given by the signs or by tunnel officials.

In congested tunnels a minor accident can soon turn into a major incident with serious or even fatal results.

13.47
*Mark **one** answer*

You are going through a tunnel. What systems are provided to warn of any accidents or congestion?

- ⊙ Double white centre lines
- ⊙ Variable message signs
- ⊙ Chevron 'distance markers'
- ⊙ Rumble strips

⊙ **Variable message signs**

Take notice of any instructions given on variable message signs or by tunnel officials. They will warn you of any accidents or congestion ahead and advise on what action to take.

13.48
*Mark **one** answer*

An accident has just happened. An injured person is lying in a busy road. What is the FIRST thing you should do to help?

- ⊙ Treat the person for shock
- ⊙ Warn other traffic
- ⊙ Place them in the recovery position
- ⊙ Make sure the injured person is kept warm

⊙ **Warn other traffic**

You could do this by

- • displaying an advance warning sign, if you have one (but not on a motorway)
- • switching on hazard warning lights
- • any other means that does not put you or anyone else at risk.

311

*Mark **two** answers*

At an accident a casualty has stopped breathing. You should

⊙ remove anything that is blocking the mouth

⊙ keep the head tilted forwards as far as possible

⊙ raise the legs to help with circulation

⊙ try to give the casualty something to drink

⊙ tilt the head back gently to clear the airway

⊙ **remove anything that is blocking the mouth**

⊙ **tilt the head back gently to clear the airway**

Unblocking the airway and gently tilting the head back will help the casualty to breathe. They will then be in the correct position if mouth-to-mouth resuscitation is required.

13.50 *Mark **four** answers*

You are at the scene of an accident. Someone is suffering from shock. You should

⊙ reassure them constantly

⊙ offer them a cigarette

⊙ keep them warm

⊙ avoid moving them if possible

⊙ avoid leaving them alone

⊙ give them a warm drink

⊙ **reassure them constantly**

⊙ **keep them warm**

⊙ **avoid moving them if possible**

⊙ **avoid leaving them alone**

The effects of trauma may not be immediately obvious. Prompt treatment can help to minimise the effects of shock.

• Lay the casualty down
• Loosen tight clothing
• Call an ambulance
• Check their breathing and pulse.

13.51 — Mark *three* answers

To start mouth to mouth on a casualty you should

- ⊙ tilt their head forward
- ⊙ clear the airway
- ⊙ turn them on their side
- ⊙ tilt their head back gently
- ⊙ pinch the nostrils together
- ⊙ put their arms across their chest

- ⊙ **clear the airway**
- ⊙ **tilt their head back gently**
- ⊙ **pinch the nostrils together**

It's important to ensure that the airways are clear before you start mouth to mouth resuscitation. Gently tilt their head back and use your finger to check for and remove any obvious obstruction in the mouth.

13.52 — Mark *one* answer

On the motorway, the hard shoulder should be used

- ⊙ to answer a mobile phone
- ⊙ when an emergency arises
- ⊙ for a short rest when tired
- ⊙ to check a road atlas

- ⊙ **when an emergency arises**

Pull onto the hard shoulder and use the emergency telephone to report your problem. The telephone connects you to police control and lets them know your exact location. They will inform the appropriate emergency services for you.

Never cross the carriageway to use the telephone on the other side.

13.53 — Mark *one* answer

There has been an accident. A motorcyclist is lying injured and unconscious. Unless it's essential, why should you usually not attempt to remove their helmet?

- ⊙ Because they may not want you to
- ⊙ This could result in more serious injury
- ⊙ They will get too cold if you do this
- ⊙ Because you could scratch the helmet

- ⊙ **This could result in more serious injury**

When someone is injured, any movement which is not absolutely necessary should be avoided since it could make injuries worse. Unless it is essential, it's generally safer to leave a motorcyclist's helmet in place.

section fourteen
MOTORCYCLE LOADING

This section covers:

- stability
- towing regulations

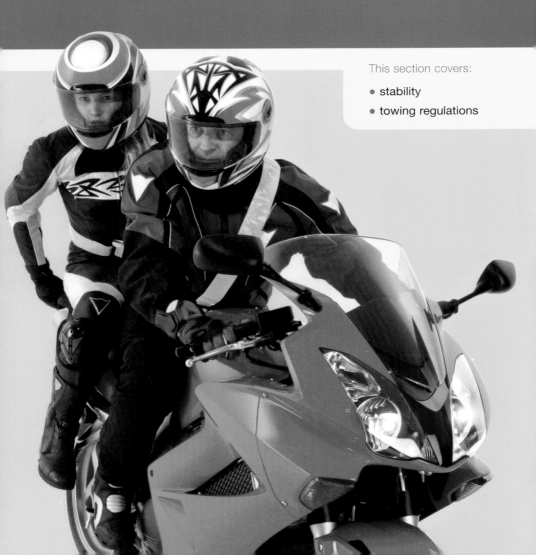

14.1 — Mark **one** answer

If a trailer swerves or snakes when you are towing it you should

- ⊙ ease off the throttle and reduce your speed
- ⊙ let go of the handlebars and let it correct itself
- ⊙ brake hard and hold the brake on
- ⊙ increase your speed as quickly as possible

⊙ **ease off the throttle and reduce your speed**

Don't be tempted to use harsh braking to stop swerving or snaking as this won't help the situation. You should reduce your speed by easing off the throttle.

14.2 — Mark **two** answers

When riding with a sidecar attached for the first time you should

- ⊙ keep your speed down
- ⊙ be able to stop more quickly
- ⊙ accelerate quickly round bends
- ⊙ approach corners more carefully

⊙ **keep your speed down**

⊙ **approach corners more carefully**

A motorcycle with a sidecar will feel very different to ride than a solo motorcycle. Keep your speed down until you get used to the outfit, especially when negotiating bends and junctions.

14.3 — Mark **one** answer

When may a learner motorcyclist carry a pillion passenger?

- ⊙ If the passenger holds a full licence
- ⊙ Not at any time
- ⊙ If the rider is undergoing training
- ⊙ If the passenger is over 21

⊙ **Not at any time**

You are not allowed to carry passenger until you hold a licence. This allows you ' riding solo before carr

14.

Any loa
rack MU.

⊙ secure
⊙ carried c
⊙ visible wh
⊙ covered wi

14.4

*Mark **three** answers*

When carrying extra weight on a motorcycle, you may need to make adjustments to the

- ⊙ headlight
- ⊙ gears
- ⊙ suspension
- ⊙ tyres
- ⊙ footrests

- ⊙ **headlight**
- ⊙ **suspension**
- ⊙ **tyres**

Carrying extra weight on your motorcycle, such as luggage or a pillion passenger, may affect the aim of the headlight and you should ensure this is adjusted so that it does not dazzle approaching traffic. Extra weight can also affect the feel and balance of your motorcycle: adjusting the suspension and tyre pressures can help overcome these problems.

14.5   NI EXEMPT   *Mark **one** answer*

To obtain the full category 'A' licence through the accelerated or direct access scheme, your motorcycle must be

- ⊙ solo with maximum power 25 kw (33 bhp)
- ⊙ solo with maximum power of 11 kw (14.6 bhp)
- ⊙ fitted with a sidecar and have minimum power of 35 kw (46.6 bhp)
-   solo with minimum power of 35 kw (46.6 bhp)

- ⊙ **solo with minimum power of 35 kw (46.6 bhp)**

From the age of 21 you may take a category A test via the Direct or Accelerated Access schemes. The motorcycle you use for your practical test under the Direct or Accelerated Access scheme is one that has an engine with a minimum power output of 35 kw (46.6 bhp).

*Mark **one** answer*

that is carried on a luggage
T be

fastened when riding

ly when strictly necessary

en you are riding

plastic sheeting

- ⊙ **securely fastened when riding**

Don't risk losing any luggage while riding: it could fall into the path of following vehicles and cause danger. It is an offence to travel with an insecure load.

14.7 · Mark **one** answer

Pillion passengers should

- ⊙ have a provisional motorcycle licence
- ⊙ be lighter than the rider
- ⊙ always wear a helmet
- ⊙ signal for the rider

⊙ **always wear a helmet**

Pillion passengers must

- sit astride the machine facing forward on a proper passenger seat
- wear a safety helmet which is correctly fastened.

14.8 · Mark **one** answer

Pillion passengers should

- ⊙ give the rider directions
- ⊙ lean with the rider when going round bends
- ⊙ check the road behind for the rider
- ⊙ give arm signals for the rider

⊙ **lean with the rider when going round bends**

When riding with a pillion passenger, your motorcycle may feel unbalanced and the acceleration and braking distance may also be affected.

Make sure your passenger knows they must lean with you while cornering. If they don't, they could cause the motorcycle to become unstable and difficult to control.

14.9 · Mark **one** answer

When you are going around a corner your pillion passenger should

- ⊙ give arm signals for you
- ⊙ check behind for other vehicles
- ⊙ lean with you on bends
- ⊙ lean to one side to see ahead

⊙ **lean with you on bends**

A pillion passenger should not giv or look round for you.

If your passenger has never ' motorcycle before, make ' that they need to lean v around bends.

Which of these may need to be adjusted when carrying a pillion passenger?

- ⊙ Indicators
- ⊙ Exhaust
- ⊙ Fairing
- ⊙ Headlight

⊙ **Headlight**

Your headlight must be properly adjusted to avoid dazzling other road users. You will probably need to do this when your motorcycle is heavily loaded or you are carrying the extra weight of a pillion passenger.

You are towing a trailer with your motorcycle. You should remember that your

- ⊙ stopping distance may increase
- ⊙ fuel consumption will improve
- ⊙ tyre grip will increase
- ⊙ stability will improve

⊙ **stopping distance may increase**

When you tow a trailer remember that you must obey the relevant speed limits. Ensure that the trailer is hitched correctly and that any load in the trailer is secure. You should also bear in mind that your stopping distance may increase.

Heavy loads in a motorcycle top box may

- ˌprove stability
- ˌˌˌ low-speed wobble
- ˌe a puncture
- ˌe braking

⊙ **cause low-speed wobble**

Carrying heavy loads in your top box could make your motorcycle unstable because the weight is high up and at the very back of the machine.

14.13
*Mark **two** answers*

Overloading your motorcycle can seriously affect the

- ⊙ gearbox
- ⊙ steering
- ⊙ handling
- ⊙ battery life
- ⊙ journey time

- ⊙ **steering**
- ⊙ **handling**

Any load can affect the handling of your motorcycle by changing its centre of gravity.

Avoid carrying heavy loads in a top box and load panniers so that the weight is spread evenly.

14.14
*Mark **one** answer*

Who is responsible for making sure that a motorcycle is not overloaded?

- ⊙ The rider of the motorcycle
- ⊙ The owner of the items being carried
- ⊙ The licensing authority
- ⊙ The owner of the motorcycle

- ⊙ **The rider of the motorcycle**

Your motorcycle must not be overloaded as this will affect the control and handling. If your motorcycle is overloaded and it causes an accident, you'll be responsible.

14.15
*Mark **one** answer*

Before fitting a sidecar to a motorcycle you should

- ⊙ have the wheels balanced
- ⊙ have the engine tuned
- ⊙ pass the extended bike test
- ⊙ check that the motorcycle is suitable

- ⊙ **check that the motorcycle is suitable**

Make sure that the sidecar is fixe_ and properly aligned. If your m_ registered on or after 1 Aug_ sidecar must be fitted on _ of the motorcycle.

14.16
*Mark **one** answer*

To carry a pillion passenger you must

- ⊙ hold a full car licence
- ⊙ hold a full motorcycle licence
- ⊙ be over the age of 21
- ⊙ be over the age of 25

- ⊙ **hold _ lice_**

The _ fo_

pc_

320

14.17
Mark **one** answer

You are using throwover saddlebags. Why is it important to make sure they are evenly loaded?

- ⊙ They will be uncomfortable for you to sit on
- ⊙ They will slow your motorcycle down
- ⊙ They could make your motorcycle unstable
- ⊙ They will be uncomfortable for a pillion passenger to sit on

⊙ **They could make your motorcycle unstable**

Panniers or saddlebags should be loaded so that you carry about the same weight in each bag. Uneven loading could affect your balance, especially when cornering.

14.18
Mark **one** answer

You are carrying a bulky tank bag. What could this affect?

- ⊙ Your ability to steer
- ⊙ Your ability to accelerate
- ⊙ Your view ahead
- ⊙ Your insurance premium

⊙ **Your ability to steer**

If your tank bag is too bulky it could get in the way of your arms or restrict the movement of the handlebars.

14.19
Mark **two** answers

You are towing a small trailer on a busy three-lane motorway. All the lanes are open. You must

- not exceed 60 mph
- not overtake
- have a stabiliser fitted
- use only the left and centre lanes

⊙ **not exceed 60 mph**

⊙ **use only the left and centre lanes**

You should be aware of the motorway regulations for vehicles towing trailers. These state that a vehicle towing a trailer must not

- use the right-hand lane of a three-lane motorway unless directed to do so, for example, at roadworks or due to a lane closure
- exceed 60 mph.

14.20
*Mark **one** answer*

When carrying a heavy load on your luggage rack, you may need to adjust your

- ⊙ carburettor
- ⊙ fuel tap
- ⊙ seating position
- ⊙ tyre pressures

- ⊙ **tyre pressures**

The load will increase the overall weight that your motorcycle is carrying. You may need to adjust your tyre pressures according to the manufacturer's instructions to allow for this. You may also need to adjust your headlight beam alignment.

14.21
*Mark **one** answer*

You are carrying a pillion passenger. When following other traffic, which of the following should you do?

- ⊙ Keep to your normal following distance
- ⊙ Get your passenger to keep checking behind
- ⊙ Keep further back than you normally would
- ⊙ Get your passenger to signal for you

- ⊙ **Keep further back than you normally would**

The extra weight of a passenger may increase your stopping distance. Allow for this when following another vehicle by increasing the separation distance.

14.22
*Mark **one** answer*

You should only carry a child as a pillion passenger when

- ⊙ they are over 14 years old
- ⊙ they are over 16 years old
- ⊙ they can reach the floor from the seat
- ⊙ they can reach the handholds and footrests

- ⊙ **they can reach the handholds and footrests**

Any passenger you carry must be able to reach footrests and handholds properly to remain safe on your machine. Ensure they are wearing protective weatherproof kit and a properly fitting helmet.

14.23

You have fitted a sidecar to your motorcycle. You should make sure that the sidecar

- ⊙ has a registration plate
- ⊙ is correctly aligned
- ⊙ has a waterproof cover
- ⊙ has a solid cover

⊙ **is correctly aligned**

If the sidecar is not correctly aligned to the mounting points it will result in the outfit being difficult to control and even dangerous.

Riding with a sidecar attached requires a different technique to riding a solo motorcycle and you should keep your speed down while learning this skill.

14.24

You are riding a motorcycle and sidecar. The extra weight

- ⊙ will allow you to corner more quickly
- ⊙ will allow you to brake later for hazards
- ⊙ may increase your stopping distance
- ⊙ will improve your fuel consumption

⊙ **may increase your stopping distance**

You will need to adapt your riding technique when riding a motorcycle fitted with a sidecar. The extra weight will affect the handling and may increase your overall stopping distance.

14.25

You are carrying a pillion passenger. To allow for the extra weight which of the following is most likely to need adjustment?

- ⊙ Preload on the front forks
- ⊙ Preload on the rear shock absorber(s)
- ⊙ The balance of the rear wheel
- ⊙ The front and rear wheel alignment

⊙ **Preload on the rear shock absorber(s)**

When carrying a passenger or other extra weight, you may need to make adjustments, particularly to the rear shock absorber(s), tyre pressures and headlight alignment. Check your owner's handbook for details.

14.26   *Mark **one** answer*

A trailer on a motorcycle must be no wider than

- ⊙ 0.5 metres (1 foot 8 inches)
- ⊙ 1 metre (3 feet 3 inches)
- ⊙ 1.5 metres (4 feet 11inches)
- ⊙ 2 metres (6 feet 6 inches)

⊙ **1 metre (3 feet 3 inches)**

When you're towing a trailer you must remember that you may not be able to filter through traffic. Don't forget that the trailer is there, especially when riding round bends and negotiating junctions.

14.27   *Mark **one** answer*

You want to tow a trailer with your motorcycle. Which one applies?

- ⊙ The motorcycle should be attached to a sidecar
- ⊙ The trailer should weigh more than the motorcycle
- ⊙ The trailer should be fitted with brakes
- ⊙ The trailer should NOT be more than 1 metre (3 feet 3 inches) wide

⊙ **The trailer should NOT be more than 1 metre (3 feet 3 inches) wide**

To tow a trailer behind a motorcycle you must have

- a full motorcycle licence
- a motorcycle with an engine larger than 125 cc.

Motorcycle trailers must not exceed 1 metre (3 feet 3 inches) in width.

14.28   *Mark **one** answer*

You have a sidecar fitted to your motorcycle. What effect will it have?

- ⊙ Reduce stability
- ⊙ Make steering lighter
- ⊙ Increase stopping distance
- ⊙ Increase fuel economy

⊙ **Increase stopping distance**

If you want to fit a sidecar to your motorcycle make sure that your motorcycle is suitable to cope with the extra load. Make sure that the sidecar is fixed correctly and properly aligned. A sidecar will alter the handling considerably. Give yourself time to adjust to the different characteristics.

Which THREE must a learner motorcyclist under 21 NOT do?

- ⊙ Ride a motorcycle with an engine capacity greater than 125 cc
- ⊙ Pull a trailer
- ⊙ Carry a pillion passenger
- ⊙ Ride faster than 30 mph
- ⊙ Use the right-hand lane on dual carriageways

- ⊙ **Ride a motorcycle with an engine capacity greater than 125 cc**
- ⊙ **Pull a trailer**
- ⊙ **Carry a pillion passenger**

Learner motorcyclists are not allowed to pull a trailer or carry a pillion passenger. In addition, if you are a learner motorcyclist under 21, you may not ride a motorcycle on the road with an engine capacity of more than 125 cc.

Carrying a heavy load in your top box may

- ⊙ cause high speed-weave
- ⊙ cause a puncture
- ⊙ use less fuel
- ⊙ improve stability

- ⊙ **cause high speed-weave**

Carrying a heavy weight high up and at the very back of the motorcycle can make it unstable, especially when travelling at high speeds.

Your motorcycle is fitted with a top box. It is unwise to carry a heavy load in the top box because it may

- ⊙ reduce stability
- ⊙ improve stability
- ⊙ make turning easier
- ⊙ cause high-speed weave
- ⊙ cause low-speed wobble
- ⊙ increase fuel economy

- ⊙ **reduce stability**
- ⊙ **cause high-speed weave**
- ⊙ **cause low-speed wobble**

Carrying a heavy weight high up and at the very back of the motorcycle can cause problems in maintaining control.

14.32
*Mark **two** answers*

You want to tow a trailer behind your motorcycle. You should

- ⊙ display a 'long vehicle' sign
- ⊙ fit a larger battery
- ⊙ have a full motorcycle licence
- ⊙ ensure that your engine is more than 125 cc
- ⊙ ensure that your motorcycle has shaft drive

⊙ **have a full motorcycle licence**

⊙ **ensure that your engine is more than 125 cc**

When you tow a trailer

- your stopping distance may be increased
- any load on the trailer must be secure
- the trailer must be fitted to the motorcycle correctly
- you must obey the speed limit restrictions that apply to all vehicles with trailers.

Any trailer towed by a motorcycle must be no wider than 1 metre, with a laden weight no greater than 150 kg or two-thirds of the kerbside weight of the motorcycle, whichever is less.

14.33
*Mark **two** answers*

To carry a pillion passenger your motorcycle should be fitted with

- ⊙ rear footrests
- ⊙ an engine of 250 cc or over
- ⊙ a top box
- ⊙ a grab handle
- ⊙ a proper pillion seat

⊙ **rear footrests**

⊙ **a proper pillion seat**

Pillion passengers should be instructed not to

- give hand signals
- lean away from the rider when cornering
- fidget or move around
- put their feet down to try and support the machine as you stop
- wear long, loose items that might get caught in the rear wheel or drive chain.

annex one
LIST OF TEST CENTRES

England

Aldershot
Barnstaple
Barrow
Basildon
Basingstoke
Bath
Berwick-upon-Tweed
Birkenhead
Birmingham
Blackpool
Bolton
Boston
Bournemouth
Bradford
Brighton
Bristol
Bury St Edmunds
Cambridge
Canterbury
Carlisle
Chatham
Chelmsford
Cheltenham
Chester
Chesterfield
Colchester
Coventry
Crawley
Derby
Doncaster
Dudley

Durham
Eastbourne
Exeter
Fareham
Gloucester
Grantham
Grimsby
Guildford
Harlow
Harrogate
Hastings
Hereford
Huddersfield
Hull
Ipswich
Isle of Wight
Isles of Scilly
King's Lynn
Leeds
Leicester
Lincoln
Liverpool
London
– Croydon
– Ilford
– Kingston
– Southgate
– Southwark
– Staines
– Uxbridge
Lowestoft
Luton

Manchester
Mansfield
Middlesbrough
Milton Keynes
Morpeth
Newcastle
Northampton
Norwich
Nottingham
Oldham
Oxford
Penzance
Peterborough
Plymouth
Portsmouth
Preston
Reading
Redditch
Runcorn
Salford
Salisbury
Scarborough
Scunthorpe
Sheffield
Shrewsbury
Sidcup
Slough
Solihull
Southampton
Southend-on-Sea
Southport
St Helens

Stevenage
Stockport
Stoke-on-Trent
Stratford-upon-Avon
Sunderland
Sutton Coldfield
Swindon
Taunton
Torquay
Truro
Watford
Weymouth
Wigan
Wolverhampton
Worcester
Workington
Worthing
Yeovil
York

Scotland
Aberdeen
Ayr
Clydebank
Dumfries
Dundee
Dunfermline
Edinburgh
Elgin
Fort William
Gairloch
Galashiels
Glasgow
Greenock
Helmsdale

Huntly
Inverness
Isle of Arran
Isle of Barra
Isle of Benbecula
Isle of Islay, Bowmore
Isle of Mull, Salen
Isle of Tiree
Kirkwall
Kyle of Lochalsh
Lerwick
Motherwell
Oban
Pitlochry
Portree
Stirling
Stornoway
Stranraer
Tarbert, Argyllshire
Tongue
Ullapool
Wick

Wales
Aberystwyth
Bangor
Builth Wells
Cardiff
Haverfordwest
Merthyr Tydfil
Newport
Rhyl
Swansea

Northern Ireland
Ballymena
Belfast
Londonderry
Newry
Omagh
Portadown

annex two
SERVICE STANDARDS

We judge our performance against the following standards (printed in our Business Plan) which we review each year

- we will improve business customer satisfaction with the overall service by 5%
- 90% of candidates will be satisfied with the overall level of service received
- 90% of customers will be satisfied with the overall level of service received
- 95% of calls to booking offices will make contact with our automated call-handling system without receiving an engaged tone
- after a call has gone through our automated call-handling system, we will answer 90% of all incoming calls to booking offices in no more than 20 seconds
- we will give 95% of candidates an appointment at their preferred centre within two weeks of their preferred date
- we will keep 99.5% of appointments
- we will answer 90% of calls to our enquiry points in no more than 30 seconds
- we will answer 97% of all letters and e-mails within 10 working days
- we will pay 95% of all refunds within 15 days of receiving a valid claim.

Complaints guide - We aim to give our customers the best possible service. Please tell us when

- we've done well
- when you aren't satisfied.

Your comments can help us to improve the service we offer.

If you have any questions about your theory test, please contact us using the numbers below.

For DSA
Tel 0870 01 01 372, fax 0870 01 04 372, minicom 0870 0106 372, Welsh speakers 0870 0100 372

For DVTA (in Northern Ireland)
Tel 0845 600 6700, fax 0870 01 04 372

If you have any complaints about how your theory test was carried out, or any aspect of our customer service, please call the Customer Services section on 0870 600 0067. Alternatively you can write to the Customer Services Manager at the following address:

Customer Services
Driving Theory Test
PO Box 381
Manchester M50 3UW

If you're dissatisfied with the reply you can write to the Managing Director at the same address.

If you're still not satisfied, you can take up your complaint with:

The Chief Executive
Driving Standards Agency
56 Stanley House
Talbot Street
Nottingham NG1 5GU

In Northern Ireland you should write to

The Chief Executive
Driver and Vehicle Testing Agency
Balmoral Road
Belfast BT12 6QL

None of this removes your right to take your complaint to your Member of Parliament, who may decide to raise your case personally with the DSA or DVTA Chief Executive, the Minister or the Parliamentary Commissioner for Administration (the Ombudsman). Please refer to our leaflet *Customer Service - a guide to our service standards*.

DSA is a Trading Fund and we are required to cover our costs from the driving test fee.

We don't have a quota for test passes or fails and if you demonstrate the standard required, you'll pass your test.

Refunding fees and expenses - DSA will normally refund the test fee, or rearrange another test at no further cost to you, if

- we cancel your test
- you cancel and give us at least three clear working days' notice
- you keep the test appointment but the test doesn't take place, or isn't finished, for a reason that isn't your fault.

We'll also repay you the expenses that you had to pay on the day of the test if we cancelled your test at short notice. We'll consider reasonable claims for

- the cost of travelling to and from the test centre
- any standard pay or earnings you lost through taking unpaid holiday leave (usually for half a day), after tax and national insurance contributions.

Please write to the address below and send a receipt showing travel costs and an employer's letter, which shows what earnings you lost. If you think you're entitled to fees and expenses write to:

Customer Services
Driving Theory Test
PO Box 381
Manchester M50 3UW

This reimbursement policy doesn't affect your existing legal rights.

DVTA has a different reimbursement policy.

WIN BIKE GEAR!

The publishers of The Official DSA range are offering you the chance to win a set of brand new leathers, gloves, boots and a helmet.

To enter, answer the three questions on the next page then tell us in 25 words or less how learning to drive will make a difference to your life. Then send this form to:

DSA Win Bike Gear Competition, TSO, Freepost, ANG 4748, Norwich NR3 1YX

The winner will be the entrant with all answers correct and the most apt and original 25 word essay, as decided by the judges.

Your opinion is important to us. In order to help us to continually improve our products please could you answer these optional questions:

* Terms and conditions apply

Name the shop or website that you bought this product from?

. . . .

. . . .

How would you improve this, or any other, DSA publication?

. . . .

. . . .

. . . .

. . . .

Questions

1 You are following a vehicle on a wet road. You should leave a time gap of at least how many seconds?

. . . .

2 What is the legal minimum depth of tread for motorcycle tyres in millimetres?

. . . .

3 Why should you check over your shoulder before turning right into a side road?

. . . .

Learning to drive will change my life . . . .

. . . .

. . . .

. . . .

Name . . . .

Address . . . .

. . . .

Daytime telephone number . . . .

E-mail address . . . .

TSO will not sell, rent or pass any of your details on to interested third parties. The details you supply will be used to allow us to administer the competition. If you would like to receive information about other Official DSA publications, please indicate how you would like us to communicate with you:

Telephone ☐   Email ☐   Post ☐

I have read, accept and agree to be bound by the Competition Rules

Signature . . . .   **Date** . . . .

Competition Rules

1. Only one entry accepted per purchase of any of the following titles: The Official DSA Guide to Learning to Ride, The Official DSA Guide to Riding - the essential skills, The Official DSA Theory Test for Motorcyclists.

2. All entries must be on official entry forms. No photocopies will be accepted.

3. Entries must be received by 7 September 2007.

4. The competition will run from 24 July 2006 to 7 September 2007 and one prize shall be awarded. All entries must be received by 7 September 2007. No responsibility can be taken by the Promoter for lost, late, misdirected or stolen entries.

5. The prize will be a set of leathers, gloves, boots and a helmet - either a set of Dainese Motordrome motorcycle leathers, a pair of Dainese Gander gloves, a Dainese D-Tour Plain helmet, a pair of Dainese Flex boots or another make of such items of similar value to be selected by the Promoter (about £1000 at the time of going to press) in its absolute discretion. Colour is subject to availability. The size of the bike gear shall be based on measurements supplied by the winner upon request by the Promoter, failing which the Promoter shall be entitled to select reasonable sizes for the winner. There will be no cash alternatives.

6. Only entrants over the age of 16 and resident in the UK are eligible.

7. The winning entry will be decided on 10 September 2007 from all correct entries received by the closing date. The winner will be notified by 24 September 2007. Only the winner will be contacted personally.

8. The winner will be contacted via the email address or telephone number they provide. The Promoter will not be held responsible if the winner cannot be contacted by the means they gave.

9. The winner's name will be published on the Promoter's website at www.tso.co.uk.

10. The prize will be made available within six weeks of the closing date.

11. By accepting any Prize, entrants consent to the use for promotional and other purposes (without further payment and except as prohibited by law) of their name, address, likeness and Prize information. The winner may be required to participate in the Promoter's reasonable marketing and promotional activities. By entering into this competition you consent to participate in the Promoter's reasonable marketing and promotional activities. The winning entrant agrees that all rights including copyright in all works created by the entrant as part of the competition entry shall be owned by the Promoter absolutely without the need for further payment being made to the entrant. Such entrant further agrees to waive unconditionally and irrevocably all moral rights pursuant to the Copyright, Designs and Patents Act of 1988 and under any similar law in force from time to time anywhere in the world in respect of all such works.

12. The Promoter reserves the right to cancel this competition at any stage, if deemed necessary in its opinion, and if circumstances arise outside of its control.

13. Entrants will be deemed to have accepted these rules and to agree to be bound by them when entering this competition.

14. This competition is not open to employees or contractors of the Promoter or the Driving Standards Agency or any person directly involved in the organisation or running of the competition, or their direct family members. The judge ' s decision is final in every situation including any not covered above and no correspondence will be entered into.

15. The Promoter is The Stationery Office Limited, St Crispins, Duke Street, Norwich, NR3 1PD (the publishers of The Official DSA Theory Test for Motorcyclists book).

The Official DSA Guide to Hazard Perception DVD

The only official fully interactive DVD for the hazard perception part of the theory test. This DVD will help boost your driving skills and prepare you for the tests and beyond.

- **The only official interactive hazard perception DVD for your DVD player, games console or your PC***

- **This easy to use DVD gives clear guidance on how to recognise and respond to hazards on the road**

- **Test your skills with the official DSA video clips. Identify the hazards using your DVD remote and receive feedback on your performance**

ISBN 0 11 5524940   **£15.99**

*Check your console manual for compatibility

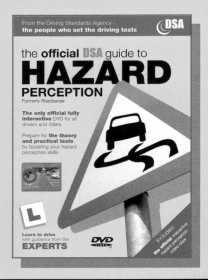

From the Driving Standards Agency -
the people who set the driving tests

DSA

the **official DSA** guide to

HAZARD
PERCEPTION
Formerly Roadsense

The only official fully interactive DVD for all drivers and riders

Prepare for **the theory and practical tests** by boosting your hazard perception skills

L

Learn to drive with guidance from the **EXPERTS**

DVD VIDEO

Includes:
the official interactive hazard perception video disk

The Official DSA Guide to Learning to Ride

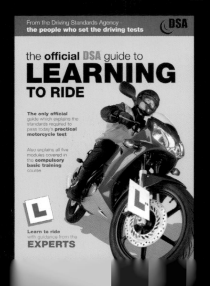

From the Driving Standards Agency -
the people who set the driving tests

DSA

the **official DSA** guide to

LEARNING
TO RIDE

The only official guide which explains the standards required to pass today's **practical motorcycle test**

Also explains all five modules covered in the **compulsory basic training** course

L   **L**

Learn to ride with guidance from the **EXPERTS**

The only official guide which explains the standards required to complete the CBT course and pass today's practical motorcycle test. Good preparation will make it more likely you will pass first time while also improving your skills for the future. This official DSA guide includes:

- **Information on all five modules covered in the compulsory basic training course**

- **The practical test syllabus and an explanation of the standard you need to reach to pass the test**

- **Explains what the examiner is looking for during your test**

ISBN 0 11 552645 5   **£7.99**